COMPETITIVE ETHNIC
RELATIONS

COMPETITIVE ETHNIC RELATIONS

Edited by

SUSAN OLZAK

Department of Sociology
Cornell University
Ithaca, New York

JOANE NAGEL

Department of Sociology
University of Kansas
Lawrence, Kansas

1986

ACADEMIC PRESS, INC.
Harcourt Brace Jovanovich, Publishers
Orlando   San Diego   New York   Austin
Boston   London   Tokyo   Toronto

ACADEMIC PRESS, INC.
Orlando, Florida 32887

United Kingdom Edition published by
ACADEMIC PRESS INC. (LONDON) LTD.
24–28 Oval Road, London NW1 7DX

Library of Congress Cataloging in Publication Data

Competitive ethnic relations.

Includes index.
1. Ethnic relations—Political aspects—Case
studies. 2. Ethnicity—Case studies. 3. Minorities
—Political activity—Case studies. 4. Competition.
I. Olzak, Susan. II. Nagel, Joane.
HM291.C624 1986   305.8   86-3457
ISBN 0—12—525890—9 (alk. paper)

PRINTED IN THE UNITED STATES OF AMERICA

86 87 88 89   9 8 7 6 5 4 3 2 1

Contents

Chapter 9
The Impact of Celtic Nationalism on Class Politics in Scotland
and Wales   199
Charles C. Ragin

Chapter 10
For God and Crown: Class, Ethnicity, and Protestant Politics in
Northern Ireland   221
Katherine O'Sullivan See

Preface

Our purpose in presenting this volume of empirical and theoretical papers on ethnicity in modern states is to address problems relevant to the persistence of ethnicity from a common theoretical perspective—that of competition theory. As researchers in the area of ethnicity and ethnic movements, we have been struck by the capacity of competition theory to account for the tenacity of ethnic boundaries. Our contributors present convincing evidence for the usefulness of competition theory to account for not only the rise of spontaneous (as well as organized) ethnic movements, but also to explain their demobilization as the result of declining levels of competition among ethnic groups.

We present here a collection of research and theory papers that employ political and economic competition as the central cause of both the persistence of ethnic group loyalties and the rise and fall of ethnic movements. The contributions cover a wide scope that crosses national as well as historical boundaries, including research on the Flemish nationalist movement during the 1960s in Belgium, ethnic conflict in South Africa during the 1970s and 1980s, Protestant movements in Northern Ireland over the past two centuries, and ethnic movements involving immigrants to American cities around the turn of the century, among many other settings. We conclude from these papers that by looking at ethnic competition in political and economic institutions, we can better understand how ethnic boundaries form organizational networks that can be transformed into viable social movements. The evidence gathered here suggests that propositions from competition theory of ethnic relations go far in explaining the dynamics of ethnic movements and the fluctuation in the stability of ethnic boundaries. But the evidence also provokes new questions, implied by the variable nature of ethnicity, which we hope will stimulate new research extending the work begun here in this collection.*

*We also wish to add that several chapters, such as those on South Africa, Belgium, and Northern Ireland, analyze ethnic relations that are constantly changing, prompting observers to revise their interpretations and predictions. Our aim here is not to provide updated accounts of current events in these volatile settings, but rather to show how sociological analysis using competition theory is relevant. It remains to be seen what will be the outcomes in such settings and whether the generalizations offered here will hold for future generations.

Introduction, Competitive Ethnic Relations: An Overview

SUSAN OLZAK
Department of Sociology
Cornell University
Ithaca, New York 14853

JOANE NAGEL
Department of Sociology
University of Kansas
Lawrence, Kansas 66045

The persistence and sometime resurgence of ethnicity in the modern world strikes many social scientists as paradoxical. Ethnic identity and conflict persist even when modern organizations based on class, such as unions, and modern political parties of the left and right exist. Why hasn't ethnicity declined as predicted by both functionalist and Marxist models of social change? The contributions to this volume address this problem using a common theoretical framework—competition theory. The chapters reformulate and extend competition theories of ethnic relations in order to clarify the persistence of ethnic boundaries in modern states.

Four empirical generalizations attesting to the perplexing nature of ethnicity in the modern world characterize the present stage of research on the relationship of modernization to ethnic identity, conflict, and social movements.[1] Modernization refers broadly to the coincident processes of industrialization, urbanization, and bureaucratization of market and political organizations. The first generalization states that *modernization tends to decrease ethnic heterogeneity*. An extensive literature notes numerous cases where economic development, state formation, and nation-building coincide with declines in the importance of ethnic

COMPETITIVE ETHNIC RELATIONS

dialects, subregional identifications, and tribal political divisions, and a concomitant rise in "modern" loyalties and politics based on class.

A second generalization casts doubt on the universality of the first one, that ethnicity tends to decline with modernization. Citing examples such as the relationship between the discovery of offshore oil in Scotland, development and industrialization in Basque provinces, and industrialization and development in Quebec, and the subsequent rise of ethnic subnationalism in each case, this tradition suggests that *modernization and development spark ethnic movements.*

A third generalization applies resource mobilization theories to cases of ethnic collective action, finding that under some conditions, modernization and development trigger ethnic movements. Despite heroic efforts on the part of the dominant ethnic group to contain ethnic fractionalism, development within a former periphery advances the bargaining position and organizational capacities of ethnic groups concentrated in peripheral regions. *When resources become initially available to an ethnic periphery, these regions are likely to mobilize against a state center.*

A fourth generalization about ethnicity focuses on the relationship between assimilation and mobilization of ethnic groups. Research on ethnic identity in the United States finds an unexpected association between degree of assimilation of immigrants or minority groups (in terms of language, occupational attainment, and residential dispersion), and strength of ethnic group loyalty and attitudes favoring the importance of ethnic traditions. Support for this relationship has been found at both ethnic group and individual levels of analysis. That is, ethnic groups with higher rates of assimilation sometimes show greater levels of ethnic awareness, mobilization, and activity than other less assimilated groups. Moreover, *within* ethnic populations, more assimilated members (in terms of education, occupation, and residential integration with the majority population) also appear more likely to support ethnic social movements than are less assimilated members of the *same* group.

The contributors to this volume use one or more of these findings as beginning points for their research. The paradoxical persistence and resurgence of ethnicity in the modern and developing world is one unifying theme of this book.

It is also organized around a theoretical perspective. The authors argue that the rise and decline in ethnic movements can be understood by examining competition between groups. Recent work stimulated by ecological perspectives in biology, sociology, anthropology, and other social sciences argues that modernization increases levels of competition for jobs, housing, and other valued resources among ethnic groups. This perspective holds that *ethnic conflict and social movements based on ethnic (rather than some other) boundaries occur when ethnic competition increases.*

Competition theories of ethnic relations, introduced by human ecologists Hawley (1945) and Park (1950), are based on the premise that mobilization along ethnic lines surfaces (or resurfaces) as ethnically distinct groups come to compete in the same labor, housing, marriage, or other kinds of markets.[2] These theories attempt to explain fluctuations in the importance of ethnic identity (see Portes, 1984), ethnic separatist parties (Nielsen, 1980; Ragin, 1979; Olzak, 1982), and ethnic collective behavior (Olzak, 1982). While they employ ecological arguments about ethnic boundaries and competition, these theories agree with resource mobilization theory that increased access to scarce resources favors political mobilization and collective action (Tilly, 1978). The central task of competition theories of ethnic relations is to explain the conditions under which *ethnic* mobilization and ethnic identity supersede other potential loyalties and political cleavages.

Competition theories suggest that economic and political modernization encourage collective action based on ethnic identity because these two processes favor organization on the basis of large-scale identities, rather than on the basis of kinship, village, tribal, or some other smaller-scale identity (Hannan, 1979). In the political realm, this means that only large groups can successfully challenge state authority as state bureaucracies penetrate, control, and administrater peripheries. Using this argument, competition theories can explain why smaller-scale tribal identities became subordinated to the larger-scale Ibo identity in the course of attempts to separate from Nigeria in the 1960s (Nagel and Olzak, 1982). It also explains why Basque and Québécois regionalism rather than small-scale (e.g., community or dialect) oppositions to nation-building mark the histories of Spain and Canada. Competition theories hold that modernization affects ethnic movements by stimulating ethnic competition within increasingly homogeneous markets, which simultaneously breaks down small-scale boundaries and increases the potential for mobilization on a larger scale.

Four propositions have been suggested by competition theorists. These propositions are:

(1) Urbanization accelerates levels of ethnic mobilization and collective action because it initiates contact and competition between ethnic populations.

(2) Expansion of industrial and service sectors of the economy increases rates of ethnic mobilization and collective action because it increases competition among ethnic groups for jobs. Ethnic competition within labor markets intensifies when ethnic segregation diminishes. Ethnic segregation declines when (1) differences in wage levels between ethnic groups decline or (2) barriers between jobs filled by ethnic groups recede.

(3) Development of peripheral regions or the discovery of resources in a periphery occupied by an ethnic population increases the probability of mobilization by the ethnic population. These changes create the potential for the emergence of subnationalist movements, ethnic political parties, and ethnic elite movements.

(4) Processes of state-building (including those following colonial independence) that implement policies targeting specific ethnic populations increase the

likelihood of ethnic collective action. Policy changes (such as instituting ethnic and racial civil rights laws, designating official lands, or implementing language rules) increase ethnic awareness and the likelihood of ethnic movements.

Empirical analyses of competition theories have generally used data on geographical units. They find that more developed, urbanized, and industrial regions support ethnic parties more than do underdeveloped ones (Olzak, 1982, 1983; Leifer, 1981; Nielsen, 1980; Ragin, 1979). Several of the chapters in Part III of this volume carry this tradition a step further by analyzing the relationship of ethnic movements to class cleavages and other kinds of cleavages within and between ethnicities.

In addition to sharing the competition perspective outlined above, the editors of this volume disagree with previous explanations of modern ethnic movements on four issues.[3]

(1) We reject the functionalist view that ethnicity is either a primordial sentiment reactivated in a modern context or a "defense of the periphery," likely to dissolve over time.

(2) We disagree with cultural division of labor theories of ethnic solidarity that portray ethnic mobilization as an outgrowth of persistent ethnic segregation and/or exploitation. Instead, we argue that intergroup competition arises when cultural divisions of labor *break down,* producing a (perhaps temporary) surge in ethnic conflict or mobilization.

(3) We also reject the related hypothesis from an internal colonialism perspective that persistent economic inequalities between center (or core) and peripheral *regions* produce ethnic mobilization. In fact, we have argued the opposite—that a reduction of inequalities between peripheral and core regions can instigate ethnic movements on the part of the formerly depressed regional group (Nagel and Olzak, 1982).

(4) We contend that theories of ethnic mobilization can be assessed meaningfully only with models that examine events and variation in ethnic loyalties or social movements *over time.* This contention is also shared by all contributors. Because the nature of ethnic mobilization involves shifts between levels of group formation marked by ethnic boundaries, only sociological methods of analysis that examine changes in independent as well as dependent variables can adequately address questions about the conditions under which ethnicity waxes and wanes as a mobilizing force. For this reason, all of the empirical chapters in this volume use research designs that span some time period and measure variables over time. The methods used to analyze these data address specifically the effects of changing levels of ethnic competition and changing levels of ethnic movements (see chapters by Olzak and Nielsen for specific examples).

Following current practice, we define ethnicity in terms of ethnic boundaries or ethnic markers, which are usually ascribed characteristics such as skin color, language, or religion. Because several levels of ethnic identity are usually available to each individual, an intriguing research question asks what conditions favor one—perhaps more inclusive—identity over another—perhaps more splintered—ethnic identity (see the chapter by Padilla for a specific example).

The contributors assume, following Barth (1969) and his associates, that ethnicity is situationally determined. While this is not a new formulation, the emphasis on situational determination of ethnicity allows researchers to address questions about the conditions that activate and deactivate ethnic boundaries rather than other social boundaries.

Each chapter extends the competition perspective on ethnic relations a step beyond previous formulations. Several chapters test hypotheses derived from the basic theory. Chapters on such diverse topics as American and English Gypsies, conflict and protest involving American ethnic immigrants, apartheid politics in South Africa, Latino identity in an American city, the Flemish movement in Belgium, and Protestant politics in Northern Ireland since 1600 suggest the flexibility and generality of a competition framework. All 10 chapters focus on the conditions under which ethnicity and ethnic relations become *more* and *less* salient in a given social system, whether they consider ethnic identity (Portes and Manning, Joane Nagel, Padilla) or ethnic collective action (Olzak, Beverly Nagel, James, Nielsen, Ragin, and See).

I. LABOR-FORCE COMPETITION AND ETHNIC COLLECTIVE ACTION

Part I examines the effects of competition in labor markets on ethnic conflict and protest (Olzak), ethnic organizational adaptations in the formation of ethnic enclaves (Portes and Manning), and ethnic political movements (Beverly Nagel). Each chapter assumes that competitive processes are likely to be activated in systems with a mobile labor force. In such situations ethnic populations (or immigrants) must either compete directly or form protective markets to mitigate disadvantages usually experienced by newcomers.

These chapters also question claims that ethnic segregation and exploitation are primary determinants of ethnic organization and social movements. Earlier theories of cultural division of labor or split labor markets proposed that segregation of ethnic (or immigrant) populations at the bottom of the occupational hierarchy or in highly isolated occupational niches encourages ethnic politics and subcultural differences. By examining the process of ethnic adaptation to competition in labor markets, Olzak, Portes and Manning, and Beverly Nagel show that not all immigrant groups face subordination and exploitation. Furthermore, these chapters suggest that economic subordination may not be the only cause of ethnic solidarity. Beverly Nagel and Portes and Manning show how ethnic enclaves that convey economic advantage to their members may reinforce ethnic identity as well.

In Chapter 1, Susan Olzak analyzes the effects of immigration and economic changes on the rates of ethnic conflict and protest in American cities around the turn of the century. Using newspaper accounts of ethnic and racial confrontations to measure the rates of ethnic collective action, Olzak also shows that event-history methods can be used to test arguments about the causes of ethnic conflict and protest. Olzak's application of event-history methods to ethnic events data constitutes a departure from more commonly used methods in studying collective action.

Olzak's formulation of competition theory holds that rising levels of immigration, rapid rates of immigration, economic contraction, and an interaction between economic hardship and immigration flows affect rates of ethnic conflict and protest. Her analysis shows consistent support for these propositions. Specifically, the flow of immigration, rates of change in immigration, and economic contraction *increase* the rates of ethnic activism. Furthermore, there is an interaction effect between the magnitude of immigration and economic contraction such that immigration *intensifies* ethnic collective action when job markets are also slack, as might be expected by the competition line of argument.

Olzak's analysis in Chapter 1 also has implications for other theories of collective protest. For example, she finds that while factors that intensify competition in labor markets raise levels of ethnic collective action, so too do indicators of the economic well-being of immigrants. Using real wages of common laborers as an indicator of such well-being, Olzak finds that rates of ethnic collective action are high when wages of common laborers are high (relative to a baseline). This finding suggests support for resource mobilization theories that hold that accumulation of resources by disadvantaged groups increases the chances that they will engage in collective action. The positive effect of laborers' wages on rates of collective action also casts doubt on theories that claim that increasing hardship for the economically disadvantaged provokes collective action.

In Chapter 2, Alejandro Portes and Robert Manning review the literature on ethnic enclaves. They identify a set of factors associated with the development and persistence of ethnic communities in the case of Japanese, Korean, Jewish, and Cuban immigrants to the United States. The factors common to all these examples are (1) presence of a substantial number of immigrants familiar with small businesses, (2) availability of sources of capital, and (3) availability of sources of cheap labor.

In reviewing case studies of ethnic enclaves, Portes and Manning show that ethnic communities having the prerequisites cited above transform small amounts of human and financial capital into enclaves linked together by paternalistic bonds, ongoing recruitment from the home country, and geographical and occupational concentration. In some cases such enclaves generate highly successful ethnic firms, creating the potential for high rates of upward mobility for group members. The case histories Portes and Manning review cast doubt on the argument that cultural factors alone explain the variations in mobility across ethnic groups. Rather, their evidence can be read to suggest the reverse is true: success of ethnic enclaves reinforces ethnic cultural identities and differences from the majority populations.

In Chapter 2, Portes and Manning suggest the proposition that high levels of assimilation depend on whether or not members of immigrant groups enter a primary market sector (contrasted here with enclave economies). That is, the authors would expect higher rates of assimilation for immigrants in America entering primary market firms (organizations that are large and monopolistic, with promotion ladders based on internal markets), compared to immigrants entering enclave economies. The importance of this proposition is that Portes and Manning point out that either of these two strategies can result in financial success and that such success may therefore vary independently from ethnic solidarity and cultural resilience.

In Chapter 3, Beverly Nagel addresses a different facet of labor markets. Building on Barth's early work, she asks how changes in the kinds of jobs filled by Gypsies and non-Gypsies affect political mobilization of Gypsies in the United States and Great Britain. Historical analysis of two ''waves'' of political mobilization of Gypsies in the United States and Great Britain shows that maintaining a specific occupational niche assists gypsies in creating boundaries around their kinship and economic organizations, but that initial breakdown of the separation between Gypsies and non-Gypsies appears to incite Gypsy political movements.

By applying the ecological concept of niche to the maintenance of ethnic boundaries in the case of Gypsies, Nagel clarifies the puzzle of the persistence of a small and almost anachronistic ethnic population. Unlike the cases of ethnic enclaves discussed in Chapter 2, Gypsies in Britain and the United States are highly dispersed and tend to avoid direct confrontations with other ethnic groups. Gypsy boundaries have been maintained by a strategy that allows them quick entry, transitory specialization, and exit. It is often economically rewarding for Gypsies to emphasize their Gypsy ethnicity, both to maintain monopolies over these temporary jobs (e.g., fortune telling, blacktop repair) and to maintain social distance from prying authorities. In contrast to more geographically stable enclaves, Gypsies emphasize their ethnicity in labor markets only when it is useful to do so. Under other conditions they may emphasize some other social boundary or even some other ethnicity.

Beverly Nagel's chapter also identifies factors responsible for protest and mobilization movements by Gypsies in the United States and Britain. A competition perspective holds that ethnic competition with non-Gypsies intensifies when niche boundaries between Gypsies and non-Gypsies initially overlap. This initial overlap produces Gypsy mobilization in the two countries.

II. POLITICAL COMPETITION AND ETHNICITY

Earlier theories of state-building identified several ways in which modern state structures create and maintain ethnicity. We have argued elsewhere that expansion of the political sector promotes ethnic mobilization to the extent that (1) establishment of national politics raises issues of national identity versus other

competing identities; (2) the expansion of political authority creates a competitive arena for distribution of state resources; and (3) there is legal recognition
of ethnicity as a basis for political resource competition (Nagel and Olzak,
1982). The chapters in Part II argue that the administrative procedures used by
modern states inadvertently create legitimate ethnic parties and organizations.
Policies of bureaucratic governments reinforce and sometimes actually redraw
ethnic boundaries. Ethnic political mobilization tends to occur when political
competition intensifies, due to shifts in methods used in distributing political
benefits.

In Chapter 4, Joane Nagel considers the political construction of ethnicity. She
identifies two ways in which political systems promote interethnic competition
and increase the likelihood of ethnic collective action. Political systems can do so
by structuring political access along ethnic lines through the administration of
ethnic or racial programs or by instituting racial quota guidelines. Political systems can also promote competition among ethnicities by adopting policies that
emphasize ethnic differences, as in laws on bilingual education or reservation
territories.

She also identifies consequences of rising political competition. Shifts in
public policy or administrative boundaries may *reinforce* existing, even relatively dormant, ethnic boundaries, providing new resources in the form of political representation (e.g., in the form of a subregional cabinet office) or access to
regionally based resources (e.g., offshore oil reserves). Moreover, shifts in
administrative boundaries or policy may create *new* ethnic boundaries, perhaps
by the merger of two or more smaller-scale groups or by the slight shift in
advantage attached to a larger-scale ethnic identity (see Chapter 7).

In Chapter 5, Crawford Young extends the argument that ideologies and
organizational politics of nationalism encourage subnationalism. This chapter,
which draws on more traditional perspectives on ethnic diversity and cultural
pluralism, considers modernization and ethnic diversity in the Third World.
Using examples from Pakistan, Nigeria, and other countries, Young argues that
modernity intensifies a variety of communal and subgroup struggles that have
been infused with the moral legitimacy of nationalism. Implicit in his argument
is the proposition that, because Third World nation-building emerged in a context of territorial anticolonialism, the possibility of further fractionalization of
former colonies into subregions always threatens national unity. Yet in discussing Third World "failures" to unify, Young also captures the spirit of earlier
(functionalist) proposals for averting conflict. That policies promoting national
integration in states such as Pakistan, Malaysia, and Lebanon had less than
peaceful consequences suggests to Young that some integrationist policies are
more likely to *activate* ethnic resistance rather than to undercut it. A most
interesting section titled Political Engineering reviews policies in Nigeria since
1979, and in India and Ethiopia. It suggests that ethnic secession and escalation
of demands may take precedence (perhaps especially) when cultural pluralism is
recognized in constitutions and in rules of representation.

South Africa provides an even more vivid example of the construction of an racial/ethnic state. In Chapter 6, Wilmot James argues that intervention by the South African state aimed at undercutting, isolating, and in some cases removing a troublesome group from the center of political action actually intensifies the ethnic struggle. Not without considerable irony, James claims South Africa's current "deracialization" policy serves to incite ethnic violence. How does "deracialization" achieve this?

According to James, the constitution of 1984, which enfranchises colored (of mixed ancestry) and Indians (of Asian–Indian descent) for the first time, clearly isolates only blacks as noncitizens. By isolating blacks, the South African state also provides them with a weapon to attack the state. Because this constitution created new representative institutions for those incorporated into the state, ethnic identity has increased in importance, in James's view. His argument rests ultimately on the proposition that all ethnic protest must take the form of antistate (and anti-status quo) radicalism because black "homelands" are administered by the South African state. As James cautions, any predictions and prognosis for opposition movements using a political construction framework must await further developments and reactions of the state as well as of other significant actors.

Parts I and II divide into chapters on the "economic" and "political" determinants of ethnic collective action. Although each contributor emphasizes one or the other, political and economic factors interact strongly. For example, peak periods of anti-Chinese activity instigated by labor market competition in the early 1880s in San Francisco led to official recognition of this collective conflict, culminating in the Chinese Exclusion Act of 1882, as well as subsequent laws limiting quotas of Chinese immigrants (see Chapter 1). Clearly these processes involve a dynamic relationship between economic and political competition that needs further investigation. For example, a natural extension of the research reported here might investigate whether the arrival of immigrants leads to political as well as economic sanctions to contain a threat. If political sanctions (including restriction of citizenship or ability to own businesses and land) succeed, they may depress ethnic conflict or attempt to segregate minority populations economically and geographically.

III. COMPETITION PERSPECTIVES ON ETHNIC POLITICAL MOVEMENTS

Part III explores the causes of movements dedicated to furthering the goals of specific ethnic or racial groups, either in response to some perceived discrimination or grievance or in reaction to state policies. The chapters in this section use data from four very different political contexts and historical settings to analyze the sources of ethnic movements: (1) mobilization of Latinos in Chicago in the mid-1970s, (2) Flemish nationalist party success from 1950 to the 1970s in Belgium, (3) Celtic nationalist support and its effects on class voting in Great

Britain during the late 1960s, and (4) Protestant collective action and political behavior in Northern Ireland from the 1600s to the present. Each study examines the usefulness of competition arguments for understanding how ethnic collective action competes (sometimes successfully) with other kinds of organizations and other potential political loyalties such as class. By asking very different kinds of research questions, each contribution highlights another facet of the paradox regarding modernization and ethnicity mentioned at the outset. Each paper systematically evaluates the utility of competition theory for understanding how competition in modern industrial states may unleash ethnic movements under some conditions.

In Chapter 7, Felix Padilla argues that an Affirmative Action program in Chicago triggered ethnic mobilization and protest organization by Hispanics as a unitary ethnic population. During the early 1970s in Chicago, two processes combined to support Latino mobilization. There were effective organizations of both Mexicans and Puerto Ricans established to combat employment discrimination against both groups. During this same period, Affirmative Action policies directed programs toward the Spanish-speaking community as a whole without regard to ethnicity. Padilla reports the chronology of protest events that followed mobilization against two Chicago employers—Illinois Bell and Jewel Tea— illustrating how these two processes interacted.

Padilla's chapter suggests that political policies that attach benefits to ethnic self-identification encourage mobilization using this new ethnic calculus. Padilla is careful not to suggest that small-scale ethnic identification (say, Puerto Rican or Mexican) disappears, but rather that ethnic identity is situationally determined. Here the context is that of city politics. Issues such as school board referenda on bilingual programs mobilize people along the larger-scale language boundary, but creation of a neighborhood youth employment program activates smaller-scale boundaries, such as Puerto Rican versus Mexican.

In Chapter 8, François Nielsen uses a general ecological model to analyze support for the Flemish nationalist party candidates, the Volksunie, in Belgium from 1950 to 1974. He compares the effects of macroeconomic and labor-force conditions on support for candidates to test hypotheses about the effects of how differences in occupations, income, and commercial development affected support for the Volksunie party.

According to Nielsen, new ethnic parties, in this case the Volksunie, have greatest likelihood of success in environments with *low political diversity*. In extending work by Pinard and others on the effects of the dominance of one party on the prospects for third parties, Nielsen explains the unexpected rise of ethnic parties in such established countries as Spain, Great Britain, and Canada, as well as Belgium.

Nielsen also uses a dynamic method of analysis of the changing context of political diversity and its impact on success of ethnic third parties. The evidence strongly supports his formulation of competition theory: in low-diversity en-

vironments, where support for the Catholic party has expanded so that it becomes
vulnerable to attack, industrial development expands support of the ethnic party.
But in high-diversity environments, the class basis of party voting remains
strong. In such high-diversity cantons, Flemish nationalism captures less support. Nielsen's results suggest an important addition to competition theory—
political complexity shapes the ways in which ethnic competition affects class
and ethnic loyalties.

In Chapter 9, Charles Ragin asks the opposite theoretical question: did the
resurgence of Celtic nationalism during the 1960s in Great Britain affect *class
politics* in this period? Considering questions generated by a series of conflicting
theories, Ragin analyzes data on the impact of support for ethnic movements
(measured by opinion poll data of class and party preference in 199 parliamentary constituencies in Great Britain in 1966) on class voting in England,
Scotland, and Wales.

Ragin finds that Celtic nationalism undermines the traditional nonmanual
bases of the Conservative party in Great Britain, while leaving support from
manual laborers for the Labour party unaffected. He argues that these results
support his hypothesis that ethnic political mobilization can result from *internal
class differentiation* within an ethnic minority.

Ragin and Nielsen characterize ethnic politics similarly. Ethnic politics are
encouraged by modernization and by low political diversity—whether measured
by one-party dominance in Belgium, or by long-term class and party relationships in Great Britain. Ragin extends the argument further by considering the
impact of ethnic politics on class politics and class mobilization. His theory of
ethnic subnationalism claims that traditional assumptions about the trade-offs
between class and ethnic politics must be reexamined. Because success of an
ethnic party erodes class politics only for the elite strata, he contends that ethnic
politics may be a strategy developed by ethnic elites to subdue class divisions
within ethnic regions.

These results from Belgium and Great Britain show promise for the competition theory in analyzing the dynamics of class support for class and ethnic
parties. A reasonable next stage is to analyze the causes of declines of ethnic
politics and the factors associated with increased class differences within ethnic
parties.

In Chapter 10, Katherine O'Sullivan See analyzes the effects of class divisions
in Northern Ireland on ethnic conflict. This historical analysis considers the
applicability of internal colonialism, split labor market, and competition theories
for various stages of Protestant (and Catholic) ethnic mobilization on the basis of
ethnicity. See suggests that the dynamics of ethnic conflict can be understood by
applying different theories to different periods in the history of Northern Ireland.

In early periods of development of Northern Ireland, models of internal colonialism appear to apply. Protestant landlords were politically and economically
dominant, while rural Catholics could only lease land from Protestant representa-

tives of the Crown. By analyzing causes of *Protestant mobilization* against
Catholics, instead of the more common method of analyzing Catholic mobilization, See is able to discover how different theories apply to mobilization by the
dominant group in Northern Ireland at different times. See suggests that ethnic
conflict by Protestants against Catholics was more likely to be aggravated by
downward mobility of Protestants in agrarian areas rather than by industrialization in the early period of colonialization. When downwardly mobile Protestants
found themselves in competition with poor Catholics, they engaged in loyalist
activity involving violence and threats to the Catholic population. However, See
concludes that internal colonialism models do describe initial stages of ethnic
dominance and subordination in Northern Ireland.

Subsequent periods of Irish history reflect factors related more to split labor
market, resource mobilization, and competition theories. Anti-Catholic activities
peak when land reform and other political changes raise the potential for Catholics
to enter farming in areas of former Protestant monopolies over agriculture and
sufficient numbers of low-level farm workers and other Protestant laborers in the
rural areas become available for recruitment into the loyalist cause. Other macroeconomic factors, including economic depressions and migrations off the land,
caused large shifts in labor supply in urban areas in subsequent periods. In both
rural and urban examples, See finds that factors related to increasing ethnic
competition in Northern Ireland are responsible for heightened conflict and
confrontations between Catholics and Protestants. Rising political competition
appears to extend this conflict in Northern Ireland even further in recent history.

IV. CONCLUSION AND IMPLICATIONS FOR
FUTURE RESEARCH

These chapters demonstrate that competition theories of the effects of changing economic and political conditions go far in explaining ethnic resurgence in
modern as well as historical situations. However, each contribution naturally
raises a series of questions. We list these as an agenda for future research on
ethnic relations.

(1)   Are there threshold levels of competition in labor, housing, or other
markets that spark conflict and collective action? At what tipping points do
natives mobilize against newcomers, or against each other? Do these thresholds
differ at different units of analysis—at the neighborhood, city, state, or country
level?

(2)   What sequences of events determine the institutionalization of specific
"official" labeling or designation of ethnic groups? That is, to what extent do
levels of prior ethnic mobilization and success, and prior levels of ethnic competition in labor and other markets, determine how the various levels of govern-

ment will respond to ethnic claims? Another way to state this question is to ask whether political construction is the *outcome* of prior success of ethnic movements. How can we develop better methods to identify the sources of state policies pertaining to ethnic groups (including discrimination laws and segregation statutes)?

(3)   What deactivates ethnic boundaries? What factors—economic, political, demographic—affect the decline of ethnic language, customs, friendship networks, and enclave communities, and how are these downward curves related to levels of subjective ethnic identification and levels of support for ethnic parties and mobilization?

(4)   Are ethnic resurgences and ethnic separatist movements, such as those in Quebec, Belgium, and the Celtic Fringe, transitory phenomena based upon sudden disequilibria of class-based and other kinds of politics, or are they enduring features of modern states? What determines the degree of persistence of such movements? Are ethnic third party movements similar in form and cause to other kinds of third party movements? Are the "protest cycles" the same along some social movement set of stages?

NOTES

[1]For reviews of these empirical generalizations, see Nagel and Olzak (1982), Olzak (1983), and Nielsen (1985).

[2]Other statements of competition theory perspectives on ethnic movements and identity can be found in Nielsen (1980, 1985), Portes (1984), Nagel and Olzak (1982), Olzak (1982), Banton (1980), Lauwagie (1979), Hannan (1979), Wilson (1978), Despres (1975), Barth (1969), Blalock (1967), and Lieberson (1961).

[3]More extensive evaluations and discussions of existing theories of ethnic mobilization and collective action are found in chapters by Olzak, Beverly Nagel, Ragin, and See in this volume.

REFERENCES

BANTON, MICHAEL (1980). *Racial and ethnic competition*. Cambridge: Cambridge University Press.

BARTH, FREDERICK (1969). *Ethnic groups and boundaries*. Boston: Little, Brown.

BLALOCK, HUBERT M. JR. (1967). *Toward a theory of minority-group relations*. New York: Capricorn Books.

DESPRES, LEO (1975). *Ethnicity and resource competition*. The Hague: Mouton Publishers.

HANNAN, MICHAEL T. (1979). The dynamics of ethnic boundaries in modern states. In *National development and the world system* (J. Meyer and M. T. Hannan, eds.), pp. 253–275. Chicago: University of Chicago Press.

HAWLEY, AMOS (1945). Dispersion versus segregation: Apropos of a solution of race problems. Papers of the Michigan Academy of Science, Arts, and Letters. Ann Arbor, Michigan: University of Michigan Press.

14 SUSAN OLZAK AND JOANE NAGEL

LAUWAGIE, BEVERLY NAGEL (1979). Ethnic boundaries in modern states: *Romano Varo-Fil* revisited. *American Sociological Review* **85**:310–337.

LEIFER, ERIC (1981). Competing models of political mobilization: The role of ethnic ties. *American Journal of Sociology* **87**:23–47.

LIEBERSON, STANLEY (1961). A societal theory of race relations. *American Sociological Review* **26**:907–908.

NAGEL, JOANE, and SUSAN OLZAK (1982). Ethnic mobilization in new and old states: An extension of the competition model. *Social Problems* **30**:127–143.

NIELSEN, FRANÇOIS (1980). The Flemish movement in Belgium after World War II: A dynamic analysis. *American Sociological Review* **45**:76–94.

NIELSEN, FRANÇOIS (1985). Toward a theory of ethnic solidarity in modern societies. *American Sociological Review* **50**:133–149.

OLZAK, SUSAN (1982). Ethnic mobilization in Quebec. *Ethnic and Racial Studies* **5**(2):253–297.

OLZAK, SUSAN (1983). Contemporary ethnic mobilization. *Annual Review of Sociology* **9**:355–374.

PARK, ROBERT (1950). *Race and culture.* Glencoe: The Free Press.

PORTES, ALEJANDRO (1984). The rise of ethnicity: Determinants of ethnic perception among Cubans in Miami. *American Sociological Review* **49**:383–397.

RAGIN, CHARLES (1979). Ethnic political mobilization: The Welsh Case. *American Sociological Review* **44**:619–635.

TILLY, CHARLES (1978). *From mobilization to revolution.* New York: Addison-Wesley.

WILSON, WILLIAM J. (1978). *The declining significance of race.* Chicago: University of Chicago Press.

Part I

Labor Force Competition and Ethnicity

1

A Competition Model of Ethnic Collective Action in American Cities, 1877–1889

SUSAN OLZAK

Department of Sociology
Cornell University
Ithaca, New York 14853

What sparks ethnic conflict against ethnic or racial groups? Why are some periods of history marked by continuous ethnic or racial protest, while others are marked by relative calm? This chapter tries to answer these questions by focusing on how the dynamics of segregation in labor markets affect rates of ethnic collective action. Ethnic collective action is collective behavior that uses a set of ethnic markers (e.g., skin color, language, nationality) as the criterion for membership in a group making distinctly ethnic claims. These claims may be based on perceived injustices due to ethnic or racial background, or they may confront another ethnic nationality group with threats or attempts to exclude or harm them.

This chapter extends theories of niche competition from classical human ecology to explain variations in ethnic collective action. It also reviews alternative explanations and outlines several significant shortcomings of the existing literature. Finally, it presents evidence on ethnic conflict and protest in American cities, 1877–1889, that provides some initial support for the argument that increasing ethnic competition produces bursts of ethnic collective action.

I. ECOLOGICAL THEORIES OF ETHNIC RELATIONS

Human ecology theories of ethnic relations begun by Hawley (1945), Park (1950), Lieberson (1961), and Barth (1969) conceptualize ethnicity in novel ways as a set of social boundaries that demarcate membership. These boundaries may be based upon language, skin color, cultural characteristics, role in productive activity (or niche), or some combination of these factors. The important contribution of this tradition is its emphasis on factors affecting the stability of ethnic boundaries (and thus the persistence of ethnicity) as well as factors causing shifts in levels and salience of boundaries.

A second important contribution of human ecology theories of ethnicity is the insight that the distribution of ethnic populations into productive roles or occupations tells us when ethnic group boundaries are favored over others in interaction. That is, human ecology formulations by Park (1950), Barth (1969), and others suggest that the coincidence of ethnic group membership with high degrees of specialization in the labor force determines *where* ethnic boundaries are drawn. A related proposition found in Barth (1969; p. 17) is that when ethnic and productive niche boundaries coincide, ethnic identity supersedes other possible ones.[1] These principles can also be applied to modern settings where niche is defined with respect to labor-force concentration in polyethnic societies (Hannan, 1979).

Here I have extended human ecology theories of ethnic boundaries to consider two instances of increasing salience of ethnicity in order to analyze the factors responsible for ethnic collective action. The first concerns *migration,* which causes groups with distinct ethnic identities to be brought into the same labor markets. Ecological theories imply that ethnic boundaries remain strong for those groups concentrated in ethnic occupations. A second instance of increasing salience of ethnicity concerns *decreasing segregation* of an ethnic group, so that the group comes to compete with other ethnicities in the same markets. In both cases, the degree of initial coincidence between ethnic identity and niche shapes the initially high level of ethnic group solidarity. Whether or not that solidarity can be transformed into collective action depends on the structural factors to be discussed in this chapter.

The argument developed here is that ethnic competition occurs when two or more ethnic populations try to acquire the same valued resources (e.g., housing, jobs, other kinds of rewards). In particular, when two or more ethnic populations *come to compete in the same markets,* ethnic collective action is likely to occur. The ethnic character of collective action directed at labor markets is determined by the persistence of strong and salient ethnic boundaries. Ethnic collective action is encouraged by two main processes common in industrial societies: (1) once-isolated minorities move across borders, as in immigration and migration, and (2) once-segregated minorities expand from their niches and come to compete on the same levels or in the same markets as other ethnic groups.

When ethnic competition produces initial confrontations among proximate ethnic groups, ethnic conflict and protest may occur. An obvious consequence of rising job competition is resistance by the dominant ethnicity or monopolizers of valued jobs to the competitive threat by organizing collectively.

A less obvious kind of ethnic collective action results from *increases* in resources of ethnic communities. Shifts in relative bargaining power due to changing resources may allow them to mobilize and protest for better living conditions, citizenship rights, or some other rewards. Competition theory implies that group mobilization occurs along ethnic lines only when there is also some degree of ethnic organizational structure or solidarity present *as well as* rising levels of competition.

Failure to distinguish the concepts of competition, conflict, and ethnic collective action may lead to the erroneous conclusion that propositions relating ethnic competition to ethnic collective action are tautological. Because this chapter consciously employs such propositions, it also draws on the important distinctions between competition and conflict formulated by Park, Burgess, and others in the human ecology tradition. As Park and Burgess stated (1921; pp. 574–575):

> Both [competition and conflict] are forms of interaction, but competition is a struggle between individuals, or groups of individuals, who are not necessarily in contact and communication; while conflict is a contest in which contact is an indispensable condition. . . . Conflict is always conscious, indeed, it evokes the deepest emotions and strongest passions and enlists the greatest concentration of attention and effort. Both competition and conflict are forms of struggle. Competition, however, is continuous and impersonal, conflict is intermittent and personal. . . .In general, then, one may say competition becomes conscious and personal in conflict. In the process of transition, competitors are transformed into rivals and enemies.

The argument that increased levels of ethnic competition cause ethnic conflict and mobilization captures this distinction. Thus this chapter asks under what conditions ethnic competition (in the economic sphere) becomes transformed into collective behavior mobilized around ethnic markers. In many ways, this question parallels Marx's question: when does a class that exists *in itself* becomes mobilized *for itself*?

A. Role of Competition in Producing Ethnic Collective Action

Generalizing from human ecology models of ethnic relations, competition theories propose that ethnic relations are likely to be stable when ethnic groups exploit segregated niches in an economy and in other spheres. Isolation may be maintained by discrimination, specialization, symbiotic market relations, or some other means. However, the important point is that interaction and contact across ethnic lines is minimized by isolation (see Blalock, 1967). As Lieberson (1980) has demonstrated, occupational concentration of ethnic populations changes drastically over time. Some populations move from isolation to dispersion throughout the occupational hierarchy. Competition theory focuses attention on the effects of these changes.

As newly arrived ethnic populations come to compete with established ones, attempts to exclude the new competitors will take place if jobs (or resources, more generally) do not expand proportionally. Attempts at exclusion (such as discrimination, deportation, antiethnic movements, and violence) may also provoke reactive movements on the part of newcomers. According to the competition perspective, both dominant and subordinate ethnic groups are likely to engage in collective action when ethnic competition in labor markets intensifies (Nielsen, 1980; Olzak, 1982; Hannan, 1979).

Changes in participation and access to labor markets that benefit disadvantaged populations can also be analyzed as types of resources associated with rising rates of collective action. Resource mobilization theory and research on social movements emphasize the importance of specifying theoretically how changing incentives, levels of resources, and organization produce ethnic collective action [see, for example, McAdam (1983)]. As Tilly (1978) has argued, the occurrence (and nonoccurrence) of a collective event is a transitory phenomenon, involving movement between stages of mobilization and nonactivity. Mobilization for collective ethnic action does not occur automatically with each migration wave. Mobilization depends on (1) the *incentives* attached to mobilization along ethnic lines compared to mobilization along some other boundaries, or nonactivity, (2) the *resources* amassed by ethnic populations, including levels of income, membership size, information networks, and (3) the *degree of organization*, including existence of formal organizations, leadership, and success of former mobilizations.

Existing theories of ethnic collective action have not yet considered the dynamics of ethnic job-market participation and changing levels of resources available to ethnic populations as causes of outbreaks of ethnic activity. What have been lacking are theoretical frameworks and research methods that capture the dynamic mechanisms at work. This chapter is a partial step toward filling that gap.

B. Definitions of Ethnic Solidarity and Ethnic Enclaves

Ethnic solidarity refers to the strength or density of ethnic social interaction. It varies at least partly independently of the likelihood of ethnic collective action. Solidary and exploited ethnic populations do not automatically organize as ethnic groups, and dispersed and socioeconomically "assimilated" ethnic populations do, on occasion, organize as ethnics. Only by distinguishing ethnic solidarity from the likelihood of collective action can these cases be explained. Ethnic enclaves illustrate one form of ethnic solidarity. An *ethnic enclave* is a structure in which members of an ethnic population exploit a common occupational niche, participate in common ethnic institutions and organizations, and form a dense interaction of network communication, information, socialization, and marital endogamy.

Consideration of the organizational base of ethnic enclaves suggests that two types of boundaries are relevant. One set of boundaries is drawn around *cultural markers,* where typical criteria for membership are language, nationality, or some behavioral characteristics. The second set of boundaries is drawn around *productive activities,* defined by occupations, sector of the economy, or industry. When the two boundaries coincide considerably, ethnic solidarity is doubly reinforced, and is maintained by economic links that are also familial and personal (Waldinger, 1983).

Ethnic enclaves can create resource bases for collective action.[2] Whether they do depends on several factors, including the number and kind of organizations involved and the length of time the organizations have been in existence. A second property of ethnic enclaves relevant to collective action is the extent to which the cultural and economic boundaries of ethnic populations coincide. In cities (or countries) in which cultural and economic boundaries overlap, ethnic identity will be a major organizing factor for all kinds of social interaction [see, for example, Bodnar *et al.* (1982)]. When cultural boundaries coincide with boundaries defined by productive activities, including job market concentration, then ethnic identity will be a central and salient identity in the labor market.

Ethnic collective action was defined earlier as activity by an ethnic group that also articulates ethnic claims. According to this definition, creation of an organization of black doctors within the American Medical Association (AMA) would not be an example of ethnic collective action if it pursued purely medical goals, but the marching of these same doctors in support of black civil rights would be.

My theoretical predictions about the role of ethnic enclaves in affecting rates of ethnic collective action concern variations in these two properties of enclaves as organizational structures—the resource base and the degree of coincidence of the two kinds of boundaries. Thus, the role of ethnic enclaves in producing ethnic collective action involves an *interaction between the strength of ethnic enclaves and the intensity of ethnic competition*. In this view, rates of ethnic collective action rise when two conditions hold: (1) existence of strong ethnic enclaves provides an organizational resource base for collective action and makes ethnic identity a strong determinant of an individual's role in productive activities and community life, and (2) economic expansion beyond the enclave boundaries increases competition with other ethnic populations.

Next, I review the research literature that bears on how patterns of economic participation of ethnic groups affect the likelihood of ethnic activity, and I suggest ways in which the shortcomings can be improved from a competition theory perspective. In the final section, I present data collected on ethnic conflict and protest in American cities, 1877–1889. The evidence substantiates my claim that competition theory provides some useful ways to model ethnic action so as to capture the effects of changing economic conditions on ethnic collective action.

II. THEORETICAL PERSPECTIVES ON ETHNIC COLLECTIVE ACTION

Several leading theoretical traditions bear directly on the question of how labor-market processes affect ethnic collective action. Three of them can be distinguished by their reliance on *economic hardship* explanations. They imply that economic and spatial segregation of a (usually exploited) ethnic population causes ethnic movements. These are the cultural division of labor (CDL), split labor market (SLM), and, more tangentially, the dual labor market (DLM) theories. Two other theoretical frameworks, resource mobilization (RM) and competition theories, hold that *increased access to resources* to ethnic populations increases the likelihood of ethnic collective action. All five perspectives regard the labor-market position of ethnic populations (whether stable or changing) as a key to understanding the process of ethnic collective action. In this section I argue that we must also use theories that specify how changes in these patterns trigger outbreaks of ethnic mobilization and action.

Although these perspectives have been reviewed more generally elsewhere (Olzak, 1983; Ragin and Davies, 1981), it is useful to note that these imply opposing hypotheses about the effects of economic hardship and ethnic labor market segregation on levels of ethnic collective action. The analysis in Section IV takes advantage of these differences to relate empirical findings to these theories.

A. Cultural Division of Labor (CDL) Theory

Cultural division of labor theories hold that ethnic solidarity is strongest when (1) ethnic groups members are segregated into subordinate economic positions, (2) ethnically homogeneous regions are underdeveloped or only weakly linked to developing or core regions, and (3) ethnic segregation in labor markets is most severe. Ethnic boundaries persist under these conditions because the majority-group employers have a continuing economic interest in maintaining a cultural division of labor, according to this argument. Moreover, strong occupational, residential, and ethnic segregation favors ethnic solidarity over class solidarity in the political sphere under these conditions (Hechter, 1975, p. 42).

Restating these propositions in rational choice terms led Hechter (1982) and Banton (1983) to conclude that participation in segregated ethnic institutions provides the organizational and self-interest bases for ethnic collective action.[3] That is, segregation of ethnic populations in work, friendship, and housing insures that ethnicity will predominate over other potential axes of mobilization:

> To the degree the members of an ethnic group are dependent on one or a small number of affiliated organizations (such as ethnic associations of various kinds) for benefits that they cannot obtain elsewhere, they are likely to be highly solidary and have the potential to engage in collective action . . . This situation occurs frequently among racial and ethnic groups that occupy distinctive positions in the stratification system [Hechter, Friedman, and Applebaum (1982), p. 421].

B. Split Labor Market (SLM) Theory

Bonacich's (1972) split labor market theory proposes that the likelihood of ethnic conflict rises when ethnic or racial groups receive different wage levels in the *same* (not segregated) labor markets for the same jobs.[4] Because employers try to minimize labor costs, they have a stake in maintaining an ethnic (or racial) wage differential according to this argument. Under these conditions, ethnic and racial conflict remains high and declines only when ethnic wage differentials diminish.

The SLM perspective assumes that *ethnic conflict is likely when capitalists can manipulate a cheap ethnic labor force.* In this view, an SLM maintains ethnic boundaries. Moreover, SLM undercuts attempts by the dominant group to build unions. The key to ethnic conflict is the availability (or threat) of a cheap labor supply, controlled by capitalist owners. Immigration, which flows to regions of higher wages, provides just such a supply.

In Bonacich's (1979) view, ethnic boundaries persist only when worker solidarity, or class identification, is blocked. If broad worker organization were successful, ethnic solidarity would be gradually eroded and replaced by class solidarity. Some argue that this proposition is consistent both with Marxist models of internal colonialism and with functionalist models of assimilation and nation-building [see Ragin and Davies (1981)]. Hannan (1979), on the other hand, claims that SLM theory is a special case of competition theory, because it depends on competition between dominant ethnic group members and a lower-wage ethnic population threatening to destabilize the dominant group's monopoly or favored status. This last point will be amplified next in discussion of the role of ethnic enclaves in creating a competitive threat.

C. Dual Labor Market (DLM) Theory

Although they do not focus on ethnic movements directly, theories positing the existence of a dual labor market also have direct implications for the theoretical questions asked here. DLM theories assume the dominance of a set of core firms or industries that are bureaucratic, diversified, and monopolistic.[5] Jobs in the core have stability because they are entered by an internal promotion market [see Doeringer and Piore (1971)]. Jobs in secondary labor markets are unstable, have lower and less steeply graded wage rates, and convey fewer fringe and other kinds of intangible benefits (Reich, Gordon, and Edwards, 1973). In this view, race and ethnic groups are more likely to work in the secondary than in primary labor market [see, for examples, Piore (1979) and Edwards (1979)].

Whether ethnic populations monopolize jobs and occupations is thus a key issue for both CDL and DLM theories.[6] Suppose that DLM theory is an accurate portrayal of ethnic stratification in the United States and other capitalist countries. Then, *to the extent that ethnic group members are concentrated in the secondary labor market, ethnic politics could be expected to divide workers against each other [see Piore (1979)].* Seen in this way, DLM theory agrees with the CDL theory about the conditions under which ethnic mobilization will take precedence over class mobilization.

D. Resource Mobilization (RM) Theory

RM theory offers two propositions about ethnic mobilization. The first links ethnic solidarity to mobilization along ethnic lines:

> If I, a Greek now, meet a new Greek, and because he's a Greek I prepare to do him favors, we have some evidence that solidarity among Greeks is high. If this sort of solidarity is high the group in question probably has a great potential capacity for collective action, all other things being equal [Tilly (1973), P. 214].

In the language of this chapter, RM theory asserts that ethnic populations with high levels of organizational solidarity (measured by membership, density, inclusivity, and other organizational factors) are likely to act collectively (along ethnic lines).

The second proposition links *changes* in access to resources to the likelihood of mobilization. Jenkins (1983, P. 532) summarizes this view: "The formation of movements is linked to improvements in the status of aggrieved groups, not because of grievances . . . but because these changes reduce the costs of mobilization and improve the likelihood of success." Applying this proposition to ethnic movements implies that increasing an ethnic group's access to valued resources increases the likelihood that the group will mobilize as ethnics.

Though the similarity of resource mobilization and competition theories of ethnic mobilization have been noted elsewhere (Nagel and Olzak, 1982), several important distinctions should be made. First, RM theory attempts to explain mobilization of all kinds and does not address directly *forms* that collective action takes. That is, it does not attempt to answer the question; under what conditions will ethnic action rather than class action occur? [See Garner and Zald (1982) for an exception.] Second, RM theory does not confront issues of timing (*when* a group is more or less likely to mobilize) directly, nor does it specify how much resources have to change to support mobilization (Tilly, 1978, P. 56).

III. COMPETITION THEORY

I have already suggested that ecological processes show how ethnic solidarity and occupational specialization strengthen ethnic boundaries in the presence of competition. This section discusses three instances of ethnic competition and their consequences for the dynamics of ethnic group boundaries and collective action. It emphasizes arguments that distinguish competition theory from those just discussed and that can be examined with available data.

A. Increases in Immigration and Migration

It is well known that migration and international immigration of ethnic populations provide a major source of change in the size and character of the labor force.[7] Although migration flows may be transitory and reversible, they tend to flow from regions of low demand and/or depressed wages toward regions of higher wages and greater demand. This increases ethnic competition, as SLM theory suggests. The voluntary (or forced) nature of migration and the skills and occupational histories of migrant workers determine how much of an actual threat is present.

Theory and research on employment of ethnic immigrants have not yet considered consequences for collective action. However, historians have noted that peak immigration flows may have inhibited one kind of collective action—union organization—around the turn of the century in the United States (Corbin, 1981; Davis, 1980; Cumbler, 1979). A large supply of cheap labor from Ireland, Germany, South Central Europe, and from the northern migration of rural blacks coincided with a period of industrialization, shifts to assembly line and production line work, and widespread attempts to unionize workers (as well as several economic depressions during this same period). In the view of many historians, as well as many nativistic movements blaming foreigners for economic problems, immigrants undercut the bargaining potential of nascent unions (Higham, 1955; Davis, 1980). Others show that the presence of immigrants contributed to a significant rise in "whites only" unions as one means to protect against the presence of foreign labor (Higham, 1955).

From this historical perspective, class mobilization and ethnic mobilization can be viewed as alternative strategies whose prevalence is shaped by the structure of work organization, the degree of segregation within factory or industry, and the wage price commanded by the various ethnic worker categories.

As immigrants or migrants enter urban labor markets (where multiple ethnic populations are more likely to reside), levels of ethnic contact and competition between immigrants and native-born increases. Furthermore, I expect that the size of the immigration or migration wave will have an independent effect on the levels of competition. The proposition suggested by this argument is:

PROPOSITION 1. *Large numbers of immigrants and migrants entering an urban labor market should initially produce rising levels of ethnic competition. To the extent that ethnic competition rises, ethnic collective action occurs.*

The argument suggested here parallels Bonacich's (1972) theory of ethnic antagonism but does not limit the conditions of the theory to those of a split labor market. Rather, the present argument implies that the impact of immigration is conditioned by an interaction effect between levels of immigration and economic well-being. The impact of increasing flows of immigrants or migrants having distinct ethnic identities on competition may intensify as economic contraction causes plant layoffs, business failures, and other widespread consequences of recessions.[8] However, the intensity of competition among ethnicities also depends on other structural factors, including shifts in the economy that *improve* immigrants' positions relative to others. The crucial point is that ethnic collective action occurs when competition levels among ethnic populations are raised so that groups come to compete in the same markets. Either downward mobility of once-favored groups or upward mobility of a disadvantaged immigrant group unleashes these competitive forces.

My argument also agrees with CDL theory *if* immigration means that a cultural division of labor develops within peripheral industries and thus creates the organizational and class bases for solidarity (Hechter, 1975). However, competition theory diverges from CDL theory because the former implies that, while economic hardship for immigrants may initially increase ethnic collective action directed against newcomers, increasing levels of wages and other resources available to immigrants may do so as well.

B. Immigration and Ethnic Enclaves

Another clue to understanding how waves of immigration trigger ethnic conflicts in open labor markets can be found in histories of ethnic enclaves. As noted above, ethnic immigrants and migrants commonly form dense interaction networks, exploit a common occupational niche, and share common institutions. In some cases, they may also gain higher than expected returns to capital investment because they can rely on a constant ethnic immigrant supply willing to work at low wages and on a captive enclave clientele (Wilson and Martin, 1982; Portes and Bach, 1985; Portes and Manning, this volume).

Ethnic immigrant enclaves are also bounded by community ties and familial networks; they were once referred to as being "institutionally complete" (Stinchcombe, 1965; Breton, 1964). This inclusiveness facilitates the use of an ethnic identity as the salient marker for loyalty in interaction of all kinds.

Waves of immigration produce considerable variation in the kinds and strength of enclave communities that are built. When institutions within the enclave are strong and can remain so for some time, the cultural boundaries around the enclave are encouraged. One way that ethnic enclaves have maintained their institutions is through continuous replacement fed by immigration flows. Enclave communities continuously face the threat of dissolution: through aging, geographical dispersion, occupational mobility, and movement of members out of the enclave. These threats of dissolution are intensified by a sudden decline in replacement of members, such as the case when most Chinese and European immigration dropped after 1924. Groups having substantial replacement flows and histories of strong ethnic institutions and community networks are far more likely to retain cultural, language, and other kinds of boundaries. The distinctiveness of ethnic boundaries is thus expected to be related to the history and size of migration and immigration flows as well as to the development of internal community institutions and organizations. In other words, I expect that immigration accelerates the rate of ethnic collective action when migrants are absorbed into already existing ethnic enclave communities. Immigration therefore has an interaction effect with the strength of ethnic organizations on the rates of ethnic collective action. When immigrant and migrant populations with strong enclaves also come to compete with other ethnic groups in the labor market, collective action along ethnic lines is likely to occur. All else being equal, I expect:

PROPOSITION 2. *Ethnic communities with ethnic enclaves can sustain longer periods of ethnic collective action than immigrant populations without enclave organizations.*

A second way in which ethnic enclaves encourage ethnic collective action is through the cumulative advantages attached to enclave capital formation and the potential for upward mobility for either enclave members or for the enclave enterprise as a whole (see Portes and Manning, this volume). Immigrant communities then can accumulate ethnic resources into marketable services or industries and eventually compete for customers with established firms. As case histories of Koreans, Japanese, Cubans, and many other groups show, favorable economic growth within enclaves can create successful intergenerational mobility for members out of the enclave. Such mobility may additionally increase ethnic conflict and competition, as former enclave members retain strong ethnic loyalties while directly competing with dominant ethnic groups for valued resources and jobs.[9]

C. Rates of Immigration

A third factor that appears to be related to bursts of ethnic conflict and protest is rapid increase in immigration. The rate of change in immigration may independently affect levels of competition in labor markets. Stated differently, a rapid influx of foreign-borns into a region has a greater impact on that region than a slow, even trickle. Competition perspectives on ethnicity imply that the rates of immigration strongly shape levels of perceived competition from incoming migrant populations and the reaction of host populations. The effect of the suddenness of arrival of a low-skilled population into a city on conflict and collective action by the native born depends on (1) the size of the native-born population and (2) availability of jobs, housing, etc.

Recent speculation from the Philadelphia Social History Project suggests that the rate of immigration interacts significantly with local, national, and international patterns of growth and decline in producing ethnic conflict [see Hershberg (1981), among others]. Rates of absorption of migrants into jobs depend on the rates of industrial expansion and on the match between jobs and skills of immigrants. The competition perspective advanced here implies that information on levels of economic success is crucial to understanding which ethnic groups experience hostility.

For economic conditions holding constant:

PROPOSITION 3. *Large and concentrated waves of immigration increase rates of ethnic collective action more than small and less concentrated waves of immigration.*

D. Economic Contraction and Tight Labor Markets

Competition theory implies that levels of competition rise when labor markets are slack, when real wages in occupations open to immigrants fall, and when depressions and recessions occur. Economic contraction shrinks the available number of jobs, so that those having achieved middle-level jobs and wages may be forced down the job queue to search for work, aggravating ethnic competition between unskilled newcomers and the downwardly mobile. Scattered evidence from studies on the location and timing of lynchings in Southern towns and rural areas suggest a similar dynamic may have been at work during peak economic crises in the Reconstruction period (Corzine, Creech, and Huff-Corzine, 1984).

This argument relates factors increasing levels of competition to levels of ethnic collective action. When jobs, wages, and business opportunities decline, ethnic competition rises and rates of ethnic collective action (at least initially) increase according to this view.

Resource mobilization theories suggest, on the other hand, that rising wage levels, particularly in jobs open to immigrants, constitute a resource for disadvantaged populations. Economic hardship theories, such as SLM and CDL theories, suggest that economic contraction increases the probability of ethnic collective action to the extent that it intensifies an ethnic division of labor.

Competition theories of ethnic collective action also imply a more complex relationship between economic hardship and competition stemming from increasing labor supply than has been noted thus far. Effects of immigration in this view become stronger when economic conditions worsen:

PROPOSITION 4. *Increasing rates and levels of immigration, therefore, interact with worsening economic conditions in affecting levels of ethnic collective action.*

To summarize, the competition theory proposed here holds that (1) increasing levels of immigration, (2) concentrated bursts of immigration, (3) economic contraction, and (4) interaction effects between economic contractions and large immigration waves increase rates of ethnic competition, which increases levels of ethnic collective action. RM models generally agree with the direction of (1) and (2), but suggest that increasing wages for immigrants may also incite ethnic collective action. Finally, economic hardship models stress that economic contractions trigger ethnic collective action when they reinforce or produce a cultural division of labor.

IV. PRELIMINARY RESULTS

This section uses data from my ongoing project on ethnic collective action to test some of the arguments already made. Here I report the first stage of the analysis, which tests arguments about the effects of ethnic competition and tight labor markets on the rates of ethnic collective action in urban America. All variables are measured at the national level. Economic indicators of tight labor markets, economic depression, and business failure rate are merged with event-histories of ethnic events in 80 cities taken together (Olzak and DiGregorio, 1985). I describe the usefulness of event-history analysis for evaluation of competition theory, and briefly discuss the estimators used to examine effects on the rate of ethnic collective action.

The time series on ethnic collective action runs from January 1, 1877, to December 31, 1889. I chose this time period because (1) immigration rates were high from 1880 through 1920 but also vary considerably within this period (see below) and (2) complete cycles of economic depression and recovery take place within the period. After consulting several census sources and National Bureau of Economic Research publications comparing various indices of business cycles, depressions and recessions, and business failures, I decided to begin the series in 1877 in order to capture the economic recovery in the latter half of 1878 following the depression of the 1870s. By beginning in 1877, I can analyze my hypotheses about economic contraction and recovery directly in this period of immigration increase.

A. Dependent Variable

Data on occurrence, participation, duration, and other dimensions of ethnic collective action have been collected for a system of 80 largest-population cities, using daily reports in *The New York Times* for the years 1877–1889. The coding instrument and coding rules have been summarized elsewhere (Olzak and Di-Gregorio, 1985). My strategy for coding collective action follows standard methodologies using newspapers to gather event counts developed by Tilly (1978), C. Tilly, L. Tilly, and R. Tilly (1975), Paige (1975), and more recently by Tarrow (1983).

A brief discussion of the definitions and operationalizations of ethnic collective action is useful before moving on to a description of the data and analysis. An *ethnic event* is judged to have occurred if (1) two or more persons are involved, in (2) a public event, that (3) makes ethnic claims, (4) based upon threats, perceived injustices, indignities, discrimination, or articulates a grievance against an ethnic or nationality group. An event is *public* when it is reported as such in a published historical newspaper account, and it is not a regularly scheduled *private* organizational meeting. Also excluded are random occurrences of violence or crime, where the participants are from different race or ethnic backgrounds but no ethnic content to the event is reported.

Note that the definition of an ethnic event includes two kinds of collective action, sometimes referred to as proactive and reactive (Tilly, 1978). I also distinguish between two kinds of events, defined with reference to the *target* or *object* of the collective action. *Ethnic conflict* is collective action involving confrontation between two or more ethnic populations. Five types of ethnic conflict have been uncovered so far: (1) spontaneous ethnic conflict instigated by native-born residents against one or more ethnic populations, (2) organized meetings of native-born residents opposing other ethnic population(s), (3) conflict between two identifiable ethnic populations, (4) conflict among more than two identifiable ethnic groups, and (5) ethnic confrontation among undifferentiated or unidentifiable ethnic groups.

The second type of collective action is *ethnic protest,* defined as collective action whose target is a government department, official, or agency, or the public at large. Event codes for protest include (1) ethnic or nationality group making a proactive claim for their civil rights, claim of discrimination, unequal treatment, or request for policy or legal change to redress the group's grievances; (2) ethnic protest meeting, having some organizational structure, making a claim for civil rights, claims of discrimination, or request to change ethnic policy or laws; and (3) ethnic protest aimed at a government office or agency.

Tables 1 and 2 report distributions of *ethnic protest events,* and Tables 3 and 4 report distributions of *ethnic conflict events* for 1877–1889. Table 1 shows that there were 28 protest events. A majority of protest events were spontaneous protests, unrelated to existing organizations or movements. An unexpected finding from this early period was that protest events constitute more than a third of all ethnic collective actions. Though we often assume that civil rights activity is a relatively recent phenomenon of the 1960s, Tables 1 and 2 dispute that claim.

Table 2 indicates the size categories of the protest events. Critics of newspapers as sources of data on events argue that newspapers are biased in favor of reporting large and violent events. Tables 2 and 3, taken together, provide some evidence against this criticism. They show that a fairly wide range of ethnic collective events was picked up by *The New York Times* in 1877–1889. Size is coded from (1) actual number of participants reported for 50% of the cases or (2) from keywords used in the newspaper account (e.g., "meeting hall," "several protesters," "hundreds of demonstrators").

TABLE 1.   Number of ethnic protest events instigated by ethnic groups, 1877–1889

| | Type of protest event | | | |
Ethnic group	Spontaneous gathering	Meeting	Collective action aimed at government	Total
Black	8	5	0	13
Chinese	1	0	0	1
British	0	2	0	2
French	0	1	0	1
French Canadian	8	0	1	9
Jewish	0	1	0	1
Irish	0	1	0	1
	17	10	1	28

TABLE 2. Size and type of ethnic protest events instigated in 1877–1889

| Size | Type of protest event | | | |
	Spontaneous gathering	Meeting	Collective action aimed at government	Total
Small group	2	1	0	3
Medium-size group	4	7	0	11
Large, mass group	7	2	1	10
Mob, large crowd	4	0	0	4
	17	10	1	28

Table 3 describes the more numerous ethnic conflict events. All but five events were instigated by white native-borns against an ethnic or racial population. Clearly the protagonist in most ethnic conflict was the native white community during this period. While most ethnic conflict events mobilized fewer than 1000 persons, five events during this period had more. Three of these large events were directed against the Chinese, during the virulent attacks against the Chinese in the 1880s in Denver, Seattle, and San Francisco. The other two events having more than 1000 participants involved interethnic conflict, between Italians and Irish in one case and Irish and native-born whites in the other. Both ethnic protest and ethnic conflict events range in size between 50 and 500

TABLE 3. Size and type of ethnic conflict events, 1877–1889

| | Size | | | | | |
	Small group	Medium-size group	Large mass assembly	Mob, crowd	Thousands	Total
Majority against Chinese	1	7	7	14	3	32
Majority against Blacks	0	4	2	2	0	8
Majority against W. Europeans	0	0	1	0	1	2
Majority against S. Europeans	0	2	0	0	0	2
Two or more ethnic groups against each other	0	2	2	0	1	5
Total	1	15	12	16	5	49

TABLE 4. Relationship of violence to type of conflict event, 1877–1889

	Violent	Nonviolent	Total
Whites against blacks or Chinese	7	33	40
Whites against foreign-born	2	2	4
Interethnic conflict	2	3	5
	11	38	49 (100%)

persons, though protests against Chinese and Blacks appear to mobilize larger numbers than other kinds of ethnic conflict events (see Table 3).

Table 4 shows the frequency of violence by type of event for conflict events. Violence is recorded if weapons were involved or if personal or property damage was reported or even threatened. Contrary to the expectation that violent events would dominate counts from *The New York Times,* Table 4 shows that most events reported were nonviolent. The ratio of violent to nonviolent event is *not* higher for blacks and Chinese than for other recipients of ethnic conflict, although the number of events in each cell is too small to compare with any confidence. Even so, it is clear that blacks and Chinese are not the sole targets of violent acts during this period.

Table 5 shows the frequency of events standardized by city population (in 10,000s). At first glance, the absolute number of events appears greatest in San Francisco and, as we might expect, in New York City. Yet when the frequency of ethnic collective action is expressed per 10,000 population in 1890, Fall River, San Francisco, and Seattle have the highest per capita incidence of ethnic activity.

B. Independent Variables

Independent variables used in this analysis include *immigration, real wage rates of common laborers,* an *interaction* term that is the product of these two variables, *the business failure rate,* and *changes in the rate of immigration (percent change).* Immigration and changes in the rate of immigration (expressed as percent change) were recorded from the *Historical Statistics of the United States* (1976).

The real wage rate is taken from David and Solar's (1977) series of the daily wages of workers in unskilled occupations divided by consumer prices.[10] This series provides an estimate of the standard of living of unskilled laborers, standardized to equal one for 1860. This measure refers to jobs most likely to be filled by immigrants. For example, my analysis of occupational segregation of foreign-borns using census data from 1870 and 1880 across 30 cities shows, for

TABLE 5. Cities experiencing ethnic collective action, 1877–1889[a]

Cities	Number of events	Number of events per capita (per 10,000 pop.)	Percent foreign parentage	Percent colored in population
Albany, NY	1	0.11	63	1
Atlanta, GA	1	0.15	7	43
Baltimore, MD	2	0.04	37	14
Charleston, NC	1	0.18	14	56
Cincinnati, OH	1	0.03	69	4
Columbus, OH	1	0.12	46	6.7
Denver, CO	2	0.19	46	4
Detroit, MI	1	0.05	77	1.6
Fall River, MA	8	1.08	83	0.2
Jersey City, NJ	1	0.06	73	1.3
Louisville, KY	3	0.19	43	18
New Orleans, LA	2	0.08	45	27
New York, NY	15	0.10	80	2
Philadelphia, PA	1	0.01	78	3
Portland, OR	2	0.43	58	11
Richmond, VA	2	0.25	11	40
St. Louis, MI	2	0.04	67	6
San Francisco, CA	24	0.80	78	9.5
Sacramento, CA	1	0.38	61	8
Seattle, WA	3	0.70	53	1.8
Worcester, MA	1	0.12	62	1
	$N = 77$			

[a]All population figures are from 1890 census, Table 16. Aggregate white, colored population distributed according to native or foreign parentage.

example, that common laborers were 59% foreign-born, while the labor force as a whole was only 39% foreign-born. Declines in wages of common laborers mean that the labor markets for immigrant workers worsen and that competition for such jobs rises.

Another set of variables measures economic downturns, indicated by the business failure rate and a dummy variable for depression years. The business failure rate was coded from the *Historical Statistics of the United States,* while the qualitative coding of depression years is from Thorp and Mitchell (1926).

Figure 1 shows counts of events by year, and Figure 2 shows the cumulative frequency of ethnic collective action in continuous time for this period. Increments in Figure 2 tell the exact times of events. The data in Figure 2 provide the basis for analyzing the effects of the independent variables on the rate of ethnic collective action. Each upward shift in the cumulative count represents an incident of ethnic collective action.

Figure 3 shows the covariation of immigration, real wage rates, and yearly

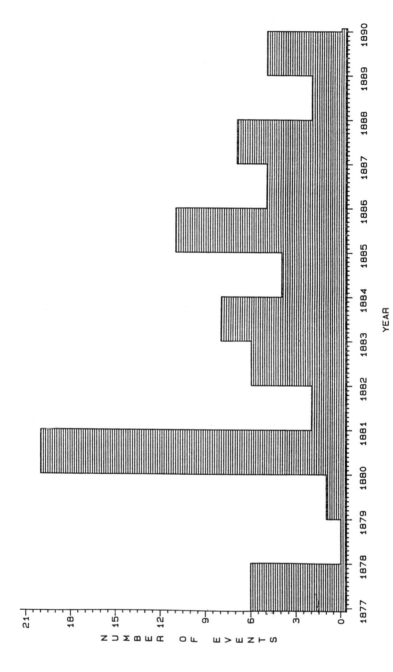

FIG. 1. Ethnic collective events by year, 1877–1889.

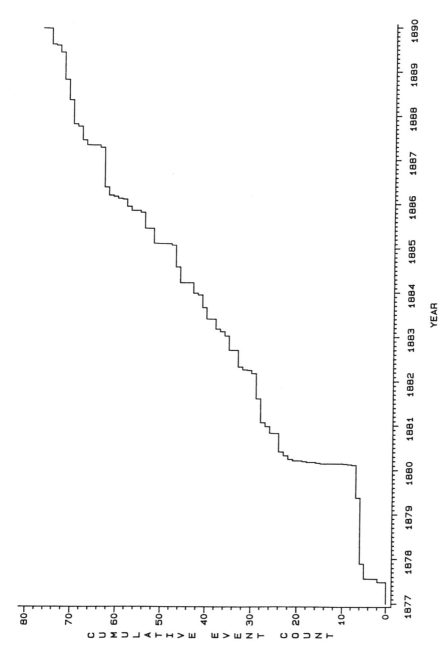

FIG. 2.   Cumulative frequency of ethnic collective events, 1877–1889.

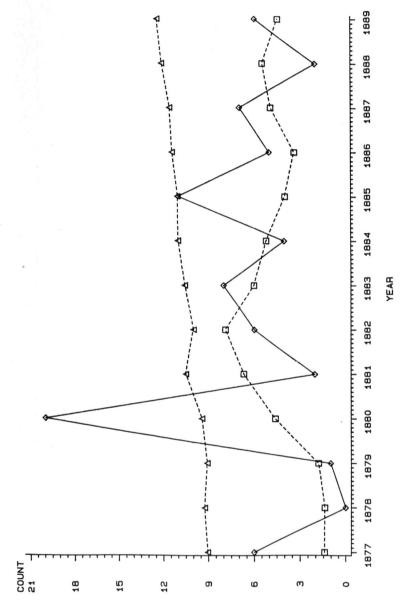

FIG. 3. Immigration, wage rates, and ethnic collective events, 1877–1889. Diamond, number of ethnic events; square, immigration in 100,000s; triangle, real wage of common laborers, ×10.

counts of ethnic collective action over the 1877–1889 period. Immigration and collective action co-vary over this period. The tables that follow show that this simple relationship holds up in multivariate analysis.

C. Models

To study the process of ethnic collective action, I have used the modeling framework developed by Coleman (1981) and Tuma and Hannan (1984), among others. The simplest model discussed here concerns the rate of undifferentiated ethnic collective action (both ethnic protest and conflict events). Four assumptions characterized the model:

(1)   Events of ethnic collective are viewed as realizations of a continuous-time stochastic process (events can occur at any time).

(2)   The transition rates governing the occurrence of collective actions depend log-linearly on observable covariates measured at the beginning of each spell (and assumed to be constant over the duration of the spell).

(3)   There is no historical variation in the rates, aside from the variation due to changing levels of the covariates; in particular, there is no period dependence.

(4)   Rates may vary with duration (time since the last event); for example, long durations between events may be related to low probabilities of future events. Since I do not know the functional form of duration-dependence, I assume that a nuisance function, defined in duration time, affects rates during each spell in the *same* way.

Taken together, these assumptions imply that the rate of ethnic collective action depends on a set of observed covariates and on an unobserved nuisance function that affects the timing of events in the same way for all spells [in the following equation this is represented by $h(t - t_n)$].

A model for the occurrences of the $(n + 1)$th event that fits these assumptions is

$$r(t - t_n) = \exp(\alpha_0 + \alpha_1 \text{ Immig}_t + \alpha_2 \text{ Real wages}_t + \alpha_3 \text{ Immig} \times \text{Real wages}_t) \cdot h(t - t_n)$$

where t is time and t_n is time of the previous (nth) event. (For concreteness, I have included what turns out to be the core set of covariates.)

My objective is to estimate the causal effects, the effects of variables such as immigration and real wages, and their interaction on the rates of ethnic collective action. The dependent variable in the following analysis is actually the instantaneous rate of occurrence of ethnic collective action. The raw data on events used to estimate the effects on the rates are the durations ("waiting time") between spells of ethnic collective action (see Figure 2). The data used to create the dependent variable are the dates of ethnic events.

D. Estimation Techniques

Given the assumptions that the process is driven by instantaneous transition rates that depend on a set of observed covariates and an unobserved nuisance function, Cox's (1975) partial likelihood estimator provides asymptotically unbiased estimates of the parameters of the kinds of models discussed above (Tuma and Hannan, 1984; Coleman, 1981, pp. 186–190).[11]

The actual estimation technique involves calculating durations ($u_n = t_{n+1} - t_n$), and associating them with levels of covariates at the beginning of a spell. This means that the covariates (such as immigration, real wage rates, etc.) are estimated to have positive effects on the rates if high levels of the covariates are associated with brief waiting times between events.

E. Results

Table 6 presents estimates of the effects of national economic and environmental variables on the rate of ethnic collective action in the set of large urban places. Many coefficients differ significantly from zero in the directions predicted by the theory just presented. Taken together, results on models including the effects of national level changes in real wage rates of common laborers, immigration flows, economic depression, and business failure rates show strong support for the hypothesis that tight labor markets and increasing levels of ethnic competition increases the rate of ethnic activity.

1. Effects of Immigration and Tight Labor Markets

Competition theory predicts that increases in levels and rates of immigration, which increase the number of workers in the labor pool, increase competition for jobs and other resources and thus stimulate ethnic collective action. The estimates of this effect in Table 6 are large and significant. So, too (in most models), is the effect of rising rates of immigration. Thus, levels *and* bursts of immigrant flows increase rates of ethnic collective action as expected by Propositions 1 and 2.[12] While variations in rates of immigration by region no doubt directly affect rates of conflict, it is clear that variations in immigration at the national level do, too.

The main effect of real wages of common laborers in Table 6 agrees with the prediction of resource mobilization theory (if increases in wage levels available to immigrant and migrant groups is considered an upward shift in resources available to the disadvantaged). Rises in real wages of common laborers *increase* rates of collective action. This finding clearly contradicts cultural division of labor theories that imply that hardship produces ethnic activity and mobilization among exploited groups. As Figure 3 suggests, the main effect of real wages of laborers is not an artifact of two time trends moving in parallel. In fact, over the 1877–1889 period, the real wage rate of common laborers varies considerably from a low of 90 to a high of 1.24 (relative to the 1860 baseline of unity).

TABLE 6. Partial likelihood estimates of effects on rates of ethnic collective action in American cities, 1877–1889[a,b]

	Model					
	(1)	(2)	(3)	(4)	(5)	(6)
Immigration, in 100s	0.0025**	0.0033**	0.0040***	0.0024*	0.0043**	0.0043**
	(0.0012)	(0.0014)	(0.0016)	(0.0014)	(0.0017)	(0.0018)
Real wage of common laborers$_t$	8.64	10.98**	14.78***	9.64**	20.72*	13.13*
	(5.36)	(5.66)	(6.66)	(5.81)	(12.74)	(6.99)
Immig × Rwage in 100s$_t$	−0.0025**	−0.0032**	−0.0038***	−0.0024*	−0.0042**	−0.0040**
	(0.0012)	(0.0014)	(0.0015)	(.0014)	(0.0017)	(0.0016)
Business failure rate$_t$		0.0079	0.0302**		0.029**	0.027*
		(0.0072)	(0.0146)		(0.015)	(0.016)
% Change in immigration			0.816*	0.433	0.815*	0.420
			(0.467)	(0.317)	(0.474)	(0.766)
Depression year$_t$				0.768**		
				(0.366)		
Linear time trend					−0.132	
					(0.234)	
Ratio of laborers/ machinists wage$_t$						2.63
						(8.73)
Chinese immig, in 100s						−0.003
						(0.003)
Number of spells	77	77	77	77	77	77
Uncensored spells	76	76	76	76	76	76
χ^2	7.40	8.78	12.08	12.25	12.39	13.40
df	3	4	5	5	6	7

[a]Asymptotic standard errors in parentheses.
[b]Significance: *$p < 0.10$, **$p < 0.05$, ***$p < 0.01$.

Competition theory predicts that the real wage of common laborers affects rates of ethnic collective action only insofar as levels of competition are affected. This argument clearly requires an interaction effect between immigration *and* an indicator of decreasing economic opportunity for those competing for scarce jobs. In other words, competition arguments (summarized in Proposition 4) suggest that immigration increases ethnic competition but only to the extent that real wages of those competing in the immigrant niche (common laborer jobs) are declining. An interaction term between real wages of common laborers and immigration levels (Immig × Rwage) is included in all models in Table 6 to capture this effect. The tables present strong evidence of this interaction. The likelihood ratio test statistic comparing models with and without this interaction term equals 6.28 with 1 degree of freedom, which is significant at the 0.02 level.[13]

Inclusion of the interaction term in Table 6 shows that *all three variables*— immigration, real wages, and the interaction between them—must be taken together to make inferences about the effects of competition on rates of ethnic collective action. For example, in model 3 of Table 6, the effect of immigration is 0.0040*** and the effect of real wages is 14.78**; however, these main effects are partly offset by a (highly significant) negative interaction effect equal to −0.0038**. As wages go from a high of 1.24 to a low of 0.90, the positive effect of immigration on the rate of ethnic collective action gets larger. Thus the implication from competition theory stated in Proposition 4, that immigration affects ethnic collective action more severely in tight labor markets, is supported in virtually all specifications in models from Table 6.

Competition and CDL theories also predict that general economic contraction increases rates of ethnic collective action. The business failure rate has been shown to be a good indicator of the economic health of the nation, especially in the nineteenth century. It also foreshadows falling demand for labor and depressions and recessions in this historical period. I argue that economic depression and tight labor markets (caused by an increase in the business failure rates) causes ethnic competition to intensify in a shrinking economy. By this argument, an increase in business failures should increase rates of ethnic collective action. Models 2, 3, 5, and 6 in Table 6 show positive and mostly significant effects of the business failure rate on rates of ethnic collective action. In models 3 and 5, the estimated effect of the business failure rate is more than twice its standard error, and it is nearly twice its standard error in model 6, Model 4 contains another specification of economic contraction, a dummy variable indicating whether or not the year was a depression year. This index also has a strong positive effect on the rate of ethnic collective action.

A question arises about why two seemingly similar indicators of economic contraction, the business failure rate and real wages of common laborers, should have opposing effects. That is, in Table 6 the business failure rate increases ethnic collective action, while declining wages decrease it. But the real wage of common laborers affects the rate as part of a system of variables. When taken together, these effects reveal a pattern consistent with the argument that factors increasing ethnic competition produce ethnic collective action, as noted above. However, the business failure rate does not interact with immigration levels (or changing immigration levels) in affecting the rate (results not shown). This suggests that the main effect of economic contraction is to increase rates of ethnic collective action as CDL theory would expect. In fact, the addition of an interaction of the business failure rate with immigration had no effect whatsoever on estimates of other variables in the models.

2. Additional Economic Effects and a Time Trend

A log-linear time trend variable was included in many of the models reported here. Models including this trend explore the possibility that the variation in rates of ethnic collective action is a function of a secular trend, increasing (or decreasing) over the observation period. Within this period, the trend has no effect either on the rate or on the effects of other explanatory variables described above. Model 5 in Table 6 gives one example.

Table 6 also includes models testing various plausible arguments about the effects of relative wages, using a measure of *the ratio of real wages of common laborers to real wages of machinists.* I suspected that when the wage gap between common laborers and machinists narrowed in this period, rates of ethnic collective action would rise. Model 6 of Table 6 shows that this ratio does not affect the rate. It is the absolute wage rate of common laborers, and its interaction with immigration, that directly affects the rate of ethnic collective action. Contrary to CDL arguments that as this ratio *decreases,* ethnic conflict rises, I find no effect of *relative* economic hardship for ethnic laborers.

To test for the possibility that the peaks in ethnic collective action can be accounted for by Chinese immigration *per se,* I estimated models that examined the levels of Chinese immigration, holding constant total immigration. Estimates of model 6 in Table 6 make clear that Chinese immigration has little effect on ethnic collective action (at the national level, at least) and that its addition to the model has no effect on the relative impact of other variables included. In model 6 in Table 6 both total immigration and the changing rate of total immigration significantly affect the rate, despite the fact that Chinese immigration rose substantially in 1879–1880. when levels of ethnic collective action peaked (see Figure 1).[14]

V. CONCLUSION

What causes ethnic collective action in American cities in the late nineteenth century? At this point, we have some preliminary answers consistent with several theories outlined above. Levels of competition caused by (1) high levels of ethnic immigration to the United States, (2) sharp increases in the influx of these immigrants, (3) increases in real wages of common laborers, the occupational niche most likely to be filled by immigrants and black migrants to American cities, and (4) tight labor markets, indicated by depressions and high numbers of business failures, all affect rates of collective action.

These findings have implications for the theories of ethnic collective action reviewed earlier in this chapter. They suggest that when wages of immigrants and migrants improve, ethnic collective action increases. These findings also support resource mobilization arguments implying that raising wages of immigrant laborers will increase the likelihood of ethnic conflict and protest. On the other hand, *general* economic contraction works in ways expected by CDL theories.

Yet the issue of ethnic competition in combination with economic hardship is more complex than existing theories have held, as the interaction effect suggest. Competition theory, with its emphasis on the dynamics of ethnic participation in various occupational niches, goes far in explaining why this interaction occurs. It is when high levels of immigration or rapid increases of immigration combine with economic contraction that the competition struggle among ethnic groups is intensified.

ACKNOWLEDGMENTS

An earlier version of the theoretical portion of this paper was presented to the Annual Meetings of the American Sociological Association in 1983. The author would like to thank Edna Bonacich, Michael Hannan, Joane Nagel, and Charles Ragin for their helpful comments and criticisms on earlier drafts. This research was funded by NSF grant SES-8420173.

NOTES

[1]Ethnic boundaries commonly attach to productive activities and forms of social organization. This is particularly true of nonindustrial societies, though Harris (1964) presented convincing evidence that *Indios* in Latin America are currently labeled primarily by what they do, rather than on skin color or some other racial/ethnic marker. Haaland (1969) describes how individuals come to adopt alternative ethnic group behaviors and productive practices, which opens the possibility for changing ethnic labels. Barth's (1969) example of herders living alongside agriculturalists in the Swat, North Pakistan, demonstrates the principle that ethnic boundaries can be stable when non-overlapping productive activities engage adjacent populations.

[2]This holds for capital investment within this enclave and mobility of members outside the enclave.

[3]See Hechter *et al.* (1982), Hechter (1982), and Banton (1983) for an application of rational choice models to issues of ethnic and other kinds of group solidarity and the likelihood of collective action. Rational choice theory predicts that *ethnic* collective action will occur when the benefits attached to ethnicity rise. The key problem for rational choice models in explaining ethnic collective

action is to specify how those costs and benefits actually occur and are weighted by individuals and groups. Rational choice models are otherwise consistent with others that argue that ethnic organizations are used to achieve ethnic collective action.

[4]The present chapter considers "ethnic antagonism," as defined by Bonacich (1972, 1976), as an instance of ethnic collective action, one in which the ethnic movement in on the part of the dominant ethnic population against some subordinate group. Bonacich (1976, p. 549) lists racism, prejudice, lynching, discrimination, segregation laws, and exclusionary movements as examples of "ethnic antagonism."

[5]See Baron and Bielby (1980), Kalleberg, Wallace, and Althauser (1981), and Hodson and Kaufman (1982) for debates over *which* level of analysis is most appropriate for distinguishing between primary and secondary labor markets.

[6]See Kluegel (1978) and Kalleberg *et al.* (1981) for empirical evidence.

[7]See, for example, the 1982 Special Issue on Theory and Methods in Migration and Ethnic Research, *International Migration Review*.

[8]Piore (1979), among others, has shown how guestworkers from Turkey, Greece, and Italy, prior to the stagflation of the 1970s, filled unskilled manual and low-level service jobs in Western Europe that were left vacant by native workers protected by unemployment compensation, health benefits, and other citizenship rights. However, when economic recession caused native workers in West Germany, France, Great Britain, and elsewhere to search for employment in niches monopolized by foreign guestworkers, violence directed toward the temporary migrants broke out, in some cases leading to cessation of the guestworker program and occasionally to deportation [see also Castels and Kosack (1975)]

[9]Which groups are more and less likely to produce such dynamics of economic growth curves remains a question of subsequent research and is outside of the scope of this chapter.

[10]David and Solar (1977, Appendix) report that the workday for such laborers was about 10–11 hours, and included such occupations as "unskilled road and canal construction workers, helpers (other than apprenticed artisans) in building trades, and some sprinkling of unskilled workers in unspecified 'mills' " (p. 58). As David and Solar report, handbills advertising such jobs simply stated the requirements as "Strong back, no previous training or experience necessary" (p. 60).

[11]The nuisance function may be defined in any measure of time. Social movement theories suggest that collective action may be a function of recent history—that is, that there may be unspecified effects of contagion, police repression, and other factors that affect the timing of events since the last event. Therefore, I define the nuisance function as a function of duration. In large samples, PL estimators have been shown to have good statistical properties (Cox, 1975; Efron, 1977). PL models also deal effectively with problems of right-censoring (see Tuma and Hannan, 1984).

[12]Addition of such variables as the number of patents issued, number of buildings constructed, and wage indexes of nonlaborer occupations do not change estimates of effects of immigration on ethnic conflict and protest (results not shown).

[13]The likelihood ratio χ^2 test statistic for each model is used (1) to compare the models to a constant rate model, that is, to a model in which exogenous variables have no effect (coefficients are 0), and (2) to compare one model against others in a series of nested models, to see if the addition of one or more variables to a baseline model improves significantly over the restricted (or more parsimonious) model. When models including additional variables show such improvement, I note this. All models presented improve significantly over a constant rate model.

[14]I suspect that the impact of specific ethnic immigration will be more powerful in my city-level analyses currently underway. For example, rates of ethnic collective action in San Francisco ought to be related to variation in Chinese immigration over this period, but this may not be so in other cities. The next stage of my research project will test this and other hypotheses about ethnic enclaves with city level data. Proposition 2 regarding the impact of established ethnic enclaves on the duration of ethnic collective action also awaits the analyses at city and ethnic group levels (Olzak and Di-Gregorio, 1985).

REFERENCES

BANTON, M. (1983). *Racial and ethnic competition*. Cambridge: Cambridge University Press.
BARON, J. N., AND BIELBY, W. T. (1980). Bringing the firms back in: Stratification, segmentation, and the organization of work. *American Sociological Review* **45**:735–765.
BARTH, FREDERIK (1969). *Ethnic groups and boundaries*. Boston: Little, Brown.
BLALOCK, H. M., JR. (1967). *Toward a theory of minority group relations*. New York: Wiley.
BODNAR, J. R., SIMON, R., and WEBER, M. P. (1982). *Lives on their own: Blacks, Italians, and Poles in Pittsburgh, 1900–1960*. Urbana: University of Illinois Press.
BONACICH, EDNA (1972). A theory of ethnic antagonism: The split labor market. *American Sociological Review* **37**:547–559.
BONACICH, EDNA (1976). Advanced capitalism and black/white relations. *American Sociological Review* **41**:31–51.
BONACICH, EDNA (1979). The past, present, and future of split labor market theory. In *Research in race and ethnic relations* (C. B. Marrett and C. Leggon, eds.), vol. 1, pp. 17–64. New York: JAI Press.
BRETON, R. (1964). Institutional completeness of ethnic communities and the personal relations of immigrants. *American Journal of Sociology* **84**:293–318.
BRIDGES, W. P. (1980). Industrial marginality and female employment: A new appraisal. *American Sociological Review* **45**:58–75.
CASTLES, S., and KOSACK, G. (1973). *Immigrant workers and class structure in Western Europe*. London: Oxford University Press.
COLEMAN, J. S. (1981). *Longitudinal data analysis*. New York: Basic Books.
CORBIN, D. A. (1981). *Life, work, and rebellion in the coal fields: The Southern West Virginia Miners, 1880–1922*. Urbana: University of Illinois Press.
CORZINE, J., CREECH, S., and HUFF-CORZINE, L. (1984). The tenant labor market and lynching in the South: A test of the split labor market theory. Paper presented to the American Sociological Association in San Antonio, Tex.
COX, D. R. (1975). Partial likelihood. *Biometrika* **62**:269–276.
CUMBLER, J. (1979). *Working-class community in industrial america*. Westport, Conn.: Greenwood Press.
DAVID, P. A., and SOLAR, P. (1977). A bicentary contribution to the history of the cost of living in America. *Research in Economic History* **2**:1–80.
DAVIS, M. (1980). Why the U.S. working class is different. *National Labor Review* (October):5–44.
DOERINGER, P., and PIORE, M. (1971). *Internal labor markets and manpower analysis*. Lexington, Mass.: Heath.
EDWARDS, R. C. (1979). *Contested terrain*. New York: Basic Books.
EFRON, B. (1977). The efficiency of Cox's likelihood function for censored data. *Journal of the American Statistical Association*. **72**:557–565.
GARNER, R. A., and ZALD, M. N. (1982). *Social movement sectors and systematic constraint: A structural theory of social movements*. Ann Arbor, Michigan: Center for Research on Social Movements, University of Michigan.
HAALAND, G. (1969). Economic determinants in ethnic processes. In *Ethnic groups and boundaries* (F. Barth, ed.), pp. 58–73. Boston: Little Brown and Company.
HANNAN, M. T. (1979). The dynamics of ethnic boundaries in modern states. In *National development and the world system* (J. Meyer and M. T. Hannan, eds.) pp. 253–275. Chicago: University of Chicago Press.
HARRIS, M. (1964). *Patterns of race in the Americas*. New York: Walker.
HAWLEY, A. (1945). Dispersion versus segregation: Apropos of a solution of race problems.

Papers of the Michigan Academy of Sciences, Arts and Letter. Ann Arbor, Michigan: University of Michigan.

HECHTER, M. (1975). *Internal colonialism.* Berkeley: University of California Press.

HECHTER, M. (1982). A theory of group solidarity. In *Choice models for buyer behavior research in marketing.* suppl. 1, pp. 285–324. New York: JAI Press.

HECHTER, M., D. FRIEDMAN, and APPLEBAUM, M. (1982). A theory of ethnic collective action. *International Migration Review* (Special issue: Theory and methods in migration and ethnic research, eds. A. Portes and C. Hirschman) **16**:412–434.

HERSCHBERG, T. (ed.) (1981). *Philadelphia: Work, space, family, and group experience in the nineteenth century.* New York: Oxford University Press.

HIGHAM, J. (1955). *Strangers in the land.* New Brunswick, New Jersey: Rutgers University Press.

HODSON, R., and KAUFMAN, R. L. (1982). Economic dualism: A critical review. *American Sociological Review* **47**:727–739.

JENKINS, J. C. (1983). Resource mobilization theory and the study of the social movements. *Annual Review of Sociology* **9**:527–553.

KALLEBERG, A. L., WALLACE, M., and ALTHAUSER, R. P. (1981). Economic segmentation, worker power, and income inequality. *American Journal of Sociology* **87**:651–683.

KLUEGEL, J. (1978). Causes and costs of racial exclusion. *American Sociological Review* **43**:285–301.

LIEBERSON, S. (1961). A societal theory of race relations. *American Sociological Review* **26**:902–908.

LIEBERSON, S. (1980). *A piece of the pie: Black and White immigrants since 1880.* New York: Academic Press.

MCADAM, D. (1983). Tactical innovation and the pace of insurgency. *American Sociological Review* **48**:735–754.

NAGEL, J., and OLZAK, S. (1982). Ethnic mobilization in new and old states: An extension of the competition model. *Social Problems* **30**:127–143.

NIELSEN, F. (1980). The Flemish movement in Belgium after World War II: A dynamic analysis. *American Sociological Review* **45**:76–94.

OLZAK, S.(1982). Ethnic mobilization in Quebec. *Ethnic and Racial Studies* **5**:253–275.

OLZAK, S. (1983). Contemporary ethnic mobilization. *Annual Review of Sociology* **9**:355–374.

OLZAK, S., and DIGREGORIO, D. (1985). Ethnic collective action. Project Manual. Department of Sociology. Cornell University, Ithaca, New York, Technical Report Series 85-1.

PAIGE, J. (1975). *AGRARIAN Agrarian revolution.* New York: Free Press.

PARK, R. (1950). *Race and culture.* Glencoe, Illinois: The Free Press.

PARK, R., and BURGESS, E. W. (1921). *Introduction to the science of sociology.* Chicago: University of Chicago Press.

PIORE, M. J. (1979). *Birds of passage: Migrant labor and industrial societies.* New York: Cambridge University Press.

PORTES, A., and BACH, R. L. (1985). *Latin journey: Cuban and Mexican immigrants in the United States.* Berkeley and Los Angeles: University of California Press.

RAGIN, C., and DAVIES, T. (1981). Welsh nationalism in context. *Research in Social Movements, Conflict and Change* **4**:215–233.

REICH, M. J., GORDON, D., and EDWARDS, R. C. (1973). Dual labor markets: A theory of labor market segmentation. *American Economic Review* **63**:359–364.

STINCHCOMBE, A. S. (1965). Social structure and organizations. In *Handbook of organizations* (J. March, ed.), pp. 142–193. Chicago: Rand McNally.

TARROW, S. (1983). *Struggling to reform.* Ithaca, N.Y.: Cornell University, Western Societies Program Series.

THORP, W. L. and MITCHELL, W. C. (1926). *Business annuals.* New York: National Bureau of Economic Research.

TILLY, C. (1973). Do communities act? *Sociological Inquiry* **43**:209–240.
TILLY, C. (1978). *From mobilization to revolution.* New York: Addison-Wesley.
TILLY, C., TILLY, L., and TILLY, R. (1975). *The rebellious century, 1830–1930.* Cambridge: Harvard University Press.
TUMA, N. B., and HANNAN, M. T. (1984). *Social dynamics.* New York: Academic Press.
WALDINGER, R. (1983). Ethnic enterprise: A critique and reformulation. Paper presented to the Annual Meeting of the American Sociological Association in Detroit.
WILSON, K., and MARTIN, W. A. (1982). Ethnic enclaves: A comparison of the Cuban and Black economies in Miami. *American Journal of Sociology* **88**:135–160.

2

The Immigrant Enclave:
Theory and Empirical
Examples

ALEJANDRO PORTES and ROBERT D. MANNING
Department of Sociology
Johns Hopkins University
Baltimore, Maryland 21218

I. INTRODUCTION

The purpose of this chapter is to review existing theories about the process of immigrant adaptation to a new society and to recapitulate the empirical findings that have led to an emerging perspective on the topic. This emerging view revolves around the concepts of different modes of structural incorporation and of the immigrant enclave as one of them. These concepts are set in explicit opposition to two previous viewpoints on the adaptation process, generally identified as assimilation theory and the segmented labor markets approach.

The study of immigrant groups in the United States has produced a copious historical and sociological literature, written mostly from the assimilation perspective. Although the experiences of particular groups varied, the common theme of these writings is the unrelenting efforts of immigrant minorities to surmount obstacles impeding their entry into the "mainstream" of American society (Handlin, 1941, 1951; Wittke, 1952; Child, 1943; Vecoli, 1977). From this perspective, the adaptation process of particular immigrant groups followed a sequential path from initial economic hardship and discrimination to eventual socioeconomic mobility arising from increasing knowledge of American culture and acceptance by the host society (Warner and Srole, 1945; Gordon, 1964; Sowell, 1981). The focus on a "core" culture, the emphasis on consensus-building, and the assumption of a basic patterned sequence of adaptation represent central elements of assimilation theory.

47

From this perspective, the failure of individual immigrants or entire ethnic groups to move up through the social hierarchies is linked either to their reluctance to shed traditional values or to the resistance of the native majority to accept them because of racial, religious, or other shortcomings. Hence, successful adaptation depends, first of all, on the willingness of immigrants to relinquish a ''backward'' way of life and, second, on their acquisition of characteristics making them acceptable to the host society (Eisenstadt, 1970). Throughout, the emphasis is placed on the social psychological processes of motivation, learning, and interaction and on the cultural values and perceptions of the immigrants themselves and those who surround them.

The second general perspective takes issue with this psychosocial and culturalist orientation as well as with the assumption of a single basic assimilation path. This alternative view begins by noting that immigrants and their descendants do not necessarily ''melt'' into the mainstream and that many groups seem not to want to do so, preferring instead to preserve their distinct ethnic identities (Greeley, 1971; Glazer and Moynihan, 1970). A number of writers have focused on the resilience of these communities and described their functions as sources of mutual support and collective political power (Suttles, 1968; Alba and Chamlin, 1983; Parenti, 1967). Others have gone beyond descriptive accounts and attempted to establish the causes of the persistence of ethnicity. Without exception, these writers have identified the roots of the phenomenon in the economic sphere and, more specifically, in the labor-market roles that immigrants have been called on to play.

Within this general perspective, several specific theoretical approaches exist. The first focuses on the situation of the so-called unmeltable ethnics—blacks, Chicanos, and American Indians—and finds the source of their plight in a history of internal colonialism during which these groups have been confined to specific areas and made to work under uniquely unfavorable conditions. In a sense, the role of colonized minorities has been to bypass the free labor market, yielding in the process distinct benefits both to direct employers of their labor and, indirectly, to other members of the dominant racial group (Blauner, 1972; Geschwender, 1978). The continuation of colonialist practices to our day explains, according to this view, the spatial isolation and occupational disadvantages of these minorities (Barrera, 1980).

A second approach attempts to explain the persistence of ethnic politics and ethnic mobilization on the basis of the organization of subordinate groups to combat a ''cultural division of labor.'' The latter confined members of specific minorities to a quasi-permanent situation of exploitation and social inferiority. Unlike the first view, this second approach does not envision the persistence of ethnicity as a consequence of continuing exploitation, but rather as a ''reactive formation'' on the part of the minority to reaffirm its identity and its interests (Hechter, 1977; Despres, 1975). For this reason, ethnic mobilizations are often most common among groups who have already abandoned the bottom of the social ladder and started to compete for positions of advantage with members of the majority (Nagel and Olzak, 1982).

A final variant focuses on the situation of contemporary immigrants to the United States. Drawing on the dual labor market literature, this approach views recent immigrants as the latest entrants into the lower tier of a segmented labor market where women and other minorities already predominate. Relative to the latter, immigrants possess the advantages of their lack of experience in the new country, their legal vulnerability, and their greater initial motivation. All of these traits translate into higher productivity and lower labor costs for the firms that employ them (Sassen-Koob, 1980). Jobs in the secondary labor market are poorly paid, require few skills, and offer limited mobility opportunities. Hence, confinement of immigrants to this sector insures that those who do not return home are relegated to a quasi-permanent status as disadvantaged and discriminated minorities (Piore, 1975, 1979).

What these various structural theories have in common is the view of resilient ethnic communities formed as the result of a consistently disadvantageous economic position and the consequent absence of a smooth path of assimilation. These situations, ranging from slave labor to permanent confinement to the secondary labor market, are not altered easily. They have given rise, in time, either to hopeless communities of ''unmeltable'' ethnics or to militant minorities, conscious of a common identity and willing to support a collective strategy of self-defense rather than rely on individual assimilation.

These structural theories have provided an effective critique of the excessively benign image of the adaptation process presented by earlier writings. However, while undermining the former, the new structural perspective may have erred in the opposite direction. The basic hypothesis advanced in this chapter is that several identifiable modes of labor-market incorporation exist and that not all of them relegate newcomers to a permanent situation of exploitation and inferiority. Thus, while agreeing with the basic thrust of structural theories, we propose several modifications that are necessary for an adequate understanding of the different types of immigrant flows and their distinct processes of adaptation.

II. MODES OF INCORPORATION

In the four decades since the end of World War II, immigration to the United States has experienced a vigorous surge reaching levels comparable only to those at the beginning of the century (National Research Council, 1985, chapter 2). Even if one restricts attention to this movement, disregarding multiple other migrations elsewhere in the world, it is not the case that the inflow has been of a homogeneous character. Low-wage labor immigration itself has taken different forms, including temporary contract flows, undocumented entries, and legal immigration. More importantly, it is not the case that all immigrants have been directed to the secondary labor market. For example, since the promulgation of the Immigration Act of 1965, thousands of professionals, technicians, and craftsmen have come to the United States, availing themselves of the occupational preference categories of the law. This type of inflow, dubbed "brain drain" in the sending nations, encompasses today sizable contingents of immigrants from such countries as India, South Korea, the Philippines, and Taiwan, each an important contributor to U.S. annual immigration.

The characteristics of this type of migration have been described in detail elsewhere (Portes, 1976, 1981). Two such traits deserve mention, however. First, occupationally skilled immigrants—including doctors, nurses, engineers, technicians, and craftsmen—generally enter the "primary" labor market; they contribute to alleviate domestic shortages in specific occupations and gain access, after a period of time, to the mobility ladders available to native workers. Second, immigration of this type does not generally give rise to spatially concentrated communities; instead, immigrants are dispersed throughout many cities and regions, following different career paths.

Another sizable contingent of entrants whose occupational future is not easily characterized a priori are political refugees. Large groups of refugees, primarily from Communist-controlled countries, have come to the United States, first after the occupation of Eastern Europe by the Soviet Army, then after the advent of Fidel Castro to power in Cuba, and finally in the aftermath of the Vietnam War. Unlike purely "economic" immigrants, refugees have often received resettlement assistance from various governmental agencies (Zolberg, 1983; Keely, 1981). The economic adaptation process of one of these groups, the Cubans, will be discussed in detail in this chapter. For the moment, it suffices to note that all the available evidence runs contrary to the notion of a uniform entry of political refugees into low-wage secondary occupations; on the contrary, there are indications of their employment in many different lines of work.

A third mode of incorporation has gained the attention of a number of scholars in recent years. It consists of small groups of immigrants who are inserted or insert themselves as commercial intermediaries in a particular country or region. These "middleman minorities" are distinct in nationality, culture, and sometimes race from both the superordinate and subordinate groups to which they relate (Bonacich, 1973; Light, 1972). They can be used by dominant elites as a buffer to deflect mass frustration and also as an instrument to conduct commercial activities in impoverished areas. Middlemen accept these risks in exchange for the opportunity to share in the commercial and financial benefits gained through such instruments as taxation, higher retail prices, and usury. Jews in feudal and early modern Europe represent the classic instance of a middleman minority. Other examples include Indian merchants in East Africa, and Chinese entrepreneurs in Southeast Asia and throughout the Pacific Basin (Bonacich and Modell, 1980, chapter 1). Contemporary examples in the United States include

Jewish, Korean, and other Oriental merchants in inner-city ghetto areas and Cubans in Puerto Rico (Kim, 1981; Cobas, 1984).

Primary labor immigration and middleman entrepreneurship represent two modes of incorporation that differ from the image of an homogeneous flow into low-wage employment. Political refugees, in turn, have followed a variety of paths, including both of the above as well as insertion into an ethnic enclave economy. The latter represents a fourth distinct mode. Although frequently confused with middleman minorities, the emergence and structure of an immigrant enclave possess distinct characteristics. The latter have significant theoretical and practical implications, for they set apart groups adopting this entry mode from those following alternative paths. We turn now to several historical and contemporary examples of immigrant enclaves to clarify their internal dynamics and causes of their emergence.

III. IMMIGRANT ENCLAVES

Immigration to the United States before World War I was, overwhelmingly, an unskilled labor movement. Impoverished peasants from southern Italy, Poland, and the eastern reaches of the Austro-Hungarian Empire settled in dilapidated and crowded areas, often immediately adjacent to their points of debarcation, and took any menial jobs available. From these harsh beginnings, immigrants commenced a slow and often painful process of acculturation and economic mobility. Theirs was the saga captured by innumerable subsequent volumes written from both the assimilation and the structural perspectives.

Two sizable immigrant groups did not follow this pattern, however. Their most apparent characteristic was the economic success of the first generation, even in the absence of extensive acculturation. On the contrary, both groups struggled fiercely to preserve their cultural identity and internal solidarity. Their approach to adaptation thus directly contradicted subsequent assimilation predictions concerning the causal priority of acculturation to economic mobility. Economic success and ''clannishness'' also earned for each minority the hostility of the surrounding population. These two immigrant groups did not have a language, religion, or even race in common and they never overlapped in significant numbers in any part of the United States. Yet, arriving at opposite ends of the continent, Jews and Japanese pursued patterns of economic adaptation that were quite similar both in content and in their eventual consequences.

A. Jews in Manhattan

The first major wave of Jewish immigration to the United States consisted of approximately 50,000 newcomers of German origin, arriving between 1840 and

1870. These immigrants went primarily into commerce and achieved, in the course of a few decades, remarkable success. By 1900, the average income of German-Jewish immigrants surpassed that of the American population (Rischin, 1962). Many individuals who started as street peddlers and small merchants had become, by that time, heads of major industrial, retail, and financial enterprises.

The second wave of Jewish immigration exhibited quite different characteristics. Between 1870 and 1914, over two million Jews left the Pale of Settlement and other Russian-dominated regions, escaping Czarist persecution. Major pogroms occurred before and during this exodus (Dinnerstein, 1977). Thus, unlike most immigrants of the period, the migration of Russian and Eastern Europe Jews was politically motivated and their move was much more permanent. In contrast to German Jews, who were relatively well educated, the Yiddish-speaking newcomers came, for the most part, from modest origins and had only a rudimentary education. Although they viewed the new Russian wave with great apprehension, German Jews promptly realized that their future as an ethnic minority depended on the successful integration of the newcomers (Rischin, 1962). Charitable societies were established to provide food, shelter, and other necessities, and private schools were set up to teach immigrants English, civics, and the customs of the new country (Howe and Libo, 1979).

Aside from its size and rapidity of arrival, turn-of-the-century Jewish immigration had two other distinct characteristics. First was its strong propensity toward commerce and self-employment in general in preference to wage labor; as German Jews before them, many Russian immigrants moved directly into street peddling and other commercial activities of the most modest sort. Second was its concentration into a single, densely populated urban area—the lower East Side of Manhattan. Within this area, those who did not become storekeepers and peddlers from the start found employment in factories owned by German Jews, learning the necessary rudiments for future self-employment (Sowell, 1981, chapter 4).

The economic activities of this population created, in the course of two decades, a dense network of industrial, commercial, and financial enterprises. Close physical proximity facilitated exchanges of information and access to credit and raw materials. Characteristic of this emerging Jewish enclave is that production and marketing of goods was not restricted to the ethnic community, but went well beyond it into the general economy. Jews entered the printing, metal, and building trades; they became increasingly prominent in jewelry and cigar-making; above all, the garment industry became the primary domain of Jewish entrepreneurship, with hundreds of firms of all sizes engaged in the trade (Rischin, 1962; Howe and Libo, 1979).

The economic success of many of these ventures did not require and did not entail rapid acculturation. Immigrants learned English and those instrumental aspects of the new culture required for economic advancement. For the rest, they preferred to remain with their own and maintained, for the most part, close adherence to their original religion, language, and values (Wirth, 1956; Howe, 1976). Jewish enclave capitalism depended, for its emergence and advancement, precisely on those resources made available by a solidaristic ethnic community: protected access to labor and markets, informal sources of credit, and business information. It was through these resources that upstart immigrant enterprises could survive and eventually compete effectively with better-established firms in the general economy.

The emergence of a Jewish enclave in East Manhattan helped this group bypass the conventional assimilation path and achieve significant economic mobility in the course of the first generation, well ahead of complete acculturation. Subsequent generations also pursued this path, but the resources accumulated through early immigrant entrepreneurship were dedicated primarily to further the education of children and their entry into the professions. It was at this point that outside hostility became most patent, as one university after another established quotas to prevent the onrush of Jewish students. The last of these quotas did not come to an end until after World War II (Dinnerstein, 1977).

Despite these and other obstacles, the movement of Jews into higher education continued. Building on the economic success of the first generation, subsequent ones achieved levels of education, occupation, and income that significantly exceed the national average (Featherman, 1971; Sowell, 1981, chapter 4). The original enclave is now only a memory, but it provided in its time the necessary platform for furthering the rapid social and economic mobility of the minority. Jews did enter the mainstream of American society, but they did not do so starting uniformly at the bottom, as most immigrant groups had done; instead, they translated resources made available by early ethnic entrepreneurship into rapid access to positions of social prestige and economic advantage.

B. Japanese on the West Coast

The specific features of Japanese immigration differ significantly from the movement of European Jews, but their subsequent adaptation and mobility patterns are similar. Beginning in 1890 and ending with the enactment of the Gentlemen's Agreement of 1908, approximately 150,000 Japanese men immigrated to the West Coast. They were followed primarily by their spouses until the Immigration Act of 1924 banned any further Asiatic immigration. Although nearly 300,000 Japanese immigrants are documented in this period (Daniels, 1977), less than half of this total remained in the United States (Petersen, 1971). This is due, in contrast to the case of the Jews, to the sojourner character of Japanese immigrants: the intention of many was to accumulate sufficient capital for purchasing farm land or settling debts in Japan. Hence this population movement included commercial and other members of the Japanese middle class who, not incidentally, were explicitly sponsored by their national government.

The residential patterns of Japanese immigrants were not as concentrated as those of Jews in Manhattan, but they were geographically clustered. Almost two-thirds of the 111,010 Japanese reported in the U.S. Census of 1920 lived in California. Further, one-third of California's Japanese residents lived in Los Angeles County in 1940, while another one-third lived in six nearby counties (Daniels, 1977). However, it was not the residential segregation of Japanese immigrants but rather their occupational patterns that eventually mobilized the hostility of the local population.

Japanese immigrants were initially welcomed and recruited as a form of cheap agricultural labor. Their reputation as thrifty and diligent workers made them preferable to other labor sources. Nativist hostilities crystallized, however, when Japanese immigrants shifted from wage labor to independent ownership and small-scale farming. This action not only reduced the supply of laborers but it also increased competition for domestic growers in the fresh-produce market. In 1900, only about 40 Japanese farmers in the entire United States leased or owned a total of 5000 acres of farmland. By 1909, the number of Japanese farmers had risen to 6000 and their collective holdings exceeded 210,000 acres (Petersen, 1971). Faced with such ''unfair'' competition, California growers turned to the political means at their disposal. In 1913, the state legislature passed the first Alien Land Law, which restricted land ownership by foreigners. This legislation did not prove sufficient, however, and, in subsequent years, the ever-accommodating legislature passed a series of acts closing other legal loopholes to Japanese farming (Petersen, 1971).

These proscriptions, which barred most of the Japanese from the lands, accelerated their entry into urban enterprise. In 1909, Japanese entrepreneurs owned almost 3000 small shops in several Western cities. Forty percent of Japanese men in Los Angeles were self-employed. They operated businesses such as dry-cleaning establishments, fisheries, lunch counters, and produce stands that marketed the production of Japanese farms (Light, 1972).

The ability of the first-generation *Issei* to escape the status of stoop labor in agriculture was based on the social cohesion of their community. Rotating credit associations offered scarce venture capital, while mutual-aid organizations provided assistance in operating farms and urban businesses. Light (1972) reports that capitalizations as high as $100,000 were financed through ethnic credit networks. Economic success was again accompanied by limited instrumental acculturation and by careful preservation of national identity and values. It was the availability of investment capital, cooperative business associations, and marketing practices (forward and backward economic linkages) within the ethnic enclave that enabled Japanese entrepreneurs to expand beyond its boundaries and compete effectively in the general economy. This is illustrated by the production and marketing of fresh produce. In 1920, the value of Japanese crops was about 10% of the total for California, when the Japanese comprised less than 1% of the state's population; many retail outlets traded exclusively with a non-Japanese clientele (Light, 1972; Petersen, 1971).

During the early 1940s, the Japanese ethnic economy was seriously disrupted but not eliminated by the property confiscations and camp internments accompanying World War II. After the war, economic prosperity and other factors combined to reduce local hostility toward the Japanese. Older *Issei* and many of their children returned to small business, while other second-generation *Nisei*, like their Jewish predecessors, pursued higher education and entered the white-collar occupations *en masse*. This mobility path was completed by the third or *Sansei* generation, with 88% of their members attending college. Other third-generation Japanese have continued, however, the entrepreneurial tradition of their parents (Bonacich and Modell, 1980). Like Jews before them, Japanese-Americans have made use of the resources made available by early immigrant entrepreneurship to enter the mainstream of society in positions of relative advantage. The mean educational and occupational attainment of the group's 600,000 members surpasses at present all other ethnic and native groups, while its average family income is exceeded among American ethnic groups only by the Jews (Sowell, 1981).

IV. CONTEMPORARY EXAMPLES

As a mode of incorporation, the immigrant enclave is not only of historical interest since there are also several contemporary examples. Enclaves continue to be, however, the exception in the post–World War II period, standing in sharp contrast to the more typical pattern of secondary labor immigration. Furthermore, there is no guarantee that the emergence and development of contemporary ethnic enclaves will have the same consequences for their members that they had among turn-of-the-century immigrants.

A. Koreans in Los Angeles

The Korean community of Los Angeles is a recent product of liberalized U.S. immigration laws and strengthened political and economic ties between the two nations. Since 1965–1968, South Korean immigration to the United States has increased sixfold, swelling the Korean population of Los Angeles from less than 9000 in 1970 to over 65,000 in 1975. Approximately 60% of Korean immigrants settle in Los Angeles. In addition to increasing the size of this population flow, U.S. immigration law has altered its class composition. Korean immigrants come predominantly from the highly educated, Westernized, Christian strata of urban Korea. Their median educational attainment of 16 years is equivalent to an undergraduate education in the United States (Kim, 1981; Portes and Mozo, 1985).

Light (1979, 1980) attributes the business impulse of Korean immigrants to their "disadvantage" in the general U.S. labor market. It derives, he argues, from their inability to speak English rather than from discrimination by American employers. Bonacich (1978; Bonacich, Light, and Wong, 1977), in comparison, describes Korean entrepreneurship as a situational response to the growing commercial vaccuum arising from the consolidation of monopoly capitalism and the subsequent decline of small business. In this view, ethnic enterprise constitutes a disguised form of cheap labor that provides inexpensive goods and services for the center economy.

The origins of Korean enterprise may be uncertain but its existence is indisputable. Bonacich estimates that 4000 or one-fourth of all Korean families in Los Angeles County owned their business in 1976. The propensity for self-employment among this minority is three times greater than among the total urban labor force of Los Angeles (Bonacich, 1978). Light consulted published Korean business directories, which are biased against firms with nonethnic clients, and arrived at a conservative estimate of 1142 Korean businesses in the Los Angeles Metropolitan Area.

Korean entrepreneurs, like Jewish and Japanese immigrants before them, are highly dependent on the social and economic resources of their ethnic community. Some immigrants managed to smuggle capital out of Korea, but most rely on individual thrift and ethnic credit systems. For instance, a Korean husband and wife may save their wages from several service and factory jobs until enough capital is accumulated to purchase a small business. This process usually takes 2 or 3 years. Rotating credit systems (*gae*), which are based on mutual trust and honor, offer another common source of venture capital. This economic institution could not exist without a high degree of social solidarity within the ethnic community. There are more than 500 community social and business associations in Los Angeles, and nearly every Korean is an active member of one or more of them. In addition, Korean businessmen have utilized public resources from the U.S. Small Business Administration as well as loans and training programs sponsored by the South Korean government (Light, 1980; Bonacich *et al.*, 1977).

The ability of the Korean community to generate a self-sustaining entrepreneurial class has had a profound impact on intraethnic labor relations and patterns of ethnic property transfers. For example, labor relations are enmeshed in extended kinship and friendship networks. In this context of ''labor paternalism,'' working in the ethnic economy frequently entails the obligation of accepting low pay and long hours in exchange for on-the-job training and possible future assistance in establishing a small business. Hence, employment in the ethnic economy possesses a potential for advancement entirely absent from comparable low-wage labor in the secondary labor market.

Along the same lines, business practices are fundamentally influenced by cultural patterns. Koreans patronize coethnic businesses and frequently rely on referrals from members of their social networks. Korean-owned businesses, moreover, tend to remain in the community through intraethnic transactions.

This is because economic mobility typically proceeds through the rapid turnover of immigrant-owned enterprises. A common pattern of succession, for instance, may begin with a business requiring a relatively small investment, such as a wig shop, and continue with the acquisition of enterprises requiring progressively larger capitalizations: grocery stores, restaurants, gas stations, liquor stores, and finally real estate. This circulation of businesses within the ethnic economy provides a continuous source of economic mobility for aspiring immigrant entrepreneurs. Table 1 presents data illustrating both the significant presence of Koreans in the liquor business in the Los Angeles area and the pattern of intra-ethnic business transfers among Koreans and other Oriental minorities.

The Korean economy is clearly thriving in Los Angeles. Its emerging entrepreneurial class and accumulating assets have created new employment opportunities for an expanding immigrant community. As in the previous historical examples, the principal characteristic of this structure is a dense network of diversified enterprises that provide goods and services both for the ethnic community and for the general market. It is this characteristic that most clearly differentiates an immigrant enclave from the assortment of restaurants and small shops commonly established by other immigrant minorities to cater to their particular cultural needs.

In 1975, Korean enterprises were overrepresented in retail trade and to a minor extent in wholesale trade (Light, 1980). This sectoral concentration no doubt reflects the recent arrival of most immigrant entrepreneurs and thus the fact that many of them are still in an early phase of business succession. Over time, however, successful Korean enterprises should be able to penetrate more highly capitalized sectors of industry and commerce. The initiation of this trend is already apparent in the presence of immigrant-owned firms in intermediate industries such as construction, manufacturing, and transportation and public utilities. Although underrepresented in these sectors due to large capital requirements and stiff outside competition, the emergence of these firms points to the

TABLE 1. Liquor license transfers in Hollywood, California, 1975[a]

| | Sellers | | | |
Buyers	Korean (%)	Chinese (%)	Japanese (%)	Buyers as percent of all buyers
Korean	79.0	18.5	16.7	15.0
Chinese	9.0	70.4	0.0	6.7
Japanese	4.0	0.0	50.0	3.9
All other	7.5	11.1	33.3	74.4
Total (%)	100.1	100.0	100.0	100.0
Number	67	27	18	641

[a]From Light (1980, pp. 33–57).

growing diversity of the ethnic economy. With continuing capital accumulation and continuing immigration from Korea, it is unlikely that this process will lose momentum in the near future.

B. Cubans in Miami

Over the past 20 years, nearly 900,000 Cubans or about 10% of the island's population have emigrated, mostly to the United States. The overwhelming proportion of the Cuban population in America, estimated at roughly 800,000, resides in the metropolitan areas of south Florida and New York (Diaz-Briquets and Perez, 1981). This movement of Cuban emigrés has not been a continuous or socially homogeneous flow. Instead, it is more accurately described as a series of "waves," marked by abrupt shifts and sudden discontinuities. This pattern has supported the emergence of an enclave economy through such features as spatial concentration, the initial arrival of a moneyed, entrepreneurial class, and subsequent replenishments of the labor pool with refugees coming from more modest class origins.

In 1959, when Fidel Castro overthrew the regime of Fulgencio Batista, the Cuban community in the United States numbered probably less than 30,000 (Jorge and Moncarz, 1982). The political upheavals of the Revolution, however, precipitated a massive emigration from the island. Not surprisingly, the Cuban propertied class, including landowners, industrialists, and former Cuban managers of U.S.-owned corporations, were the first to leave, following close in the heels of leaders of the deposed regime. In the first year of the exodus, approximately 37,000 emigrés settled in the United States; most were well-to-do and brought considerable assets with them (Thomas and Huyck, 1967). After the defeat of the exile force in the Bay of Pigs, in April 1961, Cuban emigration accelerated and its social base expanded to include the middle and urban working classes (Clark, 1977). By the end of 1962, the first phase of Cuban emigration had concluded and over 215,000 refugees had been admitted to the United States. The emerging Cuban community in south Florida, unlike earlier Japanese and contemporary Korean settlements, was thus fundamentally conditioned by political forces (Portes and Bach, 1985; Pedraza-Bailey, 1981).

Political factors continued to shape the ups and downs of Cuban emigration as well as its reception by American society over the next two decades. In this period, three additional phases can be distinguished: November 1962 to November 1965, December 1965 to April 1973, and May 1973 to November 1980, including 74,000 in the second phase, 340,000 in the third, and 124,769 in the last (Portes and Bach, 1985, chapter 3). This massive influx of refugees to south Florida generated local complaints about the social and economic strains placed in the area. Accordingly, the policy of the Cuban Refugee Program originally established by the Kennedy Administration, was oriented from the start to resettle Cubans away from Miami. Assistance to the refugees was often made contingent on their willingness to relocate. Although over 469,000 Cubans elected to move by 1978, many subsequently returned to metropolitan Miami (Clark, 1977; Boswell, 1984). There is evidence that many of these "returnees" made use of their employment in relatively high-wage Northern areas to accumulate savings with which to start new business ventures in Miami. By 1980, the Cuban-born population of the city, composed to a large extent of returnees from the North, was six times greater than the second largest Cuban concentration in New Jersey (Boswell, 1984).

Although a number of Cuban businesses appeared in Miami in the 1960s, they were mostly restaurants and ethnic shops catering to a small exile clientele. An enclave economy only emerged in the 1970s as a result of a combination of factors, including capital availability, access to low-wage labor provided by new refugee cohorts, and the increasingly tenuous hope of returning to Cuba. Cuban-owned firms in Dade County increased from 919 in 1967 to about 8000 in 1976 and approximately 12,000 in 1982. Most of these firms are small, averaging 8.1 employees in 1977, but they also include factories employing several hundred workers (Diaz-Briquets, 1985; Portes and Bach, 1985, chapter 6). Cuban firms in such sectors as light manufacturing, including apparel, footwear, beverages, cigars, and furniture, construction, agriculture (sugar), and finance and insurance have ceased supplying an exclusively ethnic clientele to become integrated into the broader local economy. Although the Cuban market in south Florida has also grown in size, the key for success among the larger immigrant-owned firms has been to make use of community resources—labor, credit, and information—to compete with better-established outside enterprises (Wilson and Martin, 1982).

This strategy seems to have paid off: between 1969 and 1977, the number of Cuban-owned manufacturing firms almost doubled and construction enterprises virtually tripled. In terms of average gross annual receipts, Cuban manufacturing firms went from a very modest $59,633 in 1969 to $639,817 in 1977, a 1067% increase. By 1972, average gross receipts of Cuban-owned enterprises in Miami exceeded that of Hispanic businesses in other cities, including Los Angeles, which has the largest concentration of such firms (Boswell, 1984; Jorge and Moncarz, 1982). With the exception of banks and other large companies, Cuban service firms continue to depend on an ethnic clientele. The latter, however, has expanded with the growth of both Cuban and other Hispanic populations in the city; service firms have become accordingly larger and more diversified, including restaurants, supermarkets, private clinics, realty offices, legal firms, funeral parlors, and private schools.

The Cuban enclave has been the subject of intense study in recent years. Jorge and Moncarz (1981, 1982) and Diaz-Briquets (1985) have reported on the size and composition of refugee-owned firms in Miami and compared them both with others in the same metropolitan area and with Hispanic enterprises elsewhere. Table 2 presents data drawn from one of these studies on the number of Cuban-

TABLE 2.   Firm ownership among Cubans, other Hispanics, and Blacks[a]

Ownership	All firms			Firms with paid employees		
	Number of firms	Firms per 100,000 population	Gross receipts per firm ($1000)	Number of firms	Firms per 100,000 population	Employees per firm
Cuban	30,336	3650.5	61.6	5888	672.4	6.6
Mexican	116,419	1467.7	44.4	22,718	286.4	4.9
Puerto Rican	13,491	740.0	43.9	1767	96.9	3.9
South Central or South American	26,301	2573.5	38.1	4900	479.4	3.0
All Spanish origin (except other Spanish)	219,355	1889.7	47.5	41,298	355.8	5.0
Black	231,203	872.9	37.4	39,968	150.9	4.1

[a]From Diaz-Briquets (1985).

owned firms and their relative size in comparison with those owned by other Hispanic groups and black Americans. Although Cuban enterprises are not the most numerous in absolute terms, they are larger on the average and more numerous relative to the respective population. Keeping in mind that sizable Cuban exile immigration started only in 1959 and that the first signs of a Cuban business community did not appear until the late 1960s, the data provide a vivid illustration of the dynamism of the process.

Along similar lines, Wilson and Martin (1982) conducted a sophisticated input–output analysis of business relationships among refugee-owned firms in south Florida and compared them with the predominant pattern among black-owned enterprises in the area. In relation to the latter, Cuban firms were shown to have a high degree of interdependence, with substantial internal "sourcing" among manufacturing and construction firms as well as heavy use of commercial and financial services. This analysis provided the first solid quantitative evidence of a dense network of enterprises at the core of the enclave economy.

These and other studies of immigrant businesses in Miami have been conducted on the basis of secondary data. Paralleling them, other research sought to examine the consequences of these activities for individual mobility through primary data collection. A longitudinal study, initiated in 1973, provided data for an extensive series of statistical analyses on the topic. By 1973 most of the Cuban upper and middle classes had left the country; thus, the 590 adult males interviewed originally in this study came overwhelmingly from lower occupational strata, mostly petty services and industrial blue collar work (Portes, Clark, and Bach, 1977). Despite these modest origins, a sizable number of sample members managed to move out of wage work and into self-employment after only a few years in the country. Between 1973 and 1976, 8% acquired their own businesses, and by 1979, 21.2% had done so. Adding the self-employed to those working in other Cuban-owned firms, almost half of the sample was found to participate in the enclave labor market in 1979 (Portes and Bach, 1985).

A discriminant analysis conducted on the basis of the 1976 follow-up survey clearly differentiated between refugees employed in enclave firms and those working in either segment of the general labor market. In addition, the analysis found a distinct and significant payoff for human capital brought from Cuba among refugees in the enclave economy (Wilson and Portes, 1980). This analysis was replicated with data from a second follow-up, conducted in 1979, yielding essentially identical results (Portes and Bach, 1985). The positive consequences of the enclave mode of incorporation for individual mobility are also reflected in other findings from the same study, three of which may be cited for illustration:

(1) Years of education in Cuba, which have little or no payoff for occupational attainment in either the primary or the secondary labor markets, have the strongest positive effect in the enclave. The same pattern holds true for the effect of occupational aspirations.

(2) Refugees employed in the enclave are not at a disadvantage with respect to those in the primary labor market either in terms of average income or rewards for human capital. The situation of both groups is far more advantageous than that of refugees employed in the secondary sector.

(3) Self-employment in the enclave is the most remunerative occupation on the average. In 1979, the median monthly earnings of employees in this sample was $974, in comparison with $1194 for the self-employed without workers, and $1924 for the self-employed with at least one salaried worker. Although the number of the latter is small, there is every indication that it is likely to increase in the future.

V. CONCLUSION: A TYPOLOGY OF THE
PROCESS OF INCORPORATION

Having reviewed several historical and contemporary examples, we can now attempt a summary description of the characteristics of immigrant enclaves and how they differ from other paths. The emergence of an ethnic enclave economy has three prerequisites: first, the presence of a substantial number of immigrants, with business experience acquired in the sending country; second, the availability of sources of capital; and third, the availability of sources of labor. The latter two conditions are not too difficult to meet. The requisite labor can usually be drawn from family members and, more commonly, from recent arrivals. Surprisingly perhaps, capital is not a major impediment either since the sums initially required are usually small. When immigrants did not bring them from abroad, they could be accumulated through individual savings or pooled resources in the community. It is the first condition that appears critical. The presence of a number of immigrants skilled in what Franklin Frazier (1949) called the art of "buying and selling" is common to all four cases reviewed above. Such an entrepreneurial–commercial class among early immigrant cohorts can usually overcome other obstacles; conversely, its absence within an immigrant community will confine the community to wage employment even if sufficient resources of capital and labor are available.

Enclave businesses typically start small and cater exclusively to an ethnic clientele. Their expansion and entry into the broader market requires, as seen above, an effective mobilization of community resources. The social mechanism at work here seems to be a strong sense of reciprocity supported by collective solidarity that transcends the purely contractual character of business transactions. For example, receipt of a loan from a rotating credit association entails the duty of continuing to make contributions so that others can have access to the same source of capital. Although, in principle, it would make sense for the individual to withdraw once his loan is received, such action would cut him off from the very sources of community support on which his future business success depends (Light, 1972).

Similarly, relations between enclave employers and employees generally transcend a contractual wage bond. It is understood by both parties that the wage paid is inferior to the value of labor contributed. This is willingly accepted by many immigrant workers because the wage is only *one* form of compensation. Use of their labor represents often the key advantage making poorly capitalized enclave firms competitive. In reciprocity, employers are expected to respond to emergency needs of their workers and to promote their advancement through such means as on-the-job training, advancement to supervisory positions, and aid when they move into self-employment. These opportunities represent the other part of the "wage" received by enclave workers. The informal mobility ladders thus created are, of course, absent in the secondary labor market where there is no primary bond between owners and workers or no common ethnic community to enforce the norm of reciprocity.

Paternalistic labor relations and strong community solidarity are also characteristic of middleman minorities. Although both modes of incorporation are similar and are thus frequently confused, there are three major structural differences between them. First, immigrant enclaves are not exclusively commercial. Unlike middleman minorities, whose economic role is to mediate commercial and financial transactions between elites and masses, enclave firms include in addition a sizable productive sector. The latter may comprise agriculture, light manufacturing, and construction enterprises; their production, marketed often by coethnic intermediaries, is directed toward the general economy and not exclusively to the immigrant community.

Second, relationships between enclave businesses and established native ones are problematic. Middleman groups tend to occupy positions complementary and subordinate to the local owning class; they fill economic niches either disdained or feared by the latter. Unlike them, enclave enterprises often enter in direct competition with existing domestic firms. There is no evidence, for example, that domestic elites deliberately established or supported the emergence of the Jewish, Japanese, Korean, or Cuban business communities as means to further their own economic interests. There is every indication, on the other hand, that this mode of incorporation was largely self-created by the immigrants, often in opposition to powerful domestic interests. Although it is true that enclave entrepreneurs have been frequently employed as subcontractors by outside firms in such activities as garment and construction (Bonacich, 1978), it is incorrect to characterize this role as the exclusive or dominant one among these enterprises.

Third, the enclave is concentrated and spatially identifiable. By the very nature of their activities, middleman minorities must often be dispersed among the mass of the population. Although the immigrants may live in certain limited areas, their businesses require proximity to their mass clientele and a measure of physical dispersion within it. It is true that middleman activities such as moneylending have been associated in several historical instances with certain streets and neighborhoods, but this is not a necessary or typical pattern. Street peddling and other forms of petty commerce require merchants to go into the areas where demand exists and avoid excessive concentration of the goods and services they offer. This is the typical pattern found today among middleman minorities in American cities (Cobas, 1984; Kim, 1981).

Enclave businesses, on the other hand, are spatially concentrated, especially in their early stages. This is so for three reasons: first, the need for proximity to the ethnic market which they initially serve; second, proximity to each other which facilitates exchange of information, access to credit, and other supportive activities; third, proximity to ethnic labor supplies on which they crucially depend. Of the four immigrant groups discussed above, only the Japanese partially departs from the pattern of high physical concentration. This can be attributed to the political persecution to which this group was subjected. Originally, Japanese concentration was a rural phenomenon based on small farms linked together by informal bonds and cooperative associations. Forced removal of this minority from the land compelled their entry into urban businesses and their partial dispersal into multiple activities.

Physical concentration of enclaves underlies their final characteristic. Once an enclave economy has fully developed, it is possible for a newcomer to live his life entirely within the confines of the community. Work, education, and access to health care, recreation, and a variety of other services can be found without leaving the bounds of the ethnic economy. This institutional completeness is what enables new immigrants to move ahead economically, despite very limited knowledge of the host culture and language. Supporting empirical evidence comes from studies showing low levels of English knowledge among enclave minorities and the absence of a net effect of knowledge of English on their average income levels (Light, 1980; Portes and Bach, 1985).

Table 3 summarizes this discussion by presenting the different modes of incorporation and their principal characteristics. Two caveats are necessary. First, this typology is not exhaustive, since other forms of adaptation have existed and will undoubtedly emerge in the future. Second, political refugees are not included, since this entry label does not necessarily entail a unique adaptation path. Instead, refugees can select or be channelled in many different directions, including self-employment, access to primary labor markets, or confinement to secondary sector occupations.

Having discussed the characteristics of enclaves and middleman minorities, a final word must be said about the third alternative to employment in the lower tier of a dual labor market. As a mode of incorporation, primary sector immigration also has distinct advantages, although they are of a different order from those pursued by "entrepreneurial" minorities. Dispersal throughout the receiving country and career mobility based on standard promotion criteria makes it imperative for immigrants in this mode to become fluent in the new language and culture (Stevens, Goodman, and Mick, 1978). Without a supporting ethnic community, the second generation also becomes thoroughly steeped in the ways of the host society. Primary sector immigration thus tends to lead to very rapid social and cultural integration. It represents the path that approximates most closely the predictions of assimilation theory with regard to (1) the necessity of acculturation for social and economic progress and (2) the subsequent rewards received by immigrants and their descendants for shedding their ethnic identities.

Clearly, however, this mode of incorporation is open only to a minority of immigrant groups. In addition, acculturation of professionals and other primary sector immigrants is qualitatively different from that undergone by others. Regardless of their differences, immigrants in other modes tend to learn the new language and culture with a heavy "local" content. Although acculturation may be slow, especially in the case of enclave groups, it carries with it elements unique to the surrounding community—its language inflections, particular traditions, and loyalties (Greeley, 1971; Suttles, 1968). On the contrary, acculturation of primary sector immigrants is of a more cosmopolitan sort. Because career requirements often entail physical mobility, the new language and culture are learned more rapidly and more generally, without strong attachments to a particular community. Thus, while minorities entering menial labor, enclave, or middleman enterprise in the United States have eventually become identified with a certain city or region, the same is not true for immigrant professionals, who tend

TABLE 3. Typology of modes of incorporation

Variable	Primary sector immigration	Secondary sector immigration	Immigrant enclaves	Middleman minorities
Size of immigrant population	Small	Large	Large	Small
Spatial concentration, national	Dispersed	Dispersed	Concentrated	Concentrated
Spatial concentration, local	Dispersed	Concentrated	Concentrated	Dispersed
Original class composition	Homogeneous: skilled workers and professionals	Homogeneous: manual laborers	Heterogeneous: entrepreneurs, professionals, and workers	Homogeneous: merchants and some professionals
Present occupational status distribution	High mean status/low variance	Low mean status/low variance	Mean status/high variance	Mean status/low variance
Mobility opportunities	High: formal promotion ladders	Low	High: informal ethnic ladders	Average: informal ethnic ladders
Institutional diversification of ethnic community	None	Low: weak social institutions	High: institutional completeness	Medium: strong social and economic institutions
Participation in ethnic organizations	Little or none	Low	High	High
Resilience of ethnic culture	Low	Average	High	High
Knowledge of host country language	High	Low	Low	High
Knowledge of host country institutions	High	Low	Average	High
Modal reaction of host community	Acceptance	Discrimination	Hostility	Mixed: elite acceptance/mass hostility

to "disappear," in a cultural sense, soon after their arrival (Stevens *et al.*, 1978; Cardona and Cruz, 1980).

Awareness of patterned differences among immigrant groups in their forms of entry and labor market incorporation represents a significant advance, in our view, from earlier undifferentiated descriptions of the adaptation process. This typology is, however, a provisional effort. Just as detailed research on the condition of particular minorities modified or replaced earlier broad generalizations, the propositions advanced here will require revision. New groups arriving in the United States at present and a revived interest in immigration should provide the required incentive for empirical studies and theoretical advances in the future.

REFERENCES

ALBA, RICHARD D., and CHAMLIN, MITCHELL B. (1983). Ethnic identification among whites. *American Sociological Review* **48**:240–47.
BARRERA, MARIO (1980). *Race and class in the Southwest: A theory of racial inequality.* Notre Dame, Indiana: Notre Dame University Press.
BLAUNER, ROBERT (1972). *Racial oppression in America.* New York: Harper and Row.
BONACICH, EDNA (1973). A theory of middleman minorities. *American Sociological Review* **38**(October):583–594.
BONACICH, EDNA (1978). U.S. capitalism and Korean immigrant small business. Riverside, California: Department of Sociology, University of California—Riverside, mimeographed.
BONACICH, EDNA, and MODELL, JOHN (1980). *The economic basis of ethnic solidarity: Small business in the Japanese–American community.* Berkeley, California: University of California Press.
BONACICH, EDNA, LIGHT, IVAN, and WONG, CHARLES CHOY (1977). Koreans in small business. *Society* **14**(October/September):54–59.
BOSWELL, THOMAS D. (1984). Cuban-Americans. In *Ethnicity in contemporary America* (J. O. McKee, ed.). Dubuque, Iowa: Kendall-Hunt.
CARDONA, RAMIRO C., and CRUZ, CARMEN I. (1980). *El exodo de Colombianos.* Bogota: Ediciones Tercer Mundo.
CHILD, IRVING L. (1943). *Italian or American? The second generation in conflict.* New Haven, Connecticut: Yale University Press.
CLARK, JUAN M. (1977). The Cuban exodus: Why? Special report. Miami: Cuban Exile Union.
COBAS, JOSE (1984). Participation in the ethnic economy, ethnic solidarity and ambivalence toward the host society: The case of Cuban emigres in Puerto Rico. Presented at the American Sociological Association Meeting, San Antonio, Texas (August).
DANIELS, ROGER (1977). The Japanese-American experience: 1890–1940. In *Uncertain Americans* (L. Dinnerstein and F. C. Jaher, eds.), pp. 250–267. New York: Oxford University Press.
DESPRES, LEO (1975). Toward a theory of ethnic phenomena. In *Ethnicity and resource competition* (Leo Despres, ed.), pp. 209–212. The Hague: Mouton.
DIAZ-BRIQUETS, SERGIO (1985). Cuban-owned businesses in the United States: A research note. *Cuban Studies* **14**(Summer):57–64.
DIAZ-BRIQUETS, SERGIO, and PEREZ, LISANDRO (1981). Cuba: The demography of revolution. *Population Bulletin* **36**(April):2–41.

DINNERSTEIN, LEONARD (1977). The East European Jewish migration. In *Uncertain Americans* (L. Dinnerstein and F. C. Jaher, eds.), pp. 216–231. New York: Oxford University Press.
EISENSTADT, S. N. (1970). The process of absorbing new immigrants in Israel. In *Integration and Development in Israel* (S. N. Eisenstadt, RivKah Bar Yosef, and Chaim Adler, eds.), pp. 341–367. Jerusalem: Israel University Press.
FEATHERMAN, DAVID L. (1971). The socio-economic achievement of white religio-ethnic subgroups: Social and psychological explanations. *American Sociological Review* 36(April):207–222.
FRAZIER, E. FRANKLIN (1949). *The Negro in the United States.* New York: MacMillan.
GESCHWENDER, JAMES A. (1978). *Racial Stratification in America.* Dubuque, Iowa: William C. Brown.
GLAZER, NATHAN, and MOYNIHAN, DANIEL P. (1970). *Beyond the melting pot: The Negroes, Puerto Ricans, Jews, Italians and Irish of New York City.* Cambridge, Massachusetts: M.I.T. Press.
GORDON, MILTON M. (1964). *Assimilation in American life: The role of race, religion, and national origins.* New York: Oxford University Press.
GREELEY, ANDREW (1971). *Why can't they be like us? America's white ethnic groups.* New York: Dutton.
HANDLIN, OSCAR (1941). *Boston's immigrants: A study of acculturation.* Cambridge: Harvard University Press.
HANDLIN, OSCAR (1951). *The uprooted: The epic story of the great migrations that made the American people.* Boston: Little Brown.
HECHTER, MICHAEL (1977). *Internal colonialism, the Celtic fringe in British national development, 1536–1966.* Berkeley, California: University of California Press.
HOWE, IRVING (1976). *World of our fathers.* New York: Harcourt, Brace, Jovanovich.
HOWE, IRVING, and LIBO, KENNETH (1979). *How we lived, a documentary history of immigrant Jews in America.* New York: Richard March.
JORGE, ANTONIO, and MONCARZ, RAUL (1981). International factor movement and complementarity: Growth and entrepreneurship under conditions of cultural variation. *R.E.M.P. Bulletin, Supplement 14 (September).*
JORGE, ANTONIO, and MONCARZ, RAUL (1982). The future of the Hispanic market: The Cuban entrepreneur and the economic development of the Miami SMSA. Discussion Paper 6, International Banking Center, Florida International University.
KEELY, CHARLES B. (1981). *Global refugee policy: The case for a development-oriented strategy.* New York: The Population Council.
KIM, ILLSOO (1981). *New urban immigrants, the Korean community in New York.* Princeton, New Jersey: Princeton University Press.
LIGHT, H. IVAN (1972). *Ethnic enterprise in America: Business and welfare among Chinese, Japanese, and Blacks.* Berkeley, California: University of California Press.
LIGHT, H. IVAN (1979). Disadvantaged minorities in self-employment. *International Journal of Comparative Sociology* XX:31–45.
LIGHT, H. IVAN (1980). Asian enterprise in America: Chinese, Japanese, and Koreans in small business. In *Self-help in urban America* (Scott Cummings, ed.) pp. 33–57. New York: Kennikat Press.
NAGEL, JOANE, and OLZAK, SUSAN (1982). Ethnic mobilization in new and old states: An extension of the competition model. *Social Problems* 30:127–143.
NATIONAL RESEARCH COUNCIL (1985). Immigration statistics: A story of neglect. Report of the Panel on Immigration Statistics. Washington, D.C.: National Academy of Sciences.
PARENTI, MICHAEL (1967). Ethnic politics and the persistence of ethnic identification. *American Political Science Review* 61:717–726.

PEDRAZA-BAILEY, SILVIA (1981). Cubans and Mexicans in the United States: The functions of political and economic migration.'' *Cuban Studies* **11**(July):79–97.

PETERSEN, WILLIAM (1971). *Japanese Americans, oppression and success.* New York: Random House.

PIORE, MICHAEL J. (1975). Notes for a theory of labor market stratification. In *Labor market segmentation* (Richard C. Edwards, Michael Reich, and David M. Gordon, eds.), pp. 125–171. Lexington, Massachusetts: Heath.

PIORE, MICHAEL J. (1979). *Birds of passage, migrant labor and industrial societies.* New York: Cambridge University Press.

PORTES, ALEJANDRO (1976). Determinants of the brain drain. *International Migration Review* **10**(Winter):489–508.

PORTES, ALEJANDRO (1981). Modes of structural incorporation and theories of labor immigration. In *Global Trends in Migration, Theory and Research on International Population Movements* (Mary M. Kritz, Charles B. Keely, and Silvano M. Tomasi, eds.), pp. 279–297. New York: Center for Migration Studies.

PORTES, ALEJANDRO, and BACH, ROBERT L. (1985). *Latin journey, Cuban and Mexican immigrants in the United States.* Berkeley, California: University of California Press.

PORTES, ALEJANDRO, and MOZO, RAFAEL (1985). The political adaptation process of Cubans and other ethnic minorities in the United States. *International Migration Review* **19**(Spring):35–63.

PORTES, ALEJANDRO, CLARK, JUAN M., and BACH, ROBERT L. (1977). The new wave: A statistical profile of recent Cuban exiles in the United States. *Cuban Studies* **7**(January):1–32.

RISCHIN, MOSES (1962). *The promised city, New York Jews 1870–1914.* Cambridge, Mass.: Harvard University Press.

SASSEN-KOOB, SASKIA (1980). Immigrant and minority workers in the organization of the labor process. *Journal of Ethnic Studies* (1/Spring):1–34.

SOWELL, THOMAS (1981). *Ethnic America: A history.* New York: Basic Books.

STEVENS, ROSEMARY, GOODMAN, LOUIS W., and MICK, STEPHEN (1978). *The alien doctors, foreign medical graduates in American hospitals.* New York: Wiley.

SUTTLES, GERALD D. (1968). *The social order of the slum, ethnicity and territory in the inner city.* Chicago: University of Chicago Press.

THOMAS, JOHN F., and HUYCK, EARL E. (1967). Resettlement of Cuban refugees in the United States. Paper presented at the Meetings of the American Sociological Association, San Francisco, (August).

VECOLI, RUDOLPH (1977). The Italian Americans. In *Uncertain Americans* (L. Dinnerstein and F. C. Jaher, eds.), pp. 201–215. New York: Oxford University Press.

WARNER, W. LLOYD, and SROLE, LEO (1945). *The social systems of American ethnic groups.* New Haven: Yale University Press.

WILSON, KENNETH, and MARTIN, W. ALLEN (1982). Ethnic enclaves: A comparison of the Cuban and Black economies in Miami. *American Journal of Sociology* **88**(July):135–160.

WILSON, KENNETH L., and PORTES, ALEJANDRO (1980). Immigrant enclaves: An analysis of the labor market experiences of Cubans in Miami. *American Journal of Sociology* **86**(September):295–319.

WIRTH, LOUIS (1956). *The ghetto.* Chicago: University of Chicago Press.

WITTKE, CARL (1952). *Refugees of revolution: The German Forty-eighters in America.* Philadelphia: University of Pennsylvania Press.

ZOLBERG, ARISTIDE (1983). Contemporary transnational migrations in historical perspective: Patterns and dilemmas. In *U.S. immigration and refugee policy* (Mary M. Kritz, ed.), pp. 15–51. Lexington, Massachusetts: Heath.

3

Gypsies in the United States and Great Britain: Ethnic Boundaries and Political Mobilization

BEVERLY NAGEL

Department of Sociology and Anthropology
Carleton College
Northfield, Minnesota 55057

I. INTRODUCTION

When discussing ethnic political activity, most people think of large, well-organized, and politically oriented movements such as the Quebecois in Canada, the Welsh movement in Great Britain, or black political organizations in the United States. It probably would not occur to anyone to think of Gypsies. In fact, most people think of Gypsies as a romantic but extinct people, today found only as fictionalized characters in the popular media. Despite this popular image, Gypsies continue to live and go about their business even in advanced industrial states like the United States and Great Britain. Their persistence is in itself surprising, since scholars and other observers have been foretelling the imminent demise of the Gypsies for over 100 years now [see, for example, Borrow (1874)].

All the more surprising, however, is the development of Gypsy political activity. Gypsies have generally sought to remain unknown to outsiders. Indeed, learned observers generally agree (as perhaps would most Gypsies) that the Gypsies have been able to persist largely as a result of their invisibility in modern states. In spite of this, there have been several instances of large-scale, ethnic-oriented political activity by Gypsies in recent times. Most notable are the formation and activities of the Red Scarf Association in the United States during

69

the Great Depression, and the Gypsy Council in Great Britain in the late 1960s and early 1970s.

This chapter examines the conditions and processes that gave rise to and shaped these recent instances of Gypsy political activity. Several explanations for the resurgence of ethnic political activity have been proposed in recent years, and there have been a number of attempts to test these models (Olzak, 1983; Hechter, 1975; Hannan, 1979; Ragin, 1979; Portes, 1984; Nielson, 1980; Leifer, 1981). My strategy is to explore key issues emerging from this debate, by seeing how these explanations can account for the seemingly quixotic political activities of Gypsies. In the following section, I briefly review key conceptual and theoretical issues that have emerged in previous research on ethnic mobilization and political activity, focusing especially on ecological theories. Then, because Gypsies remain so unfamiliar and romanticized, I will discuss the nature of Gypsy ethnicity and social organization. Finally, I examine the history of modern Gypsy political activity in the United States and Great Britain.

II. ETHNIC BOUNDARIES AND ETHNIC MOBILIZATION

An ethnic group can be said to be mobilized to the degree that it organizes around symbols of shared ethnic identity to pursue collective goals. In modern states, ethnic mobilization is often manifest by the presence of formal organizations and collective action based on ethnicity. Attempts to explain ethnic mobilization have generally focused on the economic conditions under which ethnic identities are "activated" for political purposes. In particular, concern has centered on the kinds of economic relationships between groups that are most likely to produce ethnic political activity. Some analysts have also been concerned with the way in which political institutions shape ethnic identities and determine the level at which ethnic political activity occurs (Horowitz, 1975; Nagel, 1979).

One of the key differences among models of ethnic mobilization lies in their view of the economic relations among groups that lead to ethnic political mobilization. One view holds that a segmental division of labor underlies ethnic mobilization. For example, Hechter (1975, 1978) argues that ethnic attachments intensify and political mobilization occurs when ethnic groups occupy different occupational strata within a single, hierarchically structured division of labor. In this view, ethnic identity is taken as given, and is of importance only when it coincides with occupation cleavages. Ethnic identity provides a useful symbol for facilitating group action, but is not problematic in itself (Hechter, 1978).

On the other hand, competition models, drawing on ecological theories, argue that ethnic mobilization is most likely when groups compete directly, as occurs when groups attempt to occupy the same or very similar niches in the same region (Hannan, 1979; Nielson, 1980). These ecological models define a group's niche in much broader terms than do segmental labor market models, which tend to see the productive niche narrowly as an occupation specialty. In the competition model, the productive niche of a group is defined as the set of conditions under which the group can maintain itself at some minimum level, together with the strategies it uses to exploit its environment. The pertinent conditions include not only economic resources needed by the group to survive—such as food, shelter, and jobs—but also constraints on the ability of the group to pursue necessary activities—for example, legal constraints imposed by national or local governments. Thus, competition may occur over access to economic, social, and/or political resources. According to this model, a culturally stratified occupation system is the outcome of such competition processes. The degree of mobilization should decline when one group has prevailed in this competition by successfully excluding the other group.

Ecological competition models argue furthermore that ethnicity itself is variable, and argue that modernization encourages a reorganization of the lines of conflict around larger-scale identities. Following Barth (1969), ecologists define an ethnic group by social boundaries. An ethnic boundary organizes, limits, and defines appropriate social relationships. Because this is a social boundary, culture may change, or vary internally, without implying a change in ethnic identity or interethnic relations. Ethnic identity is attributed on the basis of current behavior as well as presumed social origins, and thus is at least partially voluntary, involving both self-identification and ascription by others.

Ecologists argue that, in equilibrium, ethnic boundaries tend to coincide with the productive niches of groups. Modernization is likely to alter niche boundaries by simplifying the structure of constraints in the socioeconomic environment. At the same time, modernization increases interdependence of the various parts of the national system. In effect, this increases the size and power of the largest competitor in a social system, e.g., the state itself. Attempts by small, peripheral groups to resist this expansion are unlikely to succeed. However, attempts at mobilizing around large-scale identities, whether ethnic or not, should be more successful since large-scale identities can be used to appeal to larger populations and thus exert greater political pressure on the state. The ability to seize and hold resources vis-à-vis a powerful state center, and to resist constraints imposed by that state, depends on both the organizational and demographic resources of the group. In the political institutions of modern industrial states, large membership confers competitive advantage by providing the capacity to organize large voting blocs or by threat of substantial civil disorder.

A large-scale group may be one that retains its original identity, but is populous, but may also be based on a new group identity, uniting a number of smaller, previously distinct groups. Every individual has a variety of social identities, ranging from an identity based on family membership to large-scale, inclusive identities based on region, nationality, or race. To say that groups mobilize around larger, more inclusive identities does not imply that individuals lose their sense of identification deriving from membership in smaller groups. However, it does imply that the social identity that becomes the basis for group action is derived from more inclusive group membership. As Nagel (1979) points out, the organization of the state itself may serve as the basis for uniting previously distinct, smaller groups.

In sum, at the same time that modernization increases the likelihood of mobilization around large-scale group identities, it simultaneously reduces the salience of small-scale, local attachments, and thus may lead to the disappearance of small-scale ethnic groups. The activities of the larger-scale groups are likely to be political for two reasons. First, in modern states, economic interests are often pursued and defended through political institutions. Thus, we would expect to see this competition reflected in political activity with specifically ethnic demands. Second, the organization of the state itself can promote political activity, by defining groups and targeting them for special treatment. Thus, we can simultaneously account for the decline in the social significance of some ethnic identities and the increasing politicization of others.

Although modernization certainly affects niche structure, it does not necessarily eliminate all small-scale ethnic groups. The persistence of the Gypsies and similar groups provides evidence that the conditions under which these groups can survive remain even in advanced industrial states. Elsewhere, I have argued that Gypsies are an excellent example of ethnic "r-strategists" (Lauwagie, 1979).[1] That is, they are adapted to exploiting resources that are transitory, irregularly dispersed in space, and unpredictable in their availability. To successfully compete with other groups for these resources, ethnic r-strategists, like their counterparts in nature, employ strategies to quickly locate available resources, exploit them before other more powerful actors can do so, and, finally, avoid direct confrontation with other competing groups that are more numerous and potentially more powerful.

In the case of Gypsies, to accomplish these tasks means maintaining a flexible social organization and seminomadic lifestyle, as well as remaining unobtrusive. Though we would expect to see signs of ethnic mobilization when Gypsies compete with other groups, public political activities, such as engaged in by larger and more powerful ethnic groups, would seem quite anomolous for Gypsies. Thus, the general research question addressed here is, under what conditions do ethnic r-strategists mobilize for collective political action? The preceding theoretical discussion suggests three specific questions must be considered:

(1)   What is the nature of ethnicity, and how is the process by which ethnic boundaries are determined and maintained related to economic and political processes?

(2)   Under what economic conditions do ethnic groups mobilize? Since most models assume that mobilization is related to competing economic claims, the major issue here concerns the timing of mobilization. Is mobilization most likely

when a system of occupational segmentation has been imposed by (presumably) the most powerful group in a system, or is it most likely while resources are contested?

(3) How is ethnic mobilization catalyzed into political activity, and what determines the political strategy pursued? Clearly, ethnic activity may take various forms. Some groups organize to pursue collective goals within the legal political arena, with the objective of gaining greater control over national institutions or resources, greater autonomy, or basic civil rights. Other groups use legal or extralegal means in an attempt to achieve independent nationhood. Still others engage in nonpolitical forms of cultural separatism. The ghost dances of the late nineteenth century can be seen as a form of ethnic mobilization along nonpolitical lines, as could any revivalist or escapist movement organized around the core cultural values of an ethnic group. In sum, what are the processes by which the content of ethnic activity is determined?

III. GYPSY ETHNICITY AND SOCIAL ORGANIZATION

The term "Gypsy" as used by most people refers to a number of groups who view themselves as distinct, though in some cases related. There has been some controversy even among scholars concerning appropriate classification schemes for these groups. Those groups generally referred to as Gypsies by scholars are thought to be descendents of bands of nomads who left India approximately a thousand years ago and wandered across western Asia, eventually arriving in Europe in the fifteenth century. Within Gypsy society there are several levels of subethnic divisions. A broad division is drawn between the Sedentary Gypsies, or Sinti, and the so-called Nomad Gypsies, or Rom. The Sinti, which include the "musician" Gypsies of Hungary and Rumania and the Gitanos of Spain, have been settled for generations, and have adopted to varying degrees the language and customs of the host society in which they settled. On the other hand, even today the Nomad Gypsies generally retain something of a nomadic lifestyle, even if only moving frequently within a single urban area, and maintain distinctive cultural and social forms. They speak versions of a language known as *Romanes,* an Indo-European dialect related to Sanskrit and Prakrit.[2]

Within the Nomad Gypsies, two types of ethnic subdivisions are recognized. The first is based on "tribal" identifications, referred to by the Rom as *natsiyi* (sing. *natsia*). Four *natsiyi* consider themselves and each other Rom. These include the Machwaya, Lowara, Kalderash, and Churara. The second type of identification is based on geographic origin, rather than *natsia* (e.g., English Gypsies, Scottish Gypsies). Though these Nomad groups identify themselves as distinct groups, they may have cordial relations. However, the division between the Nomads and the Sinti is reported to be very great (Gropper, 1975).

A number of other groups also fall under the rubric of "Gypsies and Travellers." These "Travellers" include groups presumed to be of mixed ancestry, produced by intermarriage of the Rom with host populations, several groups of disputed origin, and several groups that are believed to have no genetic relationship to the Rom. These groups generally maintain a seminomadic lifestyle, their own customs, and in most cases speak a dialect distinct from that of the host society. The best known are the Irish Travellers (or "Tinkers") [see Barnes (1975), Crawford and Gmelch (1974), Rehfisch and Rehfisch (1975), and Gmelch (1985)]. This analysis focuses on the Nomad Gypsies (hereafter referred to as Gypsies) and the Travellers. The Sinti are not discussed, as their economic and political history differs significantly from that of the other groups.

A. Gypsies in the United States

Several groups of Gypsies and Travellers are found in the United States today. The largest of these groups are known as Romanichals and are descendents of Gypsy families who began arriving in North America in the mid-1800s. They speak Anglo-Romani, a dialect based on English grammar with some Romani words. According to Salo (1979, p. 79), the Romanichals estimate their number in North America at about 100,000. Groups calling themselves Rom are estimated to number around 20,000 (Salo, 1979, p. 76; Cohn, 1973, p. 23). The most numerous *natsiyi* in the United States are the Machwaya and the Kalderash, with a smaller group of recently migrated Lowara. There also appears to be a small group of Churara in the Americas. Gropper (1975) suggests that the so-called "Killer-Gypsies" are in fact Churara. Also present in the United States is a group called the Ludar, numbering several thousand, who speak a form of Rumanian. Their relationship to the Rom and Romanichals is ambiguous. [see Salo (1979)]. Salo (1979, p. 81) also reports the presence of a group of German Gypsies (called "Black Dutch") and several groups of Irish and Scottish Travellers.

Several features of Gypsy social organization and culture are pertinent to this analysis of political mobilization.[3] The Rom maintain a highly adaptable social organization, based on kinship. Each *natsia* is subdivided into *vitsi* (sing. *vitsa*), or lineages. The *vitsa* may vary in size, and it functions situationally, providing authority as well as an identificational reference point. The *vitsa* is composed of several *familiyi* (sing. *familia*), or extended cognatic families, each headed by the eldest functioning adult member.[4] The family head exerts considerable power over other family members, and leadership in the *vitsa* rests with these family heads. However, a single individual may emerge as *rom baro* ("Big Man"). The leaders of the *vitsa* exert considerable influence and can mobilize members to achieve collective economic ends, in competition with both other Gypsies and outsiders.

While the *vitsa* provides identity and authority, the residential group and most important economic group in Gypsy social structure is the *kumpania*. The *kumpania* may consist of persons from a single *vitsa,* or from several *vitsi* or even several *natsiyi*. Membership in a *kumpania* appears quite fluid, with individuals coming and going according to no set pattern. The *kumpania* can vary considerably in size, depending on the economic situation. The *kumpania* is also an important locus of internal Gypsy politics. Within the kumpania, the heads of the *familiyi* together make decisions through discussion and consensus. However, there may also emerge a *rom baro,* who can claim authority over other families in the *kumpania* and represent them in dealing with non-Gypsies, who are referred to as *gaje* (sing. *gajo*). The *rom baro*'s power may derive from the size of his *familia* within the *kumpania,* the status of his *vitsa* or *natsia,* his wealth, his age, and/or his ability to manipulate *gaje* to the advantage of his *kumpania*. Reports of Gypsy chiefs or Gypsy kings may refer to the *rom baro* of a *kumpania* or of a *vitsa*. However, a so-called Gypsy king is often a less powerful individual who functions to mask the actual leadership of the group from *gajo* hostility.

Rom cultural practices emphasize the gap between Rom and *gaje*. This gap is maintained by a number of conventions that minimize contact with *gaje* and limit the private information any *gaje* can obtain, and it is reinforced by a system of pollution taboos. This system is based on a separation of clean from unclean (*marime*), ordering parts of the body, relations between sexes, and relations between Rom and *gaje,* as well as defining rules of sanitation. To violate these rules may make an individual *marime*. Most important, it defines relations with *gaje* as *marime*—especially sexual relations. Traditionally, an individual who is *marime* by virtue of some infraction would be temporarily or permanently excluded from the group.[5]

The gap between Rom and non-Rom is further emphasized in the complementary institution known as the *kris romani* (court), a tribunal consisting of a council of elders and one or more judges. A *kris* may be convened to deal with serious infractions or injustices. Most of the cases reported by observers concern economic and marital disputes. Any Rom—and only Rom—can participate in the *kris,* reinforcing the separation of Rom from *gaje,* and even Rom from non-Rom Gypsies.

The Romanichals and Ludari appear to have a similar form of social organization and practice similar pollution taboos. Several differences in marriage patterns have been noted, however (Salo, 1979). Little is known about the cultural practices of Travellers in the United States.

The economic activities of these groups are similar in that all prefer self-employment and pursue economic activities marginal to the *gajo* economy. These occupations are marked by diversity, varying both synchronically and diachronically. A single group of individuals may pursue several occupations at once, or change occupations sequentially, as new opportunities become available and old ones disappear. Today, the main income of the Rom is from women's fortune-telling work, supplemented with income from intermittent work by the men. Rom men pursue a wide variety of occupations, including black-topping and seal-coating of driveways; auto body work; repair of hydraulic jacks, shopping carts, and similar items; carnival concessions; and dealing in scrap metal or used cars [see Salo (1981)]. Other reported sources of income for the Rom include seasonal farm labor, welfare, begging, and various scams (Sutherland, 1975; Sway, 1982). The Romanichal and Ludari practice similar occupations. However, Salo (1981) found that the men's occupations provide the main income for these groups, while women's fortune-telling is supplementary.

Thus, at one extreme, Gypsies fill a gap, albeit marginal, in the *gajo* economy. They perform needed tasks, such as repair of shopping carts and seal-coating of driveways, that under usual economic conditions are too irregular or unprofitable to be attractive to larger *gajo* enterprises. At the other extreme, Gypsies exploit the surplus of the *gajo* system of production: carnival work, fortune-telling, and even the highly touted Gypsy scams are all ways of squeezing a surplus from the larger economy. Furthermore, Gypsies are constantly in competition with other groups for a share of the work. Even fortune-telling and personal "advising/healing," long considered a mainstay of Gypsy economics, undoubtedly has more non-Gypsy practitioners than Gypsies. Gypsies use their seminomadism and flexible organization to discover and obtain jobs before *gaje* organizations can do so and to eke a living out of the margins of those trades that are too unprofitable to be of interest to the *gaje*.[6]

Of course, various strategies are available to the practitioner of most of these occupations. One can perform sheet metal work or home repairs within the confines of an established bureaucratic enterprise with a permanent location. Or, one can pursue a more informal mode of business, soliciting work independently and over a scattered geographic area. Gypsies prefer the second alternative, which allows them to maintain independence and minimize contact with *gaje*. Gypsy enterprises are generally small-scale and labor-intensive, drawing primarily on the labor of kin and other members of one's *kumpania*. Great value is placed on "living by one's wits," and on the ability to exploit unwitting *gaje*.

It should already be obvious that the distinction between "Gypsy" and "*gaje*" is central to Gypsy life. Gypsies go to great lengths to keep outsiders out. Maintaining their own language and a seminomadic lifestyle contributes to this separation. When trouble arises or *gaje* become too close, the Gypsies can simply move on. In addition, Gypsy society is insulated by the selective manipulation of ethnic identity. Knowing when to conceal and when to exaggerate one's "Gypsiness" is an important aspect of being a Gypsy (Silverman, 1982; Sutherland, 1975). In many economic pursuits, it is advantageous for Gypsies to conceal their ethnic identity from their customers. Even fortune-tellers often claim the identity of the ethnic group from which they draw customers. However, in dealing with welfare workers, Gypsies often find it advantageous to exaggerate their status as a poor minority.[7] The distinction between Gypsy and non-Gypsy is a central, shared value, common to all the groups discussed here.

However, there also exist important ethnic boundaries separating the groups from each other. The Rom, Romanichals, and Ludari generally categorize themselves and each other as "Gypsies," though recognizing the distinctiveness of each group. The Rom, however, do not consider the other two groups to be "real Gypsies," and the social distance between the Romanichals and Ludari is less than between either of those groups and the Rom. Each group harbors ambivalent feelings about the other. Salo (1979, p. 92) suggests that among all three groups, marriage with *gaje* is more common than intergroup marriages. Even within the Rom, boundaries exist between *natsiyi*. For example, Salo (1979) reports considerable social distance between the recently arrived Lowara and the other Rom groups. Sutherland (1975) reports some distance between the Machwaya and Kalderash, though Machwaya apparently preferred Kalderash daughter-in-laws, as they were seen to be more "traditional." Similar divisions exist separating the "Gypsies" from the Irish and Scottish Travellers, who do not identify themselves as Gypsies (Harper, 1971; Salo, 1979). Though each group recognizes that the others are not *gaje,* they do not see themselves as a forming a larger, homogeneous group. As Salo (1977, p. 54) put it in referring to the Rom: "The overall judgement seems to be that the others may not be quite as sharp in business as the Rom, but they do live by their wits and certainly cannot be classed as *gaze.*"

B. Gypsies and Travellers in Great Britain

Estimates of the number of Gypsies and Travellers in Great Britain vary widely, and the confusion is compounded by debates about who should and should not be counted a "Traveller." In the early 1960s, Norman Dodds, a member of Parliament and staunch defender of Travellers, estimated their number to be approximately 100,000 (Ministry of Housing, 1967, p. 7). In 1964, the government undertook a census of Travellers, using local officials and sometimes police to administer the questionnaires. The census counted about 15,000 Travellers but is acknowledged to be an undercount (Ministry of Housing, 1967; Okely, 1983, p. 22). Data provided by Acton (1974, p. 183) put the number of Travellers at between 20,000 and 30,000.

As in the United States, several groups are commonly lumped together under the term "Gypsies" or "Travellers." Among Travellers in Britain, the term Rom is generally used to refer only to a relatively small group of Kalderash from Eastern Europe. British Gypsies employ subethnic identifications based on geographic boundaries corresponding to those of the larger non-Gypsy society: e.g., referring to themselves as "Welsh Gypsies" or "English Gypsies." Other groups, such as the Scottish Travellers and Irish Travellers, are believed to be unrelated to the Rom and are generally treated as non-Gypsy but leading a similar lifestyle. Several groups are commonly presumed to be the product of miscegenation of Gypsies and non-Gypsies (called *gorgios*), and have been referred to by a variety of names, most pejorative, including Didikois, posh-rats, and Tinkers. These groups are referred to collectively as Travellers.

These Travellers are scattered throughout Great Britain, though they are somewhat more numerous in the southeastern areas. Like Gypsies in North America, until recently they were largely rural nomads, performing a variety of crafts and agricultural work, as well as telling fortunes and hawking. Their present-day concentrations are in areas on the urban fringe, and scrap dealing has become an important occupation. Nonetheless, like Gypsies in America, the Travellers simultaneously pursue a variety of occupations, including hawking of various goods, dealing in used cars and appliances, casual entertainment, agricultural work, and wagon and cart construction (Okely, 1983; Acton, 1974; Adams, Okely, Morgan, and Smith, 1975). As in the United States, it is economically important for Gypsies to know how and when to conceal their ethnic identity and when to use it to play upon *gorgio*'s stereotypes. For purposes of pursuing some occupations, Gypsies conceal their ethnic identity. For example, in dealing in antiques, they present themselves as respectable businessmen with a permanent business address, while as scrap and rag collectors, they employ an image as poor scavengers. Other occupations have been exoticised by non-Gypsies as "traditional Gypsy crafts," including fortune-telling, hawking of hand-made wooden clothes pegs and baskets, and wagon and cart construction (Okely, 1983, pp. 50–52). Here, it is an advantage for Gypsies to dramatize their identity.

Like Gypsies in the United States, Travellers usually live and work in relatively small, extended family units. According to Okely (1983), leadership among Gypsies in Great Britain is usually shared by elders, and the emergence of an individual leader like a *rom baro* is rare. Though all groups, including the Irish and Scottish Travellers, are reported to observe pollution taboos, there does not appear to be any institution similar to the *kris*. [See Gentlemen and Swift (1971), Adams *et al.* (1975), Okely (1975, 1983), Rehfisch and Rehfisch (1975), and Gmelch (1985).] Though there appears to be a bias toward endogamy, Okely (1983) reports considerable intermarriage among the groups. However, there is little sense of ethnic unity among the groups, aside from a sense of collective distinction from *gorgios* (Acton, 1974; Okely, 1983).

IV. GYPSY POLITICAL MOBILIZATION

A. The Red Scarf Association

Until the Great Depression of the 1930s, Gypsies in the United States were mainly seminomadic, relying on horse-drawn caravans for transportation, and were primarily rural, settling in forest camps or urban areas during the winter. They practiced a variety of trades, including horse dealing, smithwork, agricultural work, and fortune-telling. The 1920s and 1930s brought a number of important changes in Gypsy lifestyle. First, the automobile began to replace the horse, altering both the Gypsies' economy and their mode of transportation.

Second, with the Crash of 1929, economic resources in rural areas began to dry up, and Gypsies began to resort to towns and cities in larger numbers. This trend intensified with the election of Roosevelt, as the nation's welfare institutions expanded. Gypsies congregated in urban areas in increasing numbers in order to avail themselves of these institutions. Since at least one member of a family had to be available to welfare agencies at all times, this meant that many had to curtail their traditional nomadic lifestyle. Later, the imposition of gasoline rationing made it all the more difficult for Gypsies to travel. Thus, during the first part of this century, the lifestyle of many Gypsies in America was dramatically altered, from one of rural nomadism to life primarily in urban areas (though Gypsies still moved within and between urban areas), and from an economy based on self-employment in a variety of trades to an economy more dependent on *gajo* welfare institutions and fortune-telling.

It was against this backdrop that the Red Scarf Association emerged. Accounts of the Association first appeared in 1928. It was ostensibly established by Steve Kaslov, a Kalderash "chief" in New York.[8] Its stated purpose was the abolition of child marriage among the Rom and the establishment of a Gypsy "colony," where Rom children could be educated, where fortune-tellers could be licensed, and where the men could have a permanent workshop in which to practice their traditional trades. The colony was presented as a place where traditional Rom culture could be preserved (and possibly improved), and where non-Gypsies could become acquainted with it [see Weybright (1938)].

Initially, only Kaslov's *vitsa* was involved. However, by 1939, he managed to convince the authorities that he was in fact the "King of all New York Gypsies," sought a WPA (Works Progress Administration) grant, and began acting as liaison for the allocation of relief funds. As a result, he became a very powerful leader, and several other groups sought client status in his organization (Gropper, 1967).[9] Among these were several non-Rom groups. According to Gropper (1967), these groups began to intermarry with the Kalderash, were accepted by the Rom, and even were allowed to participate in the *kris*. In 1939, a Romani Coppersmith shop was opened, and in 1940, a WPA adult education project was launched. In order to obtain part of the funds, the Machwaya in Manhattan were forced to ally themselves with Kaslov as well.

Meanwhile, a Chicago leader, Tinia Bimbo, had arrived in New York with his *vitsa*. There followed a period of competition for leadership between Kaslov and Tinia Bimbo, and later Tinia's son Steve, with each having the other arrested on various charges. Apparently in order to avoid prosecution by *gaje*, both Steve Bimbo and Steve Kaslov eventually fled New York. Kaslov fled some time after 1942, and the Red Scarf Association for all practical purposes broke up. The disintegration of the association was hastened by the discontinuance of WPA and its replacement with Social Security and individual benefits.

Though short-lived, the Red Scarf Association was unusual in the history of the Gypsies in the United States. It was novel in that it organized an unusually large number of Gypsies into a single entity that presented itself to the political institutions of the United States as a corporate group, deserving of funding and (by extension) political recognition. It was also unusual in the degree of public attention it has received. Nonetheless, it was essentially an instance of traditional Rom economic strategy and Rom internal politics. Throughout their history in Europe, the Rom had repeatedly taken advantage of *gajo* political institutions for protection and economic advantage—for example, by requesting client status from local rulers. Even in the United States, Gypsies had devised various schemes for manipulating the welfare institutions. The Red Scarf Association does not appear to have been directed at changing the position of Rom within American society. Rather, it was an attempt to garner some economic resources from *gajo* institutions, using a novel strategy. Its stated ideology was romantic: to establish a protected "colony" where Rom culture could be preserved. Whatever its actual goals, its strategy was consistent with other smaller-scale Gypsy activities: locate and obtain whatever surplus resources are available from the larger economy.

What was different in this case was that WPA made grants to corporate groups rather than individuals or families. Thus, there were advantages in organizing at a more inclusive level than the family. Government policy, by allocating funds to corporate groups, directly influenced the level and nature of ethnic activity pursued by Gypsies. These policies simultaneously encouraged the formation of a corporate group with quasi-political aims and the shift in ethnic boundaries to a more inclusive level.

B. The Gypsy Council

The Gypsy Council of Great Britain, on the other hand, is unlike traditional Gypsy strategies in dealing with *gaje*. The conditions leading to the foundation of the Gypsy Council in 1966 had their roots in the crowding of temporary housing projects and campsites during World War II. During the war, some Traveller men were drafted, and others were pressed into public service in work brigades. The families of these men had to be housed somewhere, and since few had permanent housing of their own, they were provided with temporary housing in campsites near the bases from which the men worked. After the war, the housing situation became critical for Travellers and non-Travellers alike, and the temporary sites provided during the war became crowded with families from all backgrounds, since little regular housing was available.

Most of the competition that emerged after World War II involved local government authorities and Travellers, and focused on land use. The postwar crowding and associated public health and sanitation problems caused considerable animosity in surrounding communities. Local officials turned to the Public Health Act of 1936, which allowed them to clear out shanty towns that did not meet public health standards. The brunt of this effort fell on Gypsies and Travellers.

The situation became more critical after 1960, when the Caravan Sites and Control of Development Act was passed by Parliament. This act established rigorous licensing procedures for caravan sites. In practice, the act made it all but impossible to establish new privately owned sites. Hence, the value of established sites rose, and rents were increased. Since other earlier acts forbade camping along the roadsides, the Travellers were left with the option of trespassing if they could not find legal sites. Even if they could find licensed sites, Gypsies were often unwelcome as their presence made the camps less attractive to non-Gypsy campers. Evicted from private campsites, unwelcome at the few licensed campsites, and driven from roadsides, Travellers often congregated at county borders, driven from one jurisdiction to another by local authorities.[10]

Indirectly, these evictions affected the Travellers' economic resources, since access to campsites was necessary in order for them to continue their semi-nomadic lifestyle and pursue their most common occupations. However, more direct occupational competition also emerged. By the late 1960s, many of the rural occupations of Travellers had disappeared, and so many had turned to dealing in scrap metal. The Scrap Metal Dealers Act of 1964 and the Civic Amenities Act of 1967 regulated these activities by requiring scrap dealers to register in the locality in which they worked, and by requiring scrap to be left only in authorized places. These laws were occasionally used against Travellers by forcing them to reregister in every new area they visited and by constricting their ability to dump scrap that could not be resold. These laws were not enforced as widely as the Caravan Sites Act, however, and hence the main competition continued to focus on access to land.

Despite the increased pressure, Travellers did not initially take any sort of organized or political action to protect their interests. Early political activity on behalf of the Travellers was led mostly by non-Travellers, and it was in these early stages that the tone of future Gypsy political action was defined.[11] The earliest—and perhaps most important—figure in the political mobilization of Travellers was Norman Dodds, a Member of Parliament for Erith and Crayford, a district that contained the largest shanty towns in England during the late 1940s. Through his visits to the shanty towns, Dodds came into contact with several Gypsies and Travellers. Following his political instincts, he organized a "Gypsy Committee" together with these representatives. The Gypsy Committee eventually drew up a nine-point Gypsy Charter. Among the points were calls for adequate provision of campsites, a scheme for educating Gypsy children, and a better liaison with the Ministry of Labor, in order to make available information on jobs in the vicinity of camps. Dodds came to be the most impassioned spokesman for Travellers, bringing their concerns to Parliament, and eventually winning passage of an ammended version of the Caravan Sites Act in 1962.

After 1965, with Dodds's death, the key figure in the emerging Gypsy political movement became Grattan Puxon, a non-Traveller who became acquainted
with some Travellers while working as a freelance journalist in Ireland. In 1966,
he, together with some of his contacts in Britain, founded the Gypsy Council and
the associated National Gypsy Education Council. The initial group of about 30
individuals consisted of non-Traveller intellectuals, philanthropists, and several
leaders of Gypsy and Traveller families. Their first meeting—held in a pub with
a sign reading "No Gypsies Allowed"—called for a strong Gypsy Council that
would be controlled by Gypsies and Travellers, a code of conduct for all Travelling peoples, and provisions for the education of Traveller and Gypsy children. A
key idea was that all travelling groups, whether Rom or not, should be included.
This idea was promoted by the non-Gypsies and caused considerable dissension
(Acton, 1974, chapter 13). In fact, it nearly brought about the demise of the
Council before it had even gotten underway. One Gypsy leader withdrew from
the fledgling organization, writing to Puxon:

> With regards to the Gypsy Council, I'm afraid I must disassociate myself from it. Whilst
> wishing you and the people you are trying to help every success, I'm afraid their
> problems aren't mine, and, while I know most of the Irish Travellers and like them, they
> know and I know, that we are of different blood. I think that all we have in common is
> that we are nomadic . . . I was rather embarrassed and a little angry when it was
> suggested we had to be cleaner. I don't think Romani people in general, and myself in
> particular need lessons in hygiene. On the other hand, we both know, you and I, that
> there are 'travellers' who certainly do need lessons in the most elementary forms of
> hygienic living!!! [quoted in Acton (1974), p. 167].

The organization survived, thanks in part to Puxon's political skills and his
ability to convince all groups that their interests were best served by combining
forces, even if begrudgingly. This recognition may have been complicated by the
fact that simultaneously some *gorgio* officials were themselves drawing distinctions among travelling groups in developing official policy. Some *gorgio* authorities even suggested that the government should provide campsites for Gypsies ("true Romanies"), but not for Travellers, who are genetically unrelated to
the Rom, and therefore apparently not so deserving (Okely, 1983).

Between 1966 and 1968, the Council was involved in a number of actions.
Typically, these involved passive resistance to evictions, demonstrations, and
sending of delegations to meetings and other public forums. Several Gypsy and
Traveller schools were founded, and these usually aroused sympathy from local
populations and the press. During 1967 conflict intensified, along with alle-
gations of violence. In one instance, a caravan being towed by local authorities
was reported to have caught fire, burning several children inside (*Irish Press,* 16
Dec. 1967; *The Guardian,* 18 Dec. 1967). Finally, in response to this pressure,
Parliament enacted the 1968 Caravan Sites Act. According to this law, county
councils are required to provide sites for all Travellers residing in or resorting to
their areas. However, at the same time, the law gave local councils extra powers

of eviction. It was left to local authorities to provide adequate sites, and district councils were given considerable discretion in meeting the requirements of the new law and in approving private sites.

By 1969, the Gypsy Council had become, at least in part, what it originally had been conceived as: a representative organization, run by Gypsies and Travellers. Puxon lost power, and a Gypsy leader took over. Though the organization continued with an uneasy alliance of several travelling groups, disputes continued, especially concerning the form of education to be provided for children of Travellers and Gypsies. Disputes also continued over tactics (legal or popular) and over finances. Despite its eventual problems, for the first few years of its existence the Gypsy Council was a success in pressure politics and as an organization. Acton (1974, p. 183) estimates that by 1970, approximately one-fifth to one-fourth of eligible travelling families in Great Britain subscribed to the organization. [See also Cripps (1977) and Adams et al. (1975).] Referring to a closing and eviction that occurred in 1961, Okely quotes one Traveller as saying, "If we'd had people like the Gypsy Council in those days, it would never have happened" (1983, p. 108). Thus, it appears that the Gypsy Council had in fact won considerable recognition and support among the Gypsies and Travellers.

This does not imply that conditions markedly improved for Travellers, however. After the Act, evictions continued, and private sites continued to be closed. In 1971, the Gypsy Council estimated that the number of sites closed by the 1960 Act outnumbered those made available under the 1968 Act (Adams et al., 1975, pp. 9–10). Government policy implicitly favored a welfare approach, aimed at settling the Travellers. Wardens and social workers were assigned to campsites. Okely (1983) notes that authorities preferred to establish "permanent sites"—by which they meant sites on which Travellers would settle permanently. Despite this effort, even in 1977, some 6000 families reportedly remained illegally camped in Britain (*The Economist,* 14 May 1977). It is important to note that there is land available to create campsites. The problem is not so much land scarcity as control over access to land. It appears that today, at least, the *gorgios* have won the contest over land use.

V. DISCUSSION

The Red Scarf Association and the Gypsy Council were very different kinds of organizations in several important respects. The Red Scarf Association was rooted in traditional Rom sociopolitical structures and employed a typical survival strategy. Kaslov, like subsequent leaders of the Association, was a typical *rom baro*. The association aimed at manipulating *gajo* institutions in order to obtain resources from the *gajo* economy. The Gypsy Council, on the other hand, was formed largely at the instigation of non-Gypsies and borrowed its tactics from non-Gypsies. In fact, accounts of the Gypsy Council's early activities read much like accounts of the Civil Rights movement in the American South. Despite this, the Gypsy Council eventually won popular support from the various Gypsy and Traveller groups it sought to organize. The fact that an organization run largely by *gorgios* could attract such popular support may reflect the fact that, though the Gypsy Council's tactics were novel, its purpose was straightforward. It sought to protect Gypsy access to campsites, which was necessary in order to pursue most Gypsy economic activities and to ensure group survival.

Nonetheless, the two organizations have much in common. In both cases, Rom associated with other groups whom they would normally disdain. In both cases, this change in ethnic boundaries, albeit temporary, precipitated a change from several highly diffuse organizations to a centralized and considerably larger unit. Both organizations can be seen as strategies used by Gypsies in competing with non-Gypsies for scarce resources—in one case, government funds, and in the other, access to land. Most important, both organizations emerged at times when competition with non-Gypsies was intensifying. In the case of the Gypsy Council, the organization was primarily reactive. That is, it was formed in response to encroachment by non-Gypsies, with the purpose of protecting access to needed resources. The Red Scarf Association emerged at a time when previously exploited resources were extremely scarce and sought by many, and when a new resource (government grants) became available. In both cases, Gypsies mobilized under conditions of intensified competition, while access to resources was in dispute.

These examples of Gypsy political mobilization are surprising on two counts. First, it is surprising that ethnic boundaries shifted to incorporate groups that were previously disdainful if not suspicious of each other. In both the cases of the Red Scarf Association and the Gypsy Council, this shift in boundaries cannot be understood without understanding the constraints imposed by the national governments and the political perceptions of non-Gypsies. In the case of the Red Scarf Association, government policy clearly encouraged the formation of a larger group. Since grants under WPA were made to corporate groups, a larger group had both a better chance of winning a grant and could obtain additional funds. Thus, there were economic benefits to be obtained by forming alliances with other non-Rom groups. These alliances disintegrated once a welfare system based on individual and family benefits was in place. Constraints imposed by the federal government altered the rules of access to resources, and in doing so shifted both the boundaries of the Gypsies' economic niche and ethnic boundaries.

The process of change leading to the Gypsy Council's formation was more complex. Until the 1960 Caravan Sites Act, competition between Travellers and *gorgios* over access to land on which to camp had been steadily intensifying. However, as in earlier times, the rules by which access was obtained still varied from local community to local community. The 1960 Caravan Sites Act imposed a more uniform set of constraints on the Travellers' access to camp sites. Certainly, this helped to focus political efforts on a national level.

Though there was a shift in boundaries in both cases, this shift was neither easy nor permanent. The alliance lasted only as long as the conditions made it advantageous to organize at a more inclusive level. Furthermore, it is important to note that this shift in boundaries affected social relationships, but did not alter the cultural practices of the groups. Traditional institutions were maintained, but definitions of who could participate were altered.

Second, it is surprising that Gypsies would turn to activities likely to attract so much public attention. Superficially, it would appear that leadership of non-Travellers was an important catalyst in turning Gypsies to pressure politics. The role of leaders and their social background has been advanced as an important element in shaping the strategy and goals of ethnic political movements (Leifer, 1981). It is tempting to attribute the different purposes and styles of the Red Scarf Association and the Gypsy Council to the backgrounds of their respective leaders. Indeed, the Gypsy Council's tactics seem more typical of *gorgios* than Gypsies. However, this explanation overlooks a key point. That is, without followers, there can be no leaders. Looking especially at the Gypsy Council, it is clear that the allegiance of Travellers was won slowly and tentatively. Here, the more pertinent question is not ''Why did the leaders of the Gypsy Council choose the political strategy of pressure politics?'' but rather ''Why did Gypsies follow?'' In both the cases considered here, the mobilization of groups was in response to actions of the national government. In the case of the Red Scarf Association, government welfare policies opened up new resources. In Britain, the 1960 Caravan Sites Act simplified the system of constraints on Traveller access to land at the same time that it altered the balance of power by giving local authorities greater power in regulating caravan travel. In both cases, the nature of changes in the productive niche of Gypsies—especially in the constraints affecting Gypsy activities—tended to focus activity on the political realm. Furthermore, these changes tended to focus activity on the level of *national* rather than local politics, as in both cases the key policies were defined by the national government. Thus, despite the fact that pressure politics is not the ''traditional'' way for Gypsies to deal with *gajo* hostility and competition, even small, ''traditional'' groups like the Red Scarf Association can be prompted into such action when conditions focus competition on national political institutions.[12]

The current state of Gypsy political activity in the United States and Great Britain may provide the best evidence in support of these interpretations. In the early 1970s, branches of the International Gypsy Committee were established in the United States and Canada. Other Gypsy political organizations also emerged in the United States during the 1970s, including the American Gypsy Organization (in Indiana), the Gypsy Cultural Program (in Washington state), the Pennsylvania Gypsy Alliance (Philadelphia), and the Gypsy Society of Chicago. The latter organization involves Rom, Romanichals, and Boyash (Hancock, 1980, p. 444). In 1976, one Gypsy leader, John Tene (of Bimbo's *vitsa*), established an organization called "Romania of Massachusetts, Inc.," with the purpose of providing education for Gypsy children and adults, legal advice, health services, and job training. However these are not mass organizations, and in most cases appear to involve only one or a few *vitsi* or *kumpaniyi*.

As for the Gypsy Council, it continues to exist but has found some competition of its own. After 1971, a number of other groups representing Gypsies and Travellers were formed. These included the Romany Guild, the Association of Travelling People, the Southern Gypsy Council, and the Association of Gypsy and Romany Organisations. All competed for assistance and recognition from the national and local governments, as well as the allegiance of Travellers. Rather than representing a revolutionary uprising of Traveller nationalism as some have suggested (Kenrick and Puxon, 1972), this appears instead to represent bureaucratic fragmentation (Okely, 1983; Acton, 1985).

Thus, in both the United States and Great Britain, Gypsy political activity now appears to be fragmented, and in fact often resembles more traditional forms of activity vis-à-vis *gaje*.[13] In Britain, though conditions have not markedly improved for the Travellers, the responsibility of providing sites and meeting the national requirements has now shifted back to the county governments. Given the nature of Gypsy economics and the fact that pertinent political constraints in both countries must once again be dealt with largely on a local level, this is not surprising.

As this analysis illustrates, processes of ethnic mobilization, the definition of ethnic boundaries, and the determination of the goals and strategies employed in ethnically oriented action are intimately interrelated. Among the Gypsies, processes of political mobilization occurred when competition with non-Gypsies intensified. Increased competition results not only from changes in the absolute level of resources in an area but also from changes in the legal constraints that affect the ability of one or both groups to utilize those resources. Viewing the Gypsies' productive niche in terms of occupations alone is insufficient for explaining Gypsy ethnic activity. However, to understand the direction of this activity and the process of change in group boundaries requires that we look specifically at the activities of the national governments. The process of state expansion, and not simply the idiosyncratic characteristics of leaders, has shaped ethnic activity in modern states.

What can this analysis of Gypsy political mobilization tell us about the theoretical questions raised in Section II? Regarding the first question, it is clear that ethnic boundaries cannot be taken for granted. As others have pointed out, a major analytic issue is to account for the level at which ethnic activity occurs. There were several levels at which Gypsies could find basis for shared activity. The level at which they did unite shifted in reflection of changes in economic and political conditions. In both cases discussed here, the policies of the central state were the decisive factor influencing the level at which ethnic mobilization occurred.

Regarding the second question, Gypsies clearly cannot be said to specialize in one or a few occupations. Furthermore, they do not in most cases enjoy a monopoly of some occupation specialty, even fortune-telling. Focusing on occupational specialization misses the key features of the Gypsy economic niche. Rather, the niche must be viewed in broader terms, encompassing not just resources (or occupations) but also strategies for exploiting those resources and governmental constraints affecting the group's ability to do so. When viewed in these terms, it is clear that Gypsies mobilized when competition intensified, before questions of access to resources had been settled. In sum, ethnic political activity was most intense while the contest was on, not after it had been settled.

As for the third question, again it appears that structural conditions in the nation-state are the key to understanding the course of ethnic mobilization. The structural conditions that create competition and define the level of ethnic activity also act to shape its content. In particular, when national governments act to centralize decision-making and impose uniform policies, political activity will focus on the national level. Insofar as local governments retain decision-making ability, though, some fragmentation of ethnic political activity can be expected. Even ethnic r-strategists can be expected to pursue collective political ends when the competition for resources (or access to resources) must be waged in national political institutions.

ACKNOWLEDGMENTS

I would like to thank Matt Salo and several members of the Gypsy Lore Society, North American Chapter, for their helpful comments on earlier versions of this paper. Of course, the opinions expressed herein are those of the author.

NOTES

[1]Bioecologists describe a population by several parameters. These include the parameter K, which denotes the carrying capacity of the population's environment, and r, which refers to the population's intrinsic rate of increase. The term "r-strategist" and its counterpart "K-strategist" denote populations that maximize certain characteristics through the process of selection in order to gain a competitive advantage. A K-strategist is a species that maximizes its ability to survive and reproduce under long-term densities near the carrying capacity (K) of the environment. For such species, it is not advantageous to have a high rate of reproduction; rather, it is advantageous to be able to seize and hold resources. An r-strategist, on the other hand, maximizes its ability to quickly expand population size in order to be able to quickly locate and exploit resources before other competing populations can, then disperse in search of new resources. Which of these strategies is more effective depends on the characteristics of the environment. The K-strategists would be favored in a stable environment, while the r-strategists are favored in temporary, irregular, and unpredictable environments. These

concepts can also be applied to human groups [see Lauwagie (1979)]. A group that uses organizational and technological means to maintain control over a part of the environment's resources under long-term high densities would be a K-strategist. An r-strategist group, on the other hand, would be opportunistic, emphasizing an ability to quickly discover resources, use them, and then disperse. However, it could employ both biological and social means to quickly expand group size.

[2]The dialects spoken by Gypsies are generally divided into two categories: those reflecting considerable Eastern European influence, which have come to be known as the Vlach dialects, and the others, known simply as non-Vlach dialects. These dialects are also often referred to as "Romani." None of these are written languages, and authors have applied countless different spellings to Romani words. I have conformed to the spellings applied by Sutherland (1975), as these seem most straightforward for English-speaking audiences.

[3]Though these groups have similar forms of social and cultural organization, there are some distinctions. Since the Red Scarf Association is an outgrowth of typical Rom internal political organization, I discuss the practices of the Rom in most detail, noting differences between the groups where necessary.

[4]In general, the head of the family would be the eldest male. However, older women sometimes function as family head and can become very powerful.

[5]The consequences of violating these taboos can vary. In some cases, not only the violator but his or her entire *familia* could be temporarily or permanently excluded from Rom society. However, Sutherland (1975) reports that today, exclusion is viewed as an extreme punishment, and lesser measures are preferred.

[6]Gypsies have occasionally been referred to as "pariah" groups (Barth, 1955). This has raised the ire of numerous gypsiologists, who do not find this label "useful" (Sutherland, 1975, p. 8), and some of whom prefer to see Gypsies as providing useful services or in symbiotic relation to *gaje*. It is more accurate to view Gypsies as being in different relations to the various groups of *gaje* with whom they deal. To someone who has been the victim of a Gypsy scam, the label "pariah" may seem appropriate—although "predator" may be more accurate. To some, the Gypsies do undoubtedly provide useful services, and they should be seen as being in a symbiotic relationship with their clients. However, Gypsies are also in competition with other groups of *gaje,* competing with some to provide those useful services to the available client pool and with others to separate money from the pool of unwitting victims.

[7]Gypsies are adept at manipulating their ethnic identity to play on *gaje* stereotypes. Yoors (1967) relates incidents when Gypsies played on outsiders' notions of Gypsies as being dirty and lice infested, carrying infectious diseases, and stealing children in order to remain unknown. For example, the Gypsies would surround the camp with women and children, who would then feign to scratch themselves and cough compulsively, in order to discourage curious outsiders from coming too close. Silverman (1982) discusses the ways in which Gypsies manipulate their identity in their occupations and in daily life in the urban United States. For example, in one instance, while searching for an apartment, members of the group she studied claimed to be Jewish, while in dealing with New York City welfare officials, they claimed to be Puerto Rican. Apparently, the *gaje* were none the wiser.

[8]The Red Scarf Association is only one of the names associated with this organization, referring to the red scarf commonly worn by the Kalderash. In other instances, it is referred to as the Red Hat Association, the Red Dress Association, the American Red Dress Gypsies, and the Russian Red Bandanna Gypsies. It was officially incorporated as the Red Dress Gypsies Association, on November 22, 1927, in Passaic County, N.J. Kaslov was the leader of the Kalderash *vitsa* that dominated Manhattan at the time.

[9]For a more detailed discussion of the internal Gypsy political maneuvering behind this, see Gropper (1967) and Weybright (1938).

[10]British authorities are not the only ones to employ these tactics. State police in New England are reported to deal with Gypsies travelling through their territory in much the same fashion—by escorting them to the state line.

[11]*Gorgios* had acted on behalf of Gypsies prior to this time. International Gypsy organizations already existed. However, these appear to be supported mainly by Gypsy intellectuals and non-Gypsies.

[12]Certainly, the early leaders of the Gypsy Council—and probably the example of other ethnic nationalist movements—served as catalysts. However, given the Gypsies' prior experience with *gorgio* political figures, it is likely that they would eventually have undertaken some form of political activity themselves.

[13]Some of these activities bear a striking similarity to those of Kaslov and the Red Scarf Association. For example, according to Silverman (1982), a Gypsy leader in Oregon was invited to Ronald Reagan's Presidential Inauguration as "King of the Western North American Gypsies." A local news story said he would use the opportunity to ask Reagan to make available government grants and funds for Gypsies.

REFERENCES

ACTON, T. (1974). *Gypsy politics and social change.* Boston: Routledge and Kegan Paul.

ACTON, T. (1985). The social construction of ethnic identity of commercial nomadic groups. In *Papers from the fourth and fifth annual meetings of the Gypsy Lore Society, North American Chapter* (J. Grumet, ed.), Publications number 2, pp. 4–23. New York: Gypsy Lore Society, North American Chapter.

ADAMS, B., OKELY, J., MORGAN, D., and SMITH, D. (1975). *Gypsies and government policy in England.* London: Heinemann.

BARNES, BETTINA. (1975). Irish travelling people. In *Gypsies, Tinkers and other Travellers* (F. Rehfisch, ed.), pp. 231–256. New York: Academic Press.

BARTH, F. (1955). The social organization of a pariah group in Norway. *Norveg* **5**:125–144.

BARTH, F. (ed.). (1969). *Ethnic groups and boundaries.* Boston: Little-Brown.

BORROW, G. (1874). *Romano Lavo-Lil.* London: John Murray.

COHN, W. (1973). *The Gypsies.* Reading, Massachusetts: Addison-Wesley.

CRAWFORD, M. H., and GMELCH, G. (1974). Human biology of the Irish Tinkers: demography, ethnohistory, and genetics. *Social Biology* **21**(4):321–331.

CRIPPS, M. (1977). *Accommodation for Gypsies: A report on the working of the Caravan Sites Act 1968.* London: HMSO.

GENTLEMEN, H., and SWIFT, S. (1971). *Scotland's travelling people: Problems and solutions.* Edinburgh: HMSO.

GMELCH, G. (1985). *The Irish Tinkers: The urbanization of an itinerant people,* 2d ed. Prospect Heights, Illinois: Waveland Press.

GROPPER, R. (1967). Urban nomads: The Gypsies of New York City. *New York Academy of Sciences Transactions,* 2d ser., **29**:1050–1056.

GROPPER, R. (1975). *Gypsies in the city.* Princeton, New Jersey: Darwin.

HANCOCK, I. (1980). Gypsies. In *Harvard encyclopedia of American ethnic groups* (S. Thernstrom, ed.), pp. 440–445. Cambridge, Massachusetts: Harvard University Press.

HANNAN, M. (1979). The dynamics of ethnic boundaries in modern states. In *National development and the world system: Educational, economic, and political change 1950–1970* (J. Meyer and M. Hannan, eds.), pp. 253–275. Chicago: University of Chicago Press.

HARPER, J. (1971). 'Gypsy' research in the South. In *The not so solid South: Anthropological studies in a regional subculture* (J. Morland, ed.), pp. 16–24. Southern Anthropological Society Proceedings, 4. Athens, Georgia: Southern Anthropological Society.

HECHTER, M. (1975). *Internal colonialism: The Celtic fringe in British national development, 1536–1966.* Berkeley: University of California Press.

HECHTER, M. (1978). Group formation and the cultural division of labor. *American Journal of Sociology* **84**(2):293–318.

HOROWITZ, D. (1975). Ethnic identity. In *Ethnicity: theory and experience* (N. Glazer and D. Moynihan, eds.), pp. 111–140. Cambridge, Massachusetts: Harvard University Press.

KENRICK, D., and PUXON, G. (1972). *The destiny of Europe's Gypsies.* New York: Basic Books.

LAUWAGIE, B. (1979). Ethnic boundaries in modern states: Romano Lavo-Lil revisited. *American Journal of Sociology* **85**(2):310–337.

LEIFER, E. (1981). Competing models of political mobilization: The role of ethnic ties. *American Journal of Sociology* **87**(1):23–47.

MINISTRY OF HOUSING. (1967). *Gypsies and other Travellers.* London: HMSO.

NAGEL, J. (1979). The political construction of ethnicity. Paper presented at the 74th annual meeting of the American Sociological Association, Boston.

NIELSON, F. (1980). The Flemish movement in Belgium after World War II: A dynamic analysis. *American Sociological Review* **45**(1):76–94.

OKELY, J. (1975). Gypsies travelling in southern England. In *Gypsies, Tinkers and other Travellers* (F. Rehfisch, ed.), pp. 55–84. New York: Academic Press.

OKELY, J. (1983). *The Traveller-Gypsies.* New York: Cambridge University Press.

OLZAK, S. (1983). Contemporary ethnic mobilization. In *Annual Review of Sociology* (R. Turner and J. Short, eds.), pp. 355–374. Palo Alto, California: Annual Reviews, Inc.

PORTES, A. (1984). The rise of ethnicity: Determinants of ethnic perceptions among Cuban exiles in Miami. *American Sociological Review* **49**(3):383–397.

RAGIN, C. (1979). Ethnic political mobilization: The Welsh case. *American Sociological Review* **44**(4):619–635.

REHFISCH, A., and REHFISCH, F. (1975). Scottish Travellers or Tinkers. In *Gypsies, Tinkers and other Travellers* (F. Rehfisch, ed.), pp. 271–284. New York: Academic Press.

SALO, M. (1977). The expression of ethnicity in Rom oral tradition. *Western Folklore* **36**(1):33–56.

SALO, M. (1979). Gypsy ethnicity: Implications of native categories and interaction for ethnic classification. *Ethnicity* **6**(1):73–96.

SALO, M. (1981). Kalderas economic organization. In *The American Kalderas: Gypsies in the New World* (M. Salo, ed.), pp. 71–98. Hackettstown, New Jersey: Gypsy Lore Society, North American Chapter.

SLVERMAN, C. (1982). Everyday drama: Impression management of urban Gypsies. *Urban Anthropology* **11**(3–4):377–398.

SUTHERLAND, A. (1975). *Gypsies, the hidden Americans.* New York: Free Press.

SWAY, M. (1982). Economic adaptability? The case of the Gypsies. Paper presented at the 77th annual meeting of the American Sociological Association, San Francisco.

WEYBRIGHT, V. (1938). Who can tell the Gypsies' fortune? *Survey* **27**:142–145.

YOORS, J. (1967). *The Gypsies.* New York: Simon & Schuster.

Part II

Political Competition and Ethnicity

4

The Political Construction
of Ethnicity

Joane Nagel
Department of Sociology
University of Kansas
Lawrence, Kansas 66045

I. THE RISE AND DECLINE OF ETHNICITY

The closing decades of the twentieth century find the world's real estate, and consequently its population, divided among a heretofore unprecedented number of sovereign states.[1] In light of their often arbitrary, sometimes capricious origins, the boundaries of this state system have remained surprisingly stable. Young (1976, p. 66) comments on the anomalously successful rupture of Pakistani territorial integrity that produced Bangladesh: "It is truly stupendous that this instance stands almost alone as the breakdown of an existing post-independence state in the three decades since World War II."

What is notable about Bangladesh is only its success, since the forces that amassed in pursuit of independence were, by 1971, abundantly familiar shapes on many national horizons—Biafra, Katanga, Kurdistan, Eritrea, the Basque region, Québec, Northern Ireland, Southern Sudan, Azerbaijan, West Irian. These challenges to the postcolonial world map represented the extreme, separatist edge of a wave of subnational[2] mobilization sweeping across the world's states. The force and pervasiveness of subnationalism, not only in Asia and Africa, but in Scotland and Wales, Québec and Brittany, Flanders and Berne, found social scientists typically surprised. The presumed integrating effects of political and economic development (Deutsch, 1966; Azkin, 1964; Lipset and Rokkan, 1967)—long underway in the West and accelerating during the postindependence mobilizations in the new states—had proved more centrifugal than conjunctive. Growing urban and industrial centers had become the sites for cultural revivals, interethnic conflicts, and communal claims on resources and

COMPETITIVE ETHNIC RELATIONS

jurisdictions. Calls for devolution, autonomy, or independence had replaced the goals and rhetoric of the "integrative revolution" (Geertz, 1963). The volume and timing of the subnational mobilizations provided a rare but clear disaffirmation of a body of social science theory. The processes of state- and nation-building had failed to manufacture national identities out of local linguistic, cultural, or religious affiliations. Indeed, just the opposite had occurred. Ethnic identity and organization clearly appeared to be strengthening in the face of economic and political development. This ethnic vitality was particularly disconcerting to social scientists because it contradicted what seemed clear evidence of integration.

In both new and old states, researchers had, for some time, reported the classic signs of assimilation: increases in native language loss and intermarriage and declines in traditional religious practices. Oddly, however, these trends did not appear to produce the expected result—i.e., the formation of national-level identities. Rather, observers noted a puzzling resurgence of ethnicity, which often involved shifting the level of ethnic identification from smaller boundaries to larger-level affiliations (Glazer and Moynihan, 1963; Rudolph and Rudolph, 1967; Horowitz, 1971). For instance, the weakening of small-scale community-of-origin divisions in favor of larger linguistic identifications was reported among Italians in the United States (Child, 1943; Firey, 1947), Ibos in Nigeria (Horowitz, 1977; van den Berghe, 1971), Sindhi in Pakistan (Das Gupta, 1975), Tamils in India (Young, 1976), Malays in Malaysia (Smith, 1970–1971), and Bagisu in Uganda (Kasfir, 1979). Similarly, the amalgamation of linguistically, religiously, culturally, and geographically diverse groups into new larger-scale ethnic groupings was observed in the United States among "white ethnics" (Yancy et al., 1985), Native Americans (Enloe, 1981; Jarvenpa, 1985), and Hispanics and Latinos (Nelson and Tienda, 1985; Padilla, 1986). Cohen labeled such shifts in levels of identification, along with their apparent simultaneous weakening and strengthening of ethnic boundaries, "a sociological paradox"— that ethnic groups can appear to be "rapidly losing their cultural distinctiveness . . . [while) also emphasizing and exaggerating their cultural identity and exclusiveness" (1969, p. 1).

Hannan (1979) offers an interesting solution to this acculturation/accentuation puzzle. Drawing on ecological theory, he argues that political and economic modernization are characterized by increases in organizational scale (particularly of economic and political units) and by increased "connectedness" (through economic and political interdependence) of various population segments. These increases in connectedness and scale of organization lead to a situation where larger and larger units interact, often competitively, with increasing frequency. In order for any contender in such a system to successfully confront (oppose, bargain with, extract resources from) these large-scale economic and political organizations, the contender (e.g., an ethnic group) should find it advantageous to organize "around larger scale cultural identities" (1979, p. 271). Thus, to the extent that ethnicity is a relevant and available basis for group organization, political and economic modernization should increase the likelihood that successful ethnic mobilization will occur along broader rather than narrower subnational identities. In a sort of social selection process, the boundaries around smaller affiliations dissolve in favor of larger affiliations, thereby accounting for the concurrent decline and growth in ethnicity, and so the puzzle is solved.

A. New Ethnicity

New ethnic mobilization can be *resurgent* (i.e., enacted by recently revitalized historical groupings) as among the Basques of Spain, the Bretons of France, the Welsh of Britain, the Quebecois of Canada, or *emergent* (Yancey, Eriksen, and Juliani, 1976) (i.e., enacted by newly formed groups) as among the Ibo of Nigeria (Wolpe, 1974), the Sikhs and Tamils of India (Horowitz, 1975, p. 117; 1977, p. 12), the Native Indians of Canada (Robinson, 1985), the Begisu of Uganda (Kasfir, 1979, pp. 372–373), the North Tapanuli Batak of Indonesia (Liddle, 1970, pp. 57–60).[3]

Both resurgent and emergent[4] ethnicity remind us that religious, linguistic, cultural, or somatic differences among a population are not reliable predictors of ethnic identification or group formation. Rather, the historical variations in ethnic mobilization observable in resurgent ethnicity, and the variations in organizational bases observable in emergent ethnicity, provide evidence of the mutability of ethnic boundaries that early researchers found so puzzling. Such fluidity is less disconcerting if we view ethnicity as partly ascribed and partly volitional, as situational, and as strategic. Rather than conceive of ethnic identification, conflict, or organization as the "natural" outgrowths of primordial divisions among a population (in, say, language, religion, or culture), the view of ethnicity as new stresses the nonfixed, fluid, and situational character of ethnic identification and points to the ascriptive and strategic nature of ethnic categories. This model of ethnic boundaries as emerging from social interaction follows from the theoretical work of Barth (1969a,b) and rests on empirical research conducted over the past two decades by a number of social scientists [among others Wallerstein (1960), Epstein (1967), Zolberg (1968), Melson and Wolpe (1971), Despres (1975), Schermerhorn (1970, 1978), Harris (1964), Young (1965, 1976), Enloe (1973) and van den Berghe (1971)]. The model has as its primary tenets (1) that ethnicity is largely an ascribed status that is situationally activated and (2) that ethnic boundaries are flexible, spatially and temporally fluid, and permeable—permitting the movement of personnel across them.

The view of ethnic identity as an ascribed or assigned status can be illustrated by the phenomenon of Sikhism "conversion" described by Garnett (Nayar, 1966). In colonial India, the British preference for Sikh army recruits led to many quick conversions from Hindu to Sikhism. Garnett reports that "it was almost a daily occurrence for—say—Ram Chand to enter our office and leave it as Ram Singh—Sikh recruit" (Nayar, 1966, p. 65). Along similar lines, Haaland (1969) reports ethnic "switching" or the relabeling of individuals' ethnic affiliation as the result of changes in economic activity among Sudanese ethnic groups. That is, an individual's move from horticulture to herding was followed by a change in others' perception of his ethnicity. Both the Indian and Sudanese cases illustrate the role of external observers in determining salient ethnic identities. In fact, such outside designations can be so powerful as to supersede an individual's beliefs about his "real" ethnic affiliation. For instance, ethnic distinctions that have meaning in certain situations (e.g., national origin distinctions among American "white ethnics" in urban political wards)[5] can become esoteric or meaningless in other settings (e.g., vis-à-vis blacks in Harlem or South Boston).

This situational character of ethnicity has led Horowitz to conclude that "ascriptive identity is heavily contextual" (1975, p. 118). A Native American is a Pine Ridge Sioux in Wounded Knee, South Dakota, but an Indian in Rapid City. Similarly, an Ibo is Onitsha or Owerri in the eastern states of Nigeria, but an Ibo or an Easterner in the North, and a Kurdish-speaking Iranian is a Barzani or Baradosti in the mountains, but a Kurd in Teheran. Thus an individual's ethnic affiliation at any point in time depends on the ethnic identities available to him or her in a particular situation. Sometimes there is a choice, and sometimes not.

While ethnic categories in a society are ascriptively delimited and the shifting of flexible ethnic boundaries may originate from forces outside the group in question (i.e., be ascriptive), shifts in ethnic boundaries may also originate from forces inside the group (i.e., be strategic). The coincidence of these two forces (ascriptive and strategic utility) is an especially powerful impetus to ethnic mobilization. When there exist social and political definitions that emphasize a particular boundary or affiliation (say, "Hispanic" in the United States) *and* when members of such an identified group perceive economic and/or political advantages to be derived from emphasizing that particular boundary (instead of, say, Puerto Rican, Cuban, or Chicano), then there exists a strong likelihood of mobilization on the basis of that designated identity. Since the most powerful ascriptive force in any state is the central government, there is a strong political character to much modern ethnic mobilization [Glazer and Moynihan (1975, p. 7) refer to ethnic groups as "interest groups"]. The next sections explore the political aspect of ethnic mobilization and argue for a view of ethnicity as politically constructed.

B. Ethnicity as a Strategic Mobilization

Tilly (1978, p. 69) defines mobilization as the process by which a group acquires resources and assures their delivery in pursuit of collective ends. Organization plays an essential role in the mobilization of any group. Both the ability to acquire and to deliver resources can be seen as a function of the degree of organization. Group organization, in turn, depends on commonality of interests as well as the extent of unifying structures within the group (Tilly, 1978, p. 54). From this, ethnic mobilization can be defined as the process by which a group organizes along ethnic lines in pursuit of group ends. But when will ethnicity be selected as the basis of group organization?

The obvious answer, suggested already, is when such a choice provides social, economic, or political advantage. Stinchcombe (1975) argues that ethnic loyalty is a function of the degree to which one's ethnic affiliation provides one with necessary and important resources. But what is it about the modern world that has transformed ethnicity into a favored organizational strategy in competitive economic and political relations—into a perceived expedient and efficacious design for resource acquisition? The answer lies in the rise and expansion of national politics.

The political character of modern ethnicity has been noted by a large number of researchers, many of whom employ explicitly political indicators of ethnic mobilization [e.g., the proportion of the vote accruing to ethnically linked parties or candidates—see especially Hechter (1975), Olzak (1982), Ragin (1979)]. Despite this political approach to conceptualizing and measuring the dependent variable, the causal forces in these models are consistently economic, with such independent variables as sectoral labor distributions, economic differentiation, levels of industrial development, and standard of living indices [see especially Ragin (1979) and Neilsen (1980)]. Thus ethnic political mobilization is seen mainly as a response to the structure and operation of the economy, particularly to economic competition among mobilized ethnic contenders (Hannan, 1979; Lauwagie, 1979).

While economic organization and processes play an important role in ethnic identification, group formation, conflict, and collective action, the political orientation of much ethnic activism suggests a similarly important role played by *political* organization and processes. Further, while the relationship between the economy and polity is a complex one, as Bell notes, "competition between plural groups takes place largely in the political arena" (1975, p. 161) due to the subordination of the economy to the polity. One reason for this subordination has been the trend, in both new and old states, toward an increased concentration of power in political centers (Parson, 1957; Tilly, 1975). The growth in political power through the political control of resources, the political regulation of social sectors, and the creation of political amenities prompted Geertz to describe the central government as "a valuable new prize over which to fight and a frightening new force with which to contend" (1963, p. 120). The power of this "new force" to determine the shape and extent of ethnic mobilization within a society is discussed next.

II. THE POLITICAL CONSTRUCTION OF ETHNICITY

This rise in ethnic mobilization around the world can be seen as a result of the nationalization and expansion of politics across states (Meyer, Boli-Bennett, and Chase-Dunn, 1975; Tilly, 1975) and the increased willingness of governments to recognize ethnic groups as legitimate contenders (Glazer and Moynihan, 1975). The nationalization and expansion of politics redirects increasing proportions of societal activity (ethnic and other) toward the political center. The recognition of ethnicity as a basis for political organization and claimsmaking legitimates ethnic mobilization. Thus we see a politicization and legitimation of ethnicity in modern states.

It is important here to clarify the role of ethnicity as both an *antecedent* as well as a *consequence* of particular political processes. It is an empirical fact that most countries contain ethnically diverse populations. It is not the assertion here that such diversity is solely or even primarily the result of political processes. However, the recognition and institutionalization of ethnicity in politics (1) *increases the level* of ethnic mobilization among all ethnic groups (e.g., among those previously mobilized as well as among those who mobilize for the first time in response to the politicization of ethnicity) and (2) *determines the boundaries* along which ethnic mobilization and/or conflict will occur by setting down the rules for political participation and political access (e.g., should contenders organize on the basis of panethnic representation or on the basis of historical claims?).

Whether ethnicity is politically newly constructed or reconstructed, created or enhanced, formed or transformed, we can specify several mechanisms whereby ethnicity is politically constructed. They fall into two categories: the structure of political access and the content of political policies.

A. Political Access

PROPOSITION 1. *Within a state, ethnic mobilization is most likely when the structure of political access and participation is organized along ethnic lines.*

The structure of political access and the rules of participation can emphasize or minimize the salience of ethnicity in political contention. Both the regionalization and institutionalization of ethnic participation in the polity promote ethnic political mobilization.

1. Regionalization

HYPOTHESIS 1. *Ethnic mobilization will tend to occur along those ethnic boundaries that correspond to geographic political and administrative boundaries.*

There are two ways in which the organization of land and population within a state can promote subnational mobilization: first, by *reinforcing* existing ethnic differences, and second, by *creating* new ethnic groups.

a. *Reinforcement.*

When the boundaries of administrative or electoral units correspond to historical communal (cultural, religious, linguistic) divisions among a population, then those divisions tend to be politicized and reinforced. One reason for this is that political authorities' choice to use existing ethnoregional boundaries can be interpreted by all groups as recognition of those particular divisions of the population. In some cases the recognition can carry a positive message of uniqueness or special status as the establishment of the Armenian Republic in the U.S.S.R. in 1922 or of the Jura canton in Switzerland in 1979. In other cases, the creation of regional units for particular ethnic groups can be punitive and isolating, as the establishment of *Bantustans* ''homelands'' for black Africans in South Africa or of Indian reservations in the United States—both more like concentration camps than politically autonomous regions.

A second way ethnic mobilization can result from reinforcing existing ethnoregional boundaries by the superimposition of electoral or administrative regions is the tendency of political organization and action to occur within bounded political units. Such regional mobilization can be on the part of the majority group in the unit or by minority groups who find themselves enclosed and are fearful of majority domination. The *Partei der Deutschsprachigen Belgien* (PDB) is an example of the latter. Constitutional plans for dividing Belgium into either French or Dutch language regions ''precipitated the formation of a new language party [the PDB]'' (Kane, 1980, p. 138) when the German speakers' region was assigned to the French language category.

b. *Creation*

The imposition of administrative or electoral boundaries around a segment of the population can go beyond reinforcing extant communal differences to actually create *new* ethnic identities. The Nigerian example is an apt one. The 1960 division of the Nigerian state into three regions that competed for access to and control of the central government resulted in the creation of three major regionally based, ethnically linked political parties (and many opposition parties in each region). The resulting ethnicization of politics led to the disintegration of the Nigerian political system and the secession of the Eastern Region (Biafra). The irony in this sequence of events is that the major ethnic groups in each of the three regions (the Ibos in the East, the Yoruba in the West, the Hausa in the North) were not historically united groups possessed of regional-level identities. Rather, these linguistic groups were historically organized into community-of-origin and kinship groups whose past internal relationships had been marked more by disinterest or contention than by unity (Sklar and Whitaker, 1964, p. 621; Sklar, 1963, p. 152; Coleman, 1958, p. 343; Awolowo, 1960; Paden, 1973; Nafziger and Richter, 1976, p. 93).

In a variety of countries the creation of administration units that serve as the bases for resource distribution has frequently led to mobilization among enclosed groups and to shifts in group identification from traditional boundaries to newly created administrative boundaries (Dresang, 1974, p. 1606; van den Berghe, 1971, p. 514; Young, 1965, p. 245; Nafziger and Richter, 1976, p. 93; Mazrui,

1979, p. 260; Horowitz, 1975, p. 133; Wallerstein, 1960, p. 132). In the United States, not only does the federal Indian reservation system crosscut and ignore traditional tribal lands (U.S. Indian Claims Commission, 1980), but reservation boundaries often fail to correspond to traditional tribal identity boundaries. The massive forced movement of the American Indian population onto reservation lands during the nineteenth century resulted in the fractionalization and/or the amalgamation of many traditional tribal organization and identity boundaries. The result is a different set of Indian tribes today than the set that existed a hundred years ago. An example of *fractionalization* is the Cherokee tribe whose members were relocated (via the "Trail of Tears") to Oklahoma; most stayed, but some returned to North Carolina. Today there are two Cherokee tribes, both officially recognized by the Bureau of Indian Affairs: the Cherokee Nation of Oklahoma and the Eastern Band of Cherokee Indians of North Carolina. These two tribes now not only are separated territorially, but have evolved separate political, economic, and social systems (Department of Commerce, 1974; Bureau of Indian Affairs, 1983). Examples of *amalgamation* can be found among many of the Pacific-Northwest tribes, such as the Confederated Tribes of the Colville Reservation or the Tulalip Tribes of the Tulalip Reservation, both in Washington as well as elsewhere, as among the Confederated Tribes of the Flathead Reservation in Montana. All three communities are comprised of formerly autonomous groups that were socially, economically, politically, culturally, and linguistically diverse in varying degrees, but whose internal divisions have increasingly blurred over time to produce progressively homogeneous new tribes: the "Colville," "Tulalip," and "Flathead" tribes (Bureau of Indian Affairs, 1983; U.S. Indian Claims Commission, 1980). Horowitz (1975) provides further examples of ethnic fractionalization and amalgamation in many countries, many often the result of the organization of political administration and access.

2. Participation

HYPOTHESIS 2. *Ethnic mobilization will tend to occur along those ethnic boundaries that are officially recognized bases of participation.*

The official structuring of political participation along ethnic lines is an even more potent force in the construction of ethnicity than is regionalization. Whereas the administrative division of land and population along extant or potential communal boundaries provides a politically recognized, structurally facilitated basis for mobilization among both the enclosed groups as well as among other subpopulations, the organization of political participation along ethnic lines provides a rationale for, and indeed demands, the mobilization of political participation on the basis of ethnicity. The main reason for the rise in ethnic mobilization in states where political participation is structured ethnically is the tendency of such arrangements to transform ethnic groups into interest groups and to politicize ethnicity.

There are two main paths to ethnically structured political participation: (1) the constitutional (de jure) recognition of ethnicity as a basis for political representation [as in Belgium where electoral districts are designated as Dutch- or French-speaking (Heisler, 1977; Kane, 1980); in Fiji where an equal number of seats in the House of Representatives are assigned to Fijians and Indians (Norton, 1977); or in India where Scheduled Caste (Untouchable) groups are guaranteed a specific proportion of seats in parliament and a designated quota of civil service posts (Dushkin, 1972)]; or (2) the regionalization (de facto) of representation to adhere to ethnoregional boundaries [as in Switzerland where federal representation is officially by canton, but where cantons tend to be linguistically homogeneous (Connor, 1977); in Malaysia where electoral districts are geographically determined, but where nine states are locally ruled by hereditary Malay rulers and where there exists a Malay advantage in the calculation of parliamentary and state constituencies (Means, 1976; Musolf and Springer, 1979, p. 34); or in Sri Lanka where the representation of minorities (e.g., Ceylon Tamils and Muslims) was adjusted upward by weighting minority-dominated regions and by appointing a small number of legislators (Wilson, 1975)].

Whether explicit or de facto, recognition of religious, cultural, or linguistic affiliations as bases of political participation tends to promote ethnic group organization and to transform ethnic groups into political interest groups and thus tends to increase interethnic competition. The mobilization of the Scheduled Castes and subsequent intergroup hostility directed toward Untouchables in India illustrates this process. Untouchables represent the lowest sector of the traditional Indian (mainly Hindu) caste system. Although the group is comprised of linguistically and geographically diverse groups, special provisions for political participation and civil service representation resulted in the mobilization of these various groups into an increasingly self-aware subnational unit with a political party (the Republican Party) and a separatist fringe (Schermerhorn, 1978; Dushkin, 1972; Nayar, 1966; Rudolph and Rudolph, 1967).

The relationship between political recognition and ethnic mobilization is complex and probably more sequential than directional. The argument being made here is that of mobilization from above (Nettl, 1967, p. 271). This is not to say that ethnic political organizations and political parties are mere creations of the writers of constitutions and do not reflect prior ethnic divisions among populations. It is to say, first, that the official recognition of ethnicity as a basis of political representation legitimizes, institutionalizes, and renders more permanent prior ethnically organized political participation—for example, the continued dominance of language parties in Belgian and Canadian politics even in the face of constitutional recognition and substantial concessions to various linguistic constituencies; and second, that the official recognition of ethnicity as a basis of political representation promotes new and parallel mobilization by formerly unorganized groups that face the prospect of exclusion from an ethnically defined political arena—for example, the rise of white ethnics in the United States, of German-speakers in Belgium, or of Italian and Portuguese nationality groups in Québec.

Both of the mechanisms for structuring political access along ethnic lines—

regionalization and participation—often result in ironic, unintended consequences for the systems employing them (consequences that are repeated below
in the various policy mechanisms). The irony in ethnic mobilization is best
illustrated by the fact that such organizing principles are often conceived as a
recipe for plural harmony (Lijphart, 1977). While it is true that in some cases
these organizational strategies are adopted to deal with historical communal
hostilities, invariably they create a competitive atmosphere that encourages ethnic mobilization by both targeted groups (in order to gain access to the polity and
all that such access provides), and by nontargeted groups as well (in order to
avoid being excluded from the polity). Thus the invitation to mobilize extended
to some groups (often with admirable intentions, as in the case of the Untouchables) ethnicizes the political process and expands the arena for ethnic competition.

B. Political Policies

PROPOSITION 2. *Within a state, ethnic mobilization is most likely when political policies are implemented that recognize and institutionalize ethnic differences.*

In addition to the ethnicization of political access through regionalization and
ethnic participation provisions, there are four categories of political policy that
are especially powerful in their implications for ethnic mobilization and in their
ability to determine the boundaries along which such mobilization occurs: language policies, land policies, official designation policies, and resource distribution policies.

1. Language Policies

HYPOTHESIS 3. *Ethnic mobilization will tend to occur along those ethnic
boundaries that coincide with official language boundaries.*

Just as constitutionally guaranteed seats in parliament or positions in the civil
service act to accentuate ethnic differences, language policies institutionalize
ethnic diversity, politicizing linguistic divisions and rendering them permanent.
Language policies range in their ability to institutionalize ethnicity according to
their content. Most powerful is that of multiple official languages. While single
official languages are difficult to select and implement and invariably provoke
resistance, multiple official languages guarantee long-term or permanent linguistic division. Again, this is not to say that the adoption of several official
languages *causes* all linguistic conflict in a state or that linguistic differences or
hostilities are not present prior to the adoption. It is to say that such a policy
institutionalizes and legitimates linguistic conflict and thus maintains and per-
petuates it.

In order to fully understand the power of political policies to *create* linguistically based mobilization (rather than simply to respond to *prior* language

group demands), we must suspend familiar notions of primordial ethnicity. The speaking of a common language, say Dutch or Scottish or Yoruba, does not automatically produce ethnic unity, group identification, an organizational substructure, or a shared culture. What it does produce is the ability to communicate within the group and the appearance of uniformity to outsiders. Mutual intelligibility, ascribed (presumed) community, and particular policies pursued by political authorities explain a good deal of linguistic mobilization in the modern world. Again, India provides a clear example of the political construction of linguistic mobilization.

The Indian constitution assigns 14 languages the status of "national languages" (Das Gupta, 1970, p. 38).[6] The history of these designations began under British colonial rule with the formation of urban literary societies by educated speakers of various languages (Das Gupta, 1970, pp. 69–97). The evolution from literary societies to linguistic social movements was the result of a two-stage process beginning with British colonial administrative practices and culminating in the competition associated with the establishment of an independent Indian state. Das Gupta (1975, p. 475) reports that "fashioning relatively larger language-based ethnic communities out of a mass of disparate segmental ethnicities . . . [was] facilitated by the system of the administrative division of India into provinces" by colonial authorities. This power of administrative boundaries to unify those enclosed has been discussed above. In India,[7] these administrative units became mobilized contenders for language and state status during the nationalist mobilization of the 1940s and 1950s. The creation of ethnic unity by British colonialists was not limited to the imposition of administrative boundaries. Civil service and military recruitment policies also encouraged the formation of ethnic unity and promoted subsequent mobilization. This was particularly true of the Sikhs, whose modern demands for autonomy are tied to British policies of separate treatment (Nayar, 1966, pp. 55–74; Schermerhorn, 1978, pp. 128–153).

In addition to the power of superimposed boundaries to promote group formation, the Indian example points out the more general relationship of state-building to subnationalism. That relationship is one of competition for political advantage. Such competition is organized ethnically where the rules of access or participation are articulated in ethnic terms. And one such articulation is in language policies. As Das Gupta neatly summarizes:

> Language demands, especially in developing nations, cannot be inferred from the nature of language groups. These groups tend to make demands only when social mobilization offers competitive opportunities and values [1975, p. 487].

While preferred languages of administration, legislation, and education are generally those with official status, in some countries language policies governing education or administration are less sweeping and more situationally oriented. Bilingual education in the United States is one such case. While the United States has no official languages besides English (yet), the question of non-English language instruction has produced political mobilization among linguistic groups in favor of and opposed to bilingual education policies and has promoted parallel mobilization in school systems among language groups not initially included in bilingual programs. The debate surrounding bilingual education in the United States[8] has politicized linguistic differences among the American population and spawned a multitude of special interest organizations and official position statements from extant groups [see, for example, Novak (1978)].

2. Land Policies

HYPOTHESIS 4. *Ethnic mobilization will tend to occur along those ethnic boundaries that coincide with officially allocated lands.*

In many states, communal groups are geographically concentrated. Besides the historic demographic forces (migration, geographic isolation, economic niche boundaries) that tend to separate groups and produce independent evolution, particular land policies can produce ethnogeographic concentration. These are of several sorts. One is the tendency of geographic administrative or electoral divisions to promote mobilization among enclosed groups as described above. Another is politically orchestrated or forced migration as in the case of the Shi'i Arab population in Iraq (Dann, 1969) or the numerous refugee populations around the world (Portes and Stepick, 1985). A third involves the allocation of land to particular ethnic groups as in the case of the Caribs of Dominica (Layng, 1985), American Indian groups in Canada and the United States (Jorgensen, 1978; Ponting and Gibbons, 1980), or black Africans in South Africa (van den Berghe, 1978). A fourth includes political economic processes involving the siting and development of industries, as in the case of guestworkers in Western Europe (Mehrlaender, 1980; Rist, 1980) or urban enclaves of rural out-migrant ethnic groups in various African states (Cohen, 1974).

An example of the capacity of land policies to shift ethnic boundaries as well as to promote ethnic mobilization can be seen in the effect of U.S. Indian policy during the 1950s on pan-Indian ethnicity. Observers have noted that a good deal of American Indian political activity (protests, petitioning, lobbying) is organized along pan-Indian (e.g., Native American) rather than tribal (eg., Jicarilla Apache, Rosebud Sioux, Tuscarora) boundaries. There is some evidence that this upward shift in political organization is paralleled by complementary upward shifts in identity and culture as well [see Stewart (1972) on the Native American Church, Hertzberg (1971), on pan-Indian organizations and movements, and Corrigan (1970) on pow-wows], producing what Thomas (1968, p. 84) has labeled "a new ethnic group, a new 'nationality' in America"—the Native American.

One explanation for this upward shift in ethnic boundaries can be found in U.S. Indian policy during the "termination" period (roughly 1946–1960). During this time an effort was being made to terminate, for once and for all, the unique trust relationship between Indian tribes and the U.S. government. Since the reservation system (a legacy of earlier federal Indian land policy) was central to the maintenance of the Indian–federal relationship, the desire to weaken reservation viability by population reduction led to a program of urban relocation of reservation Indians. Beginning with the Navajo–Hopi Rehabilitation Act of 1950, and continuing throughout the decade, through various "relocation" programs, the federal government engaged in an extended effort to move Indians from reservations to urban areas where they were to be assisted by government Indian centers in finding housing and employment (Jorgensen, 1978). This population management program arising out of land policies was not incidental to the emergence of pan-Indian social and political organization among the tribally mixed populations residing in urban relocation areas. The fact that nearly half of the American Indian population is urban (U.S. Statistical Abstract, 1981) is largely the result of land policies that guaranteed impoverished reservations and provided incentives for urban migration (Nagel, Ward, and Knapp, 1986).

3. Official Designations and Resource Distribution

HYPOTHESIS 5. *Ethnic mobilization will tend to occur along those ethnic boundaries that are official ethnic designations for special treatment and/or political resource acquisition.*[9]

Policies of singling out particular ethnic groups for special treatment also tend to legitimate ethnic divisions and to emphasize certain boundaries over others. The power of official designations is obvious where negative policies such as genocide, internment, or deportation are concerned. However, neutral or positively intended official categories also operate to enhance ethnic mobilization. One fairly innocuous such designation is the census category. Horowitz (1975, p. 116) reports an emerging Yugoslav Muslim ethnic group whose legitimacy is partly based on census policy. Somewhat more powerful is the conception of "official" ethnic groups. In the U.S.S.R. one chooses an official nationality at age 16 (Glazer and Moynihan, 1975, p. 17); the choice has long-lasting economic and political implications (Allworth, 1977). In the United States certain ethnic groups "count" for particular purposes (e.g., Affirmative Action), rendering them legitimate and encouraging organization and affiliation consistent with official boundaries rather than with more traditional or culturally relevant units (e.g., "Hispanic" as opposed to Mexican-American or Puerto Rican).

In terms of strategic organization for competitive advantage, the distribution of politically controlled resources according to ethnicity is an immensely powerful factor in ethnic mobilization. Part of Untouchable mobilization in India was attributable to the distribution of education scholarships, low-interest loans, and land on the basis of membership in Scheduled Castes (Nayar, 1966, p. 319;

Rudolph and Rudolph, 1967, pp. 143–144). Dresang (1974) notes the mobilizing effects of the allocation of politically controlled jobs and resources in Zambia. And access to and control of central government resources has promoted ethnic mobilization among a variety of groups in Nigeria (Kirk-Greene, 1971), among francophones in Canada (Smiley, 1977, p. 190), and among blacks in the United States (Oberschall, 1973, pp. 237–238).

Such "affirmative action" programs produce not only mobilization among designated groups, but can also lead to communal conflict in the form of "backlashes" *against* official groups; examples can be found in the same nations listed above: India, Nigeria, Canada, and the United States.

The role of officially designated political resource distribution in ethnic mobilization is not surprising, inasmuch as it parallels an argument arrived at by a somewhat different route in the social movements literature. A central tenet of the resource mobilization perspective is that successful mobilization depends on a combination of organization and resource acquisition (Jenkins and Perrow, 1977; McCarthy and Zald, 1973, 1977; Oberschall, 1973; Tilly, 1978; Walsh, 1980). It follows that, *ceteris paribus*, those groups to whom political resources are available (set aside funds, special programs, low interest loans, etc.) are more likely to mobilize successfully than are nondesignated groups. Thus, the ethnic boundaries along which resources are distributed become the bases for mobilization.

While the power of the polity to define the "appropriate" bases for recognition and resource distribution increases the likelihood of mobilization among targeted groups, it must be remembered that to the extent that official designations are seen as advantageous, nondesignated groups will also seek recognition and expand the domain of ethnic politics. Thus recognizing and rewarding ethnicity for even one or a few groups in a state can promote parallel mobilization among nontargeted groups, and thus we see a general ethnicization of social, economic, and political life.

C. Ethnic Mobilization and the Nationalization of Politics

In addition to the role of political organization and policies in promoting ethnic mobilization, the trend in both old and new states toward national political structures encourages subnational mobilization. To the extent that ethnicity is politically constructed, the nationalization of politics should lead to increased nationally organized ethnic groups. A case in point is Guyana. In a preindependence election held in April 1953, a cross-section and majority of Guyana's subnationally mixed population [East Indians, 49%; Africans, 30%; Europeans, Amerindians, and others, 21% (Greene, 1974, p. 2)] mobilized behind the People's Progressive Party (PPP) and its left-leaning leader Cheddi Jagan. In October 1953, fearing an alleged communist takeover, British colonial authorities (at United States urging) suspended the constitution and the PPP-dominated House of Assembly (Manley, 1979, p. 6; Landis, 1974, p. 256). The PPP continued to dominate subsequent elections in 1957 and 1961, although the ethnic consensus had begun to deteriorate, aided by British and American machinations and funding programs (Greene, 1974) that strengthened the opposition party (the People's National Congress). The *coup de grace* was the introduction in the 1964 election of proportional representation, which changed the method of election to parliament from a locally focused, single-member constituency system to a nationally focused, proportional representation system. The shift to proportional representation had three results: (1) it nationalized political contention by moving campaigns out of local districts (where the party candidates stood off against one another, the winner going to parliament) to the national arena (where national proportion of the vote received by each party determined its number of representatives in parliament); (2) it centralized and nationalized political parties because campaigns became orchestrated at the national, not local, level; and (3) it ethnicized partisan politics because proportional representation refocussed the voter from his or her district (and from which candidate would best represent local interests) to the national level where parties increasingly appealed to subnational loyalties as an easy and wider-issue basis for obtaining the vote. The logic of the vote shifted from the local candidate to the national party, and over time (between 1953 and 1964) a realignment of voters occurred, producing ethnic parties (Greene, 1974) and a dramatic rise in communal conflict and hostility (Despres, 1967; Landis, 1974, p. 257).

III. CONCLUSION

It has been hypothesized and argued that the above political structural arrangements and policies promote ethnic mobilization. They provide the rationale for the selection of ethnicity as the basis for mobilization and designate the particular boundaries along which mobilization most likely occurs. Further, they provoke complementary mobilization among nondesignated groups. These structural arrangements and policies are often designed and implemented to avoid real or anticipated ethnic conflict. Whether or not they serve this end in the short term, in both the short and long term they act to spotlight diversity, to institutionalize ethnic differences, and to increase the level of ethnic mobilization and conflict.

As for the future, the political construction of ethnicity is probably no more potent a force than the political construction of nationalism. Both are situationally enhanced or diminished and rest on the same ideological bedrock of self-determination and representative government. The incentives for subnationalism appear at least as strong as those promoting nationalism at this juncture in world history, though the shifting ephemeral character of group organization must never be underestimated. The message is that ethnic nationalism is not the stuff of primordial, genetic, ancient differences, but is a child of the modern world with its multitude of fecund states and parturient political processes. The word for ethnicity is secular, not sacred.

ACKNOWLEDGMENTS

I wish to thank the following colleagues for their comments and advice in the development of these ideas: Susan Olzak, R. A. Schermerhorn, and Norman Yetman. This research was supported by National Science Foundation grant SES-8108314.

NOTES

[1]From around 75 states at the beginning of World War II, to more than 150 at the present (Crawford, 1979, p. 3).

[2]Variously called "cultural pluralism" (Young, 1976), "ethnonationalism" (Conner, 1977), "communalism" (Melson and Wolpe, 1971), "ethnicity" (Glazer and Moynihan, 1975), "eth-nopolitics" (Rothschild, 1981).

[3]Other groups described by social scientists as newly emergent are the Sinhalese of Sri Lanka (Kearney, 1967, pp. 40–51; Horowitz, 1977, p. 16) the Sindhi of Pakistan (Das Gupta, 1975, p. 472) and the Naga of India (Nag, 1968; Schermerhorn, 1978, p. 86).

[4]Kilson refers to the phenomena of resurgent and emergent ethnicity as "neoethnicity . . . the revitalization of weak ethnic collectivities" (1975, p. 236); Singer (1962) and Despres (1975) label them "ethnogenesis"—the process whereby populations become (a) culturally differentiated and (b) corporately organized on the basis of that differentiation.

[5]My thanks to Susan Olzak for this example.

[6]They are Assamese, Bengali, English, Gujarte, Hindi, Kannada, Kashmiri, Malayalam, Marathi, Oriya, Punjabi, Tamil, Telugu, and Urdu (Das Dupta, 1970, p. 46).

[7]As in Nigeria (Melson and Wolpe, 1971, p. 23), in Zaire (Young, 1965, p. 245), in Malaysia (Horowitz, 1975, p. 133), in Zambia (Dresang, 1974, p. 1605–1606), and in Iraq (Horowitz, 1977, p. 11).

[8]For instance, does bilingual education promote Spanish language retention or hinder economic advancement? The evidence is far from clear (Veltman, 1981; Rodriguez, 1981).

[9]These hypotheses can be recast to predict relative rates of ethnic mobilization among states. By the argument presented here, the following also hold: all things being equal, (1) ethnic mobilization will tend to be greatest in those states where geographic, political, and administrative boundaries coincide with linguistic, cultural, or religious divisions among the population; (2) ethnic mobilization will tend to be greatest in those states where ethnicity is designated as a legitimate basis for political representation and/or participation; (3) ethnic mobilization will tend to be greatest in those states that recognize multiple official languages; (4) ethnic mobilization will tend to be greatest in those states with ethnic land policies; (5) ethnic mobilization will tend to be greatest in those states with official ethnic groups designated for special treatment and/or for the allocation of resources.

REFERENCES

ALLWORTH, EDWARD (1977). *Nationality group survival in multi-ethnic states.* New York: Praeger.
AWOLOWO, CHIEF OBAFEMI (1960). *Awo.* London: Cambridge University Press.
AZKIN, BENJAMIN (1964). *State and nation.* London: Hutchinson University Library.
BARTH, FREDRIK (1969a). Introduction. In *Ethnic groups and boundaries* (F. Barth, ed.), pp. 9–38. Boston: Little, Brown and Company.
BARTH, FREDRIK (1969b). Ecological relationships of ethnic groups in Swat, Pakistan. In *En-*

vironment and cultural behavior (A. Vayda, ed.), pp. 362–376. Austin: University of Texas Press.

BELL, D. (1975). Ethnicity and social change. *Ethnicity: Theory and experience* (N. Glazer and D. P. Moynihan, eds.), pp. 141–166. Cambridge: Harvard University Press.

BUREAU OF INDIAN AFFAIRS (1983). Indian tribal entities recognized and eligible to receive services from the United States Bureau of Indian Affairs. *Federal Register*, Wednesday, December 10, 1983.

CHILD, IRVIN L. (1943). *Italian or American?* New Haven, Connecticut: Yale University Press.

COHEN, ABNER (1969). *Custom and politics in urban Africa.* Berkeley: University of California Press.

COHEN, ABNER (1974). *Urban ethnicity.* New York: Harper and Row.

COLEMAN, JAMES (1958). *Nigeria: Background to nationalism.* Berkeley: University of California Press.

CONNER, WALKER (1977). Ethnonationalism in the first world. In *Ethnic Pluralism and Conflict in the Western World* (Milton Esman, ed.), pp. 19–45. Ithaca, New York: Cornell University Press.

CORRIGAN, SAMUEL W. (1970). The Plains Indian powwow: Cultural integration in Manitoba and Saskatchewan. *Anthropologica* **12**:253–277.

CRAWFORD, JAMES (1979). *The creation of states in international law.* Oxford: Clarendon Press.

DANN, URIEL (1969). *Iraq under Qassem.* New York: Praeger.

DAS GUPTA, JYOTIRINDRA (1970). *Language, conflict and national development.* Berkeley: University of California Press.

DAS GUPTA, JYOTIRINDRA (1975). Ethnicity, language demands, and national development in India. In *Ethnicity: Theory and experience* (N. Glazer and D. P. Moynihan, eds.), pp. 466–488. Cambridge: Harvard University Press.

DEPARTMENT OF COMMERCE (1974). Federal and state Indian reservations and Indian trust areas. Washington, D.C.: Government Printing Office.

DESPRES, LEO (1967). *Cultural pluralism and nationalist politics in British Guiana.* Chicago: Rand-McNally.

DESPRES, LEO (1975). Toward a theory of ethnic phenomena. In *Ethnicity and resource competition* (L. Despres, ed.), pp. 186–207. The Hague: Mouton.

DEUTSCH, KARL (1966). Nation-building and national development. In *Nation-building* (K. Deutch and W. Foltz, eds.), pp. 1–16. New York: Atherton.

DRESANG, DENNIS (1974). Ethnic politics, representative bureaucracy, and development administration: The Zambian case. *American Political Science Review* **69**:1605–1625.

DUSHKIN, LELAH (1972). Scheduled caste politics. In *The Untouchables in contemporary India* (J. Michael Mahan, ed.), pp. 165–226. Tucson: The University of Arizona Press.

ENLOE, CYNTHIA (1973). *Ethnic development and political conflict.* Boston: Little, Brown and Company.

ENLOE, CYNTHIA (1981). The growth of the state and ethnic mobilization: the American experience. *Ethnic and Racial Studies* **4**(April):123–136.

EPSTEIN, A. L. (1967). Urbanization and social change in Africa. *Current Anthropology* (October):275–295.

FIREY, WALTER (1947). *Land use in central Boston.* Cambridge: Harvard University Press.

GEERTZ, CLIFFORD (1963). The integrative revolution: Primordial sentiments and civil politics in the new states. In *Old societies and new states* (G. Geertz, ed.), pp. 105–157. New York: Free Press.

GLAZER, NATHAN, and MOYNIHAN, DANIEL P. (1963). *Beyond the melting pot.* Cambridge, Massachusetts: Harvard University Press.

GLAZER, NATHAN, and MOYNIHAN, DANIEL P. (1975). Introduction. In *Ethnicity: Theory and experience* (N. Glazer and D. P. Moynihan, eds.), pp. 1–26. Cambridge: Harvard University Press.

GREENE, J. E. (1974). *Race vs. politics in Guyana*. Jamaica: Institute of Social and Economic Research, University of the West Indies.

HAALAND, G. (1969). Economic determinants in ethnic processes. In *Ethnic groups and boundaries* (F. Barth, ed.), pp. 58–73. Boston: Little, Brown.

HANNAN, MICHAEL T. (1979). The dynamics of ethnic boundaries in modern states. In *National development and the world system* (J. Meyer and M. T. Hannan, eds.), pp. 253–275. Chicago: University of Chicago Press.

HARRIS, MARVIN (1964). *Patterns of race in the Americas*. New York: Norton.

HECHTER, MICHAEL (1975). *Internal colonialism*. Berkeley: University of California Press.

HEISLER, MARTIN (1977). Managing ethnic conflict in Belgium. *Annals* **433**(September):32–46.

HERTZBERG, HAZEL W. (1971). *The search for an American Indian identity. Modern pan-Indian movements*. Syracuse: Syracuse University Press.

HOROWITZ, DONALD (1971). Three dimensions of ethnic politics. *World Politics* **XXIII**-(January):232–244.

HOROWITZ, DONALD (1975). Ethnic identity In *Ethnicity: Theory and Experience* (N. Glazer and D. Moynihan, eds.), pp. 111–140. Cambridge: Harvard University Press.

HOROWITZ, DONALD (1977). Cultural movements and ethnic change. *Annals* **433**(September:6–18.

JARVENPA, ROBERT (1985). The political economy and political ethnicity of American Indian adaptations and identities. *Ethnic and Racial Studies* **8**(January):29–48.

JENKINS, J. CRAIG, and PERROW, CHARLES (1977). Insurgency of the powerless: Farm worker movements (1946–1972). *American Sociological Review* **42**(April):249–268.

JORGENSEN, J. G. (1978). A century of political economic effects on American Indian society, 1880–1980. *The Journal of Ethnic Studies* **6**:1–82.

KANE, JEAN ELLEN (1980). Flemish and Walloon nationalism: Devolution of a previously unitary state. In *Ethnic resurgence in modern democratic states* (U. Ra'anan, ed.), pp. 122–171. New York: Pergamon.

KASFIR, NELSON (1979). Explaining ethnic political participation. *World Politics* (March)365–388.

KIRK-GREENE, A. H. M. (1971). *Crisis and conflict in Nigeria*, Vols. I and II. London: Oxford University Press.

LANDIS, JOSEPH B. (1974). Racial polarization and political conflict in Guyana. In *Ethnicity and nation-building: Comparative, international and historical perspectives* (W. Bell and Walter R. Freeman, eds.), pp. 255–267. Beverly Hills, California: Sage.

LAUWAGIE, B. (1979). Ethnic boundaries in modern states. *American Journal of Sociology* **85**(September):310–337.

LAYNG, ANTHONY (1985). The Caribs of Dominica: prospects for structural assimilation of a territorial minority. *Ethnic Groups* **6**(February):209–221.

LIDDLE, R. WILLIAM. (1970). *Ethnicity, party, and national integration*. New Haven, Connecticut: Yale University Press.

LIJPHART, ARENDT (1977). *Democracy in plural societies*. New Haven, Connecticut: Yale University Press.

LIPSET, SEYMOUR M., and ROKKAN, STEIN (1967). *Party systems and voter alignments*. New York: Free Press.

MANLEY, ROBERT H. (1979). *Guyana emergent*. Boston: Hall.

MAZRUI, ALI A. (1979). Soldiers as traditionalizers: Military rule and the re-Africanization of Africa. *World Politics* (January):246–272.

MCCARTHY, JOHN, and ZALD, MAYER (1973). *The trend of social movements in America: Professionalization and resource mobilization*. Morristown, New Jersey: General Learning Press.

MCCARTHY, JOHN, and ZALD, MAYER (1977). Resource mobilization and social movements: A partial theory. *American Journal of Sociology* **82**:1212–1241.

MEANS, GORDON P. (1976). *Malaysian politics*. London: Hodder and Stoughton.

MEHRLAENDER, URSULA (1980). The 'human resource' problem in Europe: Migrant labor in the Federal Republic of Germany. In *Ethnic resurgence in modern democratic states* (Uri Ra'anan, ed.), pp. 77–100. New York: Pergamon.

MELSON, ROBERT, and WOLPE, HOWARD (eds.) (1971). *Nigeria: Modernization and the politics of communalism*. East Lansing, Michigan: Michigan State University Press.

MEYER, JOHN W., BOLI-BENNETT, JOHN, and CHASE-DUNN, CHRISTOPHER (1975). Convergence and divergence in development. *Annual Review of Sociology* **1**:223–246.

MUSOLF, LLOYD D., and SPRINGER, J. FREDERICK (1979). *Malaysia's parliamentary system: Representative politics and policy-making in a divided society*. Boulder, Colorado: Westview Press.

NAFZIGER, W., and RICHTER, W. (1976). Biafra and Bangladesh: The political economy of secessionist conflict. *Journal of Peace Research* **XIII**:91–109.

NAGEL, JOANE, WARD, CAROL, and KNAPP, TIMOTHY (1986). The politics of American Indian economic development: The reservation/Urban Nexus. In *American Indian economic development: Policy impacts and unresolved problems* (Matthew Snipp, ed.). Albuquerque: University of New Mexico Press.

NAYAR, BALDEV RAJ (1966). *Politics in the Punjab*. New Haven: Yale University Press.

NEILSEN, FRANCOIS (1980). The Flemish movement in Belgium after World War II. *American Sociological Review* **45**(February):76–94.

NELSON, CANDACE, and TIENDA, MARTA (1985). The structuring of Hispanic identity: historical and contemporary perspectives. *Ethnic and Racial Studies* **8**(January):49–74.

NETTL, J. P. (1967). *Political mobilization*. London: Faber and Faber.

NORTON, ROBERT (1977). *Race and politics in Fiji*. New York: St. Martin's Press.

NOVACK, MICHAEL (ed.) (1978). *Novack Report on the New Ethnicity*. 918 F Street, N.W., Suite 410, Washington, D.C. 20004.

OBERSCHALL, ANTHONY (1973). *Social conflict and social movements*. Englewood Cliffs, New Jersey: Prentice-Hall.

OLZAK, S. (1982). Ethnic mobilization in Quebec. *Ethnic and Racial Studies* (July):253–275.

PADEN, JOHN (1973). *Religion and political culture in Kano*. Berkeley: University of California Press.

PADILLA, FELIX (1986). Latino ethnicity in the city of Chicago. In *Competitive Ethnic Relations* (Susan Olzak and Joane-Nagel, eds.), pp. 153–117. New York: Academic Press.

PARSONS, TALCOTT (1957). The distribution of power in American society. *World Politics* **10**:123–143.

PONTING, J. RICK, and GIBBONS, ROGER (1980). *Out of irrelevance*. Toronto: Butterworths.

PORTES, ALEJANDRO, and STEPICK, ALEX (1985). Unwelcome immigrants: the labor market experiences of 1980 (Mariel) Cuban and Haitian refugees in South Florida. *American Sociological Review* **50**(4):493–514.

RAGIN, C. (1979). Ethnic political mobilization: The Welsh case. *American Sociological Review* **44**(August):619–635.

RIST, RAY C. (1980). Guestworkers and post-World War II European migrations. *Studies in Comparative International Development* **14**(Fall):28–53.

ROBINSON, PATRICIA (1985). Language retention among Canadian Indians: a simultaneous equations model with dichotomous endogenous variable. *American Sociological Review* **50**(4):515–529.

RODRIGUEZ, RICHARD (1981). *Hunger of memory*. New York: Godine.

ROTHSCHILD, JOSEPH (1981). *Ethnopolitics*. New York: Columbia University Press.

RUDOLPH, LLOYD, and RUDOLPH, SUSANNE (1967). *The modernity of tradition: Political development in India*. Chicago: University of Chicago Press.

SCHERMERHORN, R. A. (1970). *Comparative ethnic relations*. New York: Random House.

SCHERMERHORN, R. A. (1978). *Ethnic plurality in India*. Tucson: University of Arizona Press.

SINGER, LESTER (1962). Ethnogenesis and Negro-Americans today. *Social Research* (Winter):422–432.

SKLAR, RICHARD (1963). *Nigerian political parties.* Princeton, New Jersey: Princeton University Press.

SKLAR, RICHARD, and WHITAKER, C. S. JR. (1964). Nigeria. In *Political parties and national integration in tropical Africa* (J. Coleman and C. Rosberg, eds.), pp. 597–654. Berkeley: University of California Press.

SMILEY, DONALD V. (1977). French-English relations in Canada and consociational democracy. In *Ethnic conflict in the western world* (Milton J. Esman, ed.), pp. 179–203. Ithaca, New York: Cornell University Press.

SMITH, R. T. (1970–1971). Race and political conflict in Guyana. *Race* **12:**415–427.

STEWART, OMER C. (1972). The Native American Church and the law. In *The emergent Native Americans* (D. Walker, ed.), pp. 382–396. Boston: Little, Brown.

STINCHCOMBE, ARTHUR (1975). Social structure and politics. In *Handbook of political science,* Vol. 3, (F. Greenstein and N. Polsky, eds.), pp. 557–622. Reading, Massachusetts: Addison-Wesley.

THOMAS, ROBERT K. (1968). Pan-Indianism. In *The American Indian today* (Stuart Levine and Nancy O. Lurie, eds.), pp. 77–85. Deland, Florida: Everett/Edwards.

TILLY, CHARLES, (ed.) (1975). *The formation of national states in Europe.* Princeton, New Jersey: Princeton University Press.

TILLY, CHARLES, (ed.) (1978). *From mobilization to revolution.* Reading, Massachusetts: Addison-Wesley.

U.S. INDIAN CLAIMS COMMISSION. (1980). Final Report. House Report no. 96-383. Washington, D.C.: Government Printing Office.

UNITED STATES STATISTICAL ABSTRACT. (1981). Washington, D.C.: Government Printing Office.

VAN DEN BERGHE, PIERRE L. (1971). Ethnicity: the African experience. *International Social Science Journal* **23:**507–518.

VAN DEN BERGHE, PIERRE L. (1978). *Race and racism,* 2d ed. New York: John Wiley.

VELTMAN, CALVIN (1981). Language planning in the United States: The politics of ignorance. Paper presented at the annual meeting of the American Sociological Association, August 24–28, Toronto.

WALLERSTEIN, IMMANUEL (1960). Ethnicity and national integration. *Cahiers d'Etudes Africaines* **3**(Oct):129–138.

WALSH, E. J. (1980). Resource mobilization theory and the dynamics of local anti-nuclear coalition formation in the wake of the Three-Mile Island accident. Paper presented at the annual meeting of the American Sociological Association, August 27–31, New York.

WILSON, A. JEYARATNAM (1975). *Electoral politics in an emergent state.* Cambridge: Cambridge University Press.

WOLPE, HOWARD (1974). *Urban politics in Nigeria.* Los Angeles: University of California Press.

YANCEY, WM., ERIKSEN, E., and JULIANI, R. (1976). Emergent ethnicity: A review and reformulation. *American Sociological Review* (June):391–402.

YANCEY, WILLIAM L., ERICKSEN, EUGENE P., and LEON, GEORGE H. (1985). The structure of pluralism: "We're all Italian around here, aren't we Mrs. O'Brien?" *Ethnic and Racial Studies* **8**(January):94–116.

YOUNG, CRAWFORD (1976). *The politics of cultural pluralism.* Madison: University of Wisconsin Press.

ZOLBERG, ARISTIDE (1968). The structure of political conflict in new states of tropical Africa. *American Political Science Review* **62**(March):70–87.

5

Cultural Pluralism in the Third World

M. CRAWFORD YOUNG
Department of Political Science
University of Wisconsin
Madison, Wisconsin 53706

I. INTRODUCTORY REMARKS

In 1944, a new word entered the language: genocide, or the annihilation of an entire national or cultural group. The genesis of the word lay in the holocaust that overwhelmed European Jewry under Nazi rule, but the term quickly came to have much broader application and widespread currency. Coined by one Raphael Lemkin, "genocide" was clearly a word whose time had come.

Reflection on the instant linguistic reception of the concept will serve to introduce the themes we wish to pursue in this essay. Lethal physical assault upon a human group objectified as stigmatized "other" is the ultimate breakdown in civility within a nation-state. The anarchical character of international society has meant that the sovereign state units that comprise it have frequently resorted to violent conflict. However, genocide is different: this occurs within the boundaries of an organized political system, within which order is presumed normal. Genocidal episodes within states illustrate the grisly capacity of human communities to form collective representations of elements within their political environment that condense powerful passions of hostility, and in extreme cases bring about bestial massacres, tolerated or even organized by the state.

Genocidal incidents have been sufficiently frequent in the contemporary world to earn a generic label (Isaacs, 1975; Kuper, 1981). Moreover, it is not simply accidental that the word was recently coined. Although violence perpetrated by one human collectivity upon another within a given society doubtless extends back to the origin of the species, the scale and frequency of such episodes is distinctly characteristic of the modern world.

COMPETITIVE ETHNIC RELATIONS

Nor, we might add, is it entirely coincidental that no analogous word has appeared to characterize murderous class warfare. Vast and flourishing intellectual industries exist, devoted to the analysis of class conflict. Properly so: class and cultural pluralism, we believe, constitute the two most crucial lines of cleavage in contemporary political societies, and the tensions engendered by the competitive struggles across these battlelines of polarization supply much of the motor force in modern social process. However, paradigms founded upon social class have not found necessary a word like "classcide." In this lexical contrast we find illuminated more profound aspects of the relationship between class and cultural pluralism, to which we will return. The absence of the term betokens an important contrast between class and cultural pluralism as bases for conflict.

Genocide represents the extreme and limiting case of a much more general phenomenon: relations of competition and tension between self-aware collectivities based on ethnicity, language, religion, race, caste, or region contained within a sovereign political entity—patterns for which we employ the generic term "cultural pluralism." Such forms of consciousness may be traced back into the mists of the past, as Armstrong (1982) has done in masterful style for the region from Samarkand to Seville. But the basic character of the political process in the modern world, we would suggest, has transformed the nature and impact of cultural pluralism. The increased scale of social mobilization, the sharpened ideological articulation of communal solidarities, the expanded zones of competition and encounter with other groups, and the rising stakes in the action of the state have all served to deepen the impact of cultural pluralism. Modern politics constitutes communal groups as political actors. Solidary cultural groups, politically activated and ideologically mobilized, become a qualitatively different force within the nation-state arena than "nations before nationalism."

Significant elements of cultural pluralism characterize an overwhelming majority of nation-states; the truly homogeneous polity, such as the two Koreas, is the deviant rather than the normal case. And, though our regional focus in this discussion is that elusive and disparate domain recently denominated as the "Third World," the issues considered here are by no means distinctive to this zone. Indeed, some of the most acute crises, calling into question long unchallenged political arrangements, are occurring in the "first" and "second" world. The Ulster crisis simmers on, with no end in view. The future unity of Canada is problematic. The end of authoritarianism in Spain has posed far-reaching questions of redefinition of the nation-state with respect to Galicians, Catalans, and above all an aggressive Basque movement. Far-reaching decentralization has occured in Yugoslavia in the past decade, in the quest for a durable single polity compatible with highly mobilized "nationality" sentiments. The world's two leading superpowers each face major challenges of ethnodemographic change for the balance of this century: the United States from the prospective scale of uncontrollable influx of Mexicans and others from the Caribbean area, and the Soviet Union from the tremendous disparity between birthrates in European Russia and non-Slav areas of Central Asia. In all corners of our shrinking globe, once-dominant assumptions of inexorable integrative trends toward the national cores of the contemporary state system have fallen by the wayside. Formerly fashionable metaphors, such as "melting pot" in the United States or "merging" of nationalities in the Soviet Union, have lost both credibility and utility (although Yuri Andropov revived the incendiary "merger" term in a December 1982 speech).

Thus, in our "Third World" focus, we consider a regional variant of a broader phenomenon, not processes distinctive to the developing world. We lay particular stress on the central impact of the political realm on cultural pluralism (Rothschild, 1981; Keyes, 1981). We share the view of Nagel and Olzak (1982, p. 2) as to "the distinctly *political* nature of ethnic movements."

In this essay, we propose an overview of the crucial dimensions of cultural pluralism in contemporary politics, focusing upon the "Third World" (using the conventional geographic meaning of this term, to refer to Africa, Asia, and Latin America). We will examine (1) the nation-state as political arena, (2) social class and cultural pluralism, (3) the impact of modernization, and (4) the political management of cultural pluralism. We do not at all wish to argue that all contemporary political conflict is reducible to cultural pluralism, or that a viable framework for grasping this dimension of politics constitutes some comprehensive "paradigm" of the political system. We do, however, hope to demonstrate that in many, perhaps most, contemporary polities, comprehensive analysis must incorporate understanding of the communal cleavages in society. Cultural pluralism involves an essentially autonomous set of vectors that interact with other determinants (character of the nation-state, social class configuration, political parties and groups, corporatist social forces, and the like) but are not simply a residual aspect of some other dimension (such as social class).

II. NATION–STATE AS POLITICAL ARENA

Cultural pluralism derives its current potency from the very nature of the modern nation-state, which defines the political arena within which it operates. It is a curious fact in the intellectual history of the discipline that, beyond the particular issue of cultural pluralism, the state, an entity analogous in importance to markets for economists or space for geographers, has received remarkably little attention in the most influential paradigms of recent times. Stepan (1978), reviewing the contents of two leading political science journals from 1958 to 1972, found only one article directly concerned with the state. For structural functionalists, state was merely the "black box" between inputs and outputs; Easton (1965) was able to entirely avoid use of the term in his 500-page treatise on the "political system." For behavioralists, it is reduced to a residual arena within which social psychology hypotheses are carefully measured. Marxists long relegated the state to a passive status as an instrument of class domination. Especially since the late 1970s, "state" is resurgent as conceptual focus in

116   M. CRAWFORD YOUNG

most paradigms (Poggi, 1978; Skocpol, 1979; Nordlinger, 1981; Gold, Lo, and Wright, 1975; Jessop, 1982). This timely reawakening is of great value to the comparative study of cultural pluralism; nation-state is the determinant political field which conditions its activation and operation. Certain characteristics of the modern nation-state tend to bring it into conflict with plural segments of the society contained within its borders. The tremendous expansion in the scope of state activity has raised enormously the stakes in social competition mediated through the state. The doctrines, ideology, and organizational form of the state profoundly shape the nature of cultural pluralism within the political field that it constitutes.

The nation-state, as we know it, emerges in mature form only in Europe and the Americas in the nineteenth century, then is extended to the entire globe by the imperial partition of the world and the anticolonial revolt that eventually overthrew European domination (Tilly, 1975; Anderson, 1974; Seton-Watson, 1977; Dyson, 1980). However, the foundations of the modern state were built gradually. Protostates, of course, extend back to the neolithic revolution, and vast empires developed in ancient times. Important changes in the structure, resources, and doctrines defining the state occurred in the sixteenth to eighteenth centuries, changes that vastly enlarged its scope and significance. Institutionalized bureaucracies extended its regulatory capacities. Legal systems were elaborated, codifying its commands as jurisprudence, and standing armies—and, from the nineteenth century, police forces—transformed the reach of its enforcement. Fiscal instruments were developed that vastly increased its revenue flow and provided the financial base for its ramifying institutional infrastructure.

Crucial changes occurred in the juridical and philosophical foundations of the state that were essential to its subsequent expansion (Passerin d'Entreves, 1967). The first task was to detach the state from the religious domain, and in particular from the confining limits of natural law doctrines. In the process, the concept of sovereignty was gradually developed, with philosophers such as Bodin, Hobbes, and Rousseau offering powerful reformulations. By the beginning of the nineteenth century, this task was essentially complete; further, the state was no longer the personal emanation of the sovereign, but an impersonal entity carrying mystical sanction as embodiment of the community (Shennan, 1974).

The ideology of the contemporary polity was completed by fusing the doctrine of the state, endowed theoretically with the plenitude of sovereign powers, with the idea of the nation, investing the community ruled by the state with a wholly new moral significance. The quite extraordinary scope of this concept is illustrated in the definition proposed by one of the most influential students of nationality, Hans Kohn (1968):

> Nationalism is a political creed that underlies the cohesion of modern societies, and legitimizes their claim to authority. Nationalism centers the supreme loyalty of the overwhelming majority of the people upon the nation-state, whether existing or desired. The nation-state is regarded not only as the ideal, 'natural,' or 'normal' form of political

organization but also as the indispensable framework for all social, cultural, and economic activities.

The idea of nationalism was at first associated with existing European states. However, it became rapidly assimilated by various communities that advanced ideologies of affinity and solidarity, based on shared language, culture, historical standing, and religion (not necessarily all of these elements). Such movements were particularly numerous in the sprawling, multicultural domains assembled before the idea of nationalism sprang forth in the early nineteenth century.

A crucial new concept now congealed within the penumbra of nationalism: self-determination. Nationhood found fulfillment in statehood: if a community met the criteria of nationality, by that very token it had a sacred right to constitute itself as a sovereign state. The doctrine of self-determination won its first major triumphs in the German and Italian unification movements. The large-scale redrawing of European maps brought about by the World War I collapse of the Austro-Hungarian, Russian, and Ottoman Empires and such cognate events as the Irish and Norwegian independence movements enshrined ethnolinguistic self-determination as an ascendant (though not universally applied) international norm within Europe, duly appointed by the Versailles peace treaty.

By the late nineteenth century, the idea of nationalism began to permeate Asia, and a little later Africa (Emerson, 1960). At first, it was an anti-imperial doctrine adopted by ancient states to mobilize their defenses against European empire-building (Japan, China, Thailand). For those that succumbed to European sub-jugation, nationalism was joined to the creed of self-determination, as justification for anticolonial revolt. As the struggle for liquidation of imperial rule could, in practice, only be conducted within the territorial units created by imperial partition, these became the units of sovereignty once the combat was won. Despite the high order of cultural plurality of many of these units, the nation-state concept as model was embraced with full enthusiasm. Political leaders were well aware of the gap that stood between their polities and full realization of the concept of nationhood. Bridging this chasm became a universally acclaimed priority of independence, under the slogans of "nation-building" and "national integration."

Particular note need be taken of the unitarian implications of the nation-state concept. In symbol and slogan, the oneness and the indivisibility of the nation is celebrated. Lurking behind the ideal of unity was the chimera of homogeneity, an unattainable and, for many plural polities, self-destructive objective that shimmers no less as a distant holy grail.

The concept of the nation-state thus stands, virtually unchallenged, as ideolog-ical charter for the contemporary polity. More, it stands as a normative model of the world, the more potent in its effects in the generality of its acceptance. Within the chrysalis of the nation-state is found the golden gift of modernity; the moral imperative of nation-building is not to be denied.

Here we encounter a crucial paradox of many Third World polities. The founding charter of the sovereign state was territorial anticolonialism, rather than an intrinsic cultural commonality discovered as nationality. The prototypical examples are India or Nigeria, rather than Poland or Ireland. Because such states are not "nations" in the Polish or Irish sense, a number of observers argue that the "nation-state" designation should be denied to them (Connor, 1978). We would prefer to retain the nation-state label, precisely because the notion that the state achieves validation, security, and permanency only by becoming a nation is sacred liturgy to virtually all Third World polities: hence the imperative of "nation-building," however arduous and lengthy a task this may be.

The unitarian impulses of the nation-state carry high risks, depending on the manner of their pursuit. Profoundly unsettling issues of cultural survival may arise from national unity strategies that imply imposing one culture unwillingly upon another. Examples abound of the mortal dangers in the blind pursuit of unity. In Pakistan, the campaign to force through Urdu as sole national language was a fatal error: East Pakistan viewed Urdu as a West Pakistan language and a cultural threat to the status of Bengali. Not only did the campaign fail, but ransom was the discrediting of much of the pro-Pakistan elite in East Bengal. In Sudan, civil war in the south from 1955 to 1972 was sustained by the concept of national integration as Arabization and may be reawakened by new threats of Islamization in the 1980s. In Chad, first Prime Minister Pierre Tombalbaye met his death in 1975 in reaction to bitter resentments triggered by his effort to enforce an arduous initiation rite associated with the *yondo* cult of his Sara ethnic community upon young people from other areas, in the name of national integration.

Cultural pluralism, as we have defined it, is a condition constituted by the nation-state. A fundamental characteristic of a state is territoriality: boundaries enclose it, and its sovereign power is exercised over the human communities contained within its frontiers. Thus bounded, the nation-state is the authoritative arena for interaction, encounter, cooperation, conflict, and struggle over the exercise of power and distribution of societal resources. The existence of different linguistic, religious, or racial groups becomes a matter of high politics when they are located within the same political community.

The mere existence of a plurality of cultural groups within a nation-state does not automatically make communal politics central; in many times and places, low-temperature politics of cultural pluralism have prevailed, for example, in Senegal, Morocco, or Thailand. The nature of the nation-state is one important factor: its ability to construct a public ideology in which all cultural groups find a place, its capacity to sustain its legitimacy by at least minimal levels of performance, its skill in managing the public domain with perceived "fairness," and above all in avoiding actions that arouse deep anxieties and fears about communal survival among particular cultural segments. The character of cultural pluralism as well can vary widely; we return to this point in Section IV.

III. SOCIAL CLASS AND CULTURAL PLURALISM

As argued at the outset, the two most important patterns of cleavage in Third World states are social class and cultural pluralism, not necessarily in that order. Indeed, one of the unresolved theoretical challenges is to adequately define the interrelationship between these two macrovariables. For the most part, analysis of these two domains has followed separate paths and has been governed by divergent epistomologies. Some students of ethnicity, such as Glazer, assert that ethnicity "seems to become a more fundamental source of stratification" than class and property (Glazer and Moynihan, 1975, p. 17). Students of social class, particularly those within the Marxist tradition, tend to regard cultural pluralism as a secondary phenomenon or a disguised artifact of class relations ("false consciousness").

Van den Berghe (Despres, 1975, p. 72) suggests a useful set of propositions on the class–ethnicity relationship, which we would take as point of departure:

(1) Ethnicity and class are interrelated but analytically distinct: even though social classes have subcultural differences, or ethnic groups are commonly arranged in a hierarchy of wealth and power, class is not reducible to ethnicity, nor vice versa.

(2) Class–ethnicity interaction differs in each case, making *a priori* judgments risky.

(3) Ethnicity is both an objective and subjective phenomenon.

(4) Both ethnic and class conflict come from unequal distribution of resources; class and ethnic cleavage often occur simultaneously, though the specific lines of cleavage may be different.

There are, indeed, a remarkable gamut of different outcomes in the class–ethnicity symbiosis. On one extreme lie polities such as Peru or Mexico, where the social basis for high-saliency ethnic cleavage is present but the singular lack of mobilization of Indian solidarity makes class division far more important. At the other lie countries like Malaysia or Cyprus, where class pales into residual significance relative to the potency of communal division.

The driving forces behind both classes and ethniciiy as political variables are inequalities on the one hand and the commanding moral force of egalitarian precepts on the other. Coleman expresses this well in placing the equality drive in the center of his "development syndrome":

> Whether viewed as a factual trend, a perceived technological possibility, or simply as the dominant aspiration underlying the drive for change, egalitarianism pervades all aspects of modern political life and culture and all forms of modern political ideology [Binder *et al.*, (1971, p. 76)].

Inequalities within the national arena relate to distribution of public resources, opportunity for economic well-being and social mobility, and legal standing before the state. Egalitarianism as a creed stigmatizes deviations from equity and from evenness in these allocations.

While doctrines of radical egalitarianism may be found early in Christian and Islamic thought and some strands of classic Chinese philosophy and African cosmologies, such views were always politically marginal until the modern era. The moral power of egalitarianism takes on entirely new significance with the rise of such philosophies as democracy, liberalism, and socialism. While the liberal tradition tended to conceive of egalitarianism in essentially individual terms, the rise of Marxist and other socialist doctrines roots its condemnation of inequality in structural categories. Somewhat later, social theory incorporates structural inequality on cultural criteria into a critique of injustice; such a presumption is implicit in many self-determination movements, although the romantic component of nationalist thought was often more salient. Perhaps we may suggest that, in mature form, the paradigm of ethnic inequalities first appears fully developed in the "cultural pluralism" school of J. S. Furnivall and his followers (Furnivall, 1948). In recent decades, class and ethnicity constitute the two most important collective metaphors within which inequality is perceived.

The transcendant norm of egalitarianism thus clothes both class and ethnicity with the garments of morality in the pursuit of material interest. The idea of equality itself is sufficiently multifaceted and ambiguous to permit different contending groups to simultaneously perceive disadvantage; perceptually, politics may well be a negative-sum game. Or, astute casuistry may convert evident inequality into justified differentiation not incompatible with egalitarian ideals. Cecil Rhodes launched the aphorism "equality for civilized men," long an article of faith among Rhodesian whites who were therefore conveniently able to restrict operation of the concept to all Europeans and a tiny handpicked handful of Africans. Or we may note the argument of members of the politico-mercantile elite in remarkably inegalitarian *Nouveau Régime* Zaire, who argue that equality should be understood simply as elimination of racial distinctions between salaries accorded to highly remunerated expatriate personnel and top Zairian cadres. On the ethnic dimension, members of groups historically favored in access to education will fervently argue that equality can only mean application of pure "merit" criteria to allocation of state favors, while spokesmen for communities who believe they labor under structural disabilities will claim that equality can only be accomplished through policies of ethnic preference by "affirmative action."

The particular blend of ethnicity and class as organizing focus for the struggle over resources depends, we would suggest, on the relative saliency of these metaphors of social structure within a given polity. Cultural pluralism becomes a political variable to the extent that communal solidarity is mobilized and activated; the mere existence of actual differences of language, race, or religion within a polity is not in itself a sufficient condition to produce manifest conflict. There are both long-run and short-term aspects to this phenomenon; cultural identify congeals into effective consciousness to the extent that it acquires ideological elaboration over time. In a more immediate sense, the impact of communal cleavages depends on situational factors, which articulate potential consciousness into activated group solidarity when a specific context is perceived as threatening group interests. Collective self-awareness is also indispensible to meaningful class political action; absent consciousness a social category is akin to the legendary "sack of potatoes" that Marx found French peasantry to be in the *Eighteenth Brumaire*. The mere existence of rural small holders, an urban working force, or stratifaction by occupation and income does not in and of itself create politics of social class.

Enormous differences exist in the relative significance of class and ethnicity in the social consciousness of various polities. These depend on the nature of political sequences, historically established patterns of competition in the political realm (for example, the political party system), and the predominant social ideologies. Dominant metaphors of society, once well rooted, have their own momentum and inertial force; Ossowoski (1963, p. 38) eloquently expresses this point, writing: "facts are powerless against stereotypes supported by emotional motivations. An intellectual scheme that is rooted in the social consciousness may within certain limits successfully withstand the test of reality."

Generally speaking, social class metaphors were relatively strong in Latin America and much weaker in most African and Asian nation-states. In the Ibero-American instance, class-based ideologies have tended to dominate; at the same time, the well-established pattern of cultural incorporation of socially mobile Indians into Hispanic identity prevented the crystallization of Indian collective awareness. Thus absorption into class roles is not diluted by ethnic consciousness; Magill (1972) demonstrates in the instance of the Bolivian mines the socialization processes by which the rural Indian recruit becomes a class-conscious worker through the impact of workplace experience and the doctrinal education by the powerful union. The ultraleftist Sendero Luminoso movement in Peru in the early 1980s seemed to reflect Indian social revolt articulated in Maoist class ideology. In contrast, the uprisings in the Western Highlands of Guatemala that gathered force after 1979 were more closely founded on Indian consciousness (Smith, 1984). In Africa, while there is a process of class formation in course, its ultimate direction is uncertain, and the categories remain quite fluid. A dominant power-holding group, above all defined by its relationship to the state, comes closest to meeting criteria of self-consciousness; the diversity of labels applied to this group in the social class literature is symptomatic of its yet indeterminate character as collective metaphor.

Cultural mobilization, on the other hand, has gone farthest in Asia, particularly in countries such as Malaysia, India, Sri Lanka, and Pakistan (though not in the Philippines). Ethnicity in sub-Saharan Africa has frequently been politicized, but is generally not invested with such highly elaborated cultural ideologies (Young, 1976). The Mahgreb follows a model of very low cultural mobilization for the numerically important "Berber" groups quite parallel to Latin America.

Gellner (Gellner and Micaud, 1972, p. 13) captures well the essence of un-mobilized identity:

> It would of course be an exaggeration to say that Berbers and their language are an
> invisible social fact. You cannot ignore . . . something as conspicuous as that a man
> speaks, or even speaks exclusively, an unintelligible and difficult language. The urban
> Arab notes it with contempt, irritation, or sometimes, fear. But the displeasure does not
> congeal around some permanent and central idea. . . . So, the difference which exists in
> linguistic fact and history is not underscored, for it lacks a connection with any of those
> ideas in terms of which men do see their world. . . . There are of course limits to what
> 'our thinking can make so' or what it can obscure. But it can 'make so' a good
> deal. . . . The Berber sees himself as a member of this or that tribe, within an Islamical-
> ly conceived and permeated world—and not as a member of a linguistically defined
> ethnic group.

There appears one crucial distinction between class and ethnicity as solidarity systems: the symbolic resources available for communal mobilization are more powerful and involve more intensely felt emotions and fears than are likely to arise within the class framework. Bell argues that contemporary ethnicity is more salient than class "because it can combine an interest with an affective tie" (Glazer and Moynihan, 1975, p. 169). The violent civil conflicts of recent decades have for the most part been organized along communal lines (India in 1947, Nigeria 1967–1970, Burundi in 1972, Lebanon after 1975). Epochal conflicts in the cultural domain may well have a very high symbolic–expressive content and relate very little to concrete material interests. The angry debates over the Sharia courts in framing the new Nigerian constitution are one example; the 1964 Kashmir crisis over the theft of a hair from the Prophet's beard from a Muslim shrine is another. Such conflicts may awaken the deepest anxieties about the innermost attachments of people and indeed their survival, evocative of a passion that is less likely to pervade class conflict.

The instrumental and affective dimensions of ethnic behavior become readily intertwined. The temptation for leaders of cultural groups to enforce their public claims by active mobilization of their cultural clientele is often irresistible. When this occurs, the appeal to interest blends with manipulation of emotion-laden and anxiety-creating symbols. Interest, in turn, may be seen at two levels: the instru-mental goals of the group, and the ambitions of the leadership. There can be little doubt, in the history of electoral politics in Africa, that many politicians have found the ethnic pathway to clientele-creation irresistible as the surest and swiftest way to consolidate a following.

Not only does cultural pluralism tend to have a larger reservoir of affective symbols for subjective mobilization in many settings, but political claims and action by communal segments tend to have high visibility. Because cultural pluralism frequently rests on readily perceived markers—language, phenotypical stereotypes, publicly observed rituals—on the crucial issues of overall resource allocations and domination of public institutions, communal imbalances are swift to be recognized and have more immediate emotional impact.

Nigeria is an instructive case in point. All observers of the Nigerian scene agree that class differentiation is—at an analytical level—important and growing. Yet open political competition in the 1979–1983 period resulted in five parties of virtually identical multiclass composition and a clear regional personality. The battle between those parties, in the apt Nigerian metaphor, concerned "cutting the national cake," an intriguing image of political power that conceptualizes it as sweet to the taste, intended to be eaten, and divisible into discrete slices. Politics, for self-aware communities, was about the size of the slices and who was to do the cutting. Class, too, was involved in "cutting the cake"; the political barons and public contractors received heaping portions, while urban poor and farmers had only the crumbs. However, public discussion of "cutting the national cake" invariably evoked ethnic images about the relative size of the slices.

In some instances cleavages of class and ethnicity may cumulate, producing the potential for high conflict. The dominance of a given cultural segment and social class may be preserved over long periods by prescriptive belief, external support, or simple coercion. At those points of historical rupture when these institutions of domination dissolve, there is a high possibility of violent confrontation, as social revolution is fused to communal animosities. Rwanda in 1959 and Zanzibar in 1964 are cases in point; at some future point, so will be South Africa. In these circumstances, class and cultural pluralism become impossible to disentangle analytically.

In sum, we would suggest that the interconnection of class and cultural pluralism is determined above all by the degree of mobilization on each of these axes, the class and communal configuration of the nation-state and its authoritative organs, the class and communal content of dominant ideologies and social beliefs, and cultural inequalities. The specificity of each political arena is crucial with a wide range of possible variation in outcome.

IV. THE IMPACT OF MODERNIZATION

With respect to modernization, we would suggest, as a general proposition, that the increasing saliency of communal cleavages in recent decades is directly related to the cluster of processes generally implied by the term "modernity." However unevenly this occurs in particular areas, it would appear that the "modernization" dynamic is both irreversible and probably accelerating. Whether we attribute this, with Wallerstein (1976), to the progressive penetration of "the world capitalist system" or follow Pye (1966) in identifying a "world culture of modernity" that has become a universal norm, the practical conclusion is identical: technology, communication, urbanization, literacy, and the cash economy inexorably spread, with major consequences for the social order.

The creed of "modernization" is espoused by virtually all regimes in the contemporary era, however divergent may be their strategies for attaining it. States enlarge their own communications resources to propagate their legitimacy. They build roads to facilitate their control of rural areas as well as to respond to local demands. The schoolhouse, quintessential symbol of "modernity", is extended to the village as fast as resources permit, both because of the presumed (though debatable) relationship between mass education and development and universal clamor for this "amenity." Even though not all countries succeed in keeping literacy expansion up with population growth, everywhere the absolute number of literate persons is increasing. The collective efforts of organized society, then, are consciously engaged in the task of "modernization." It is not something that simply "happens," but is a central political project of the contemporary state.

The conjunction of activist developmentalism and popular welfare demands together yield a truly extraordinary expansion in the scale of state activity. Bell (Glazer and Moynihan, 1975, p. 147) suggests that the "revolution of rising expectations" subtly verges into a sustained demand for rising entitlements. One relevant measure of the scale of state-expansion is through level of government expenditure. Two examples may be cited, Ghana and Zaire. In the former case public outlays were only £6,630,000 on the heels of World War II, a figure that had only doubled during the previous 35 years. In the final colonial decade, however, Ghana state disbursement multiplied 10-fold (Bourret, 1960, p. 28). In Zaire, government outlays increased by 15-fold between 1939 and 1950, tripled again in the final decade of Belgian rule, then were multiplied by four during the Mobutu era, totalling over half the Gross Domestic Product by 1976 (Young and Turner, 1985).

The imperatives of modernization thus enlarge the authoritative arena for social interaction and conflict: the integrating, penetrating, extracting, and redistributing nation-state. The developmentalist, unity-seeking polity fixes high stakes for the ongoing game of group competition for collective advantage. Through the state the rules of competition will be set. Few of the major policy decisions of the state are wholly neutral in the distribution of costs and benefits among groups. If for no other reason than cultural self-defense, mobilized communal groups will closely monitor state action, propelled by the conviction that rival groups are doing likewise.

The processes also continue through the momentum of forces quite beyond the control of states. Local communities throw up primary school buildings even if the state will not, and they eventually secure teachers for the schools; the equation of education equals social mobility is so powerfully fixed that literacy expansion adds its own momentum to the considerable role of the state. The advent of the transistor radio in the 1960s was the basis for a profound communications revolution; the radios were not tied to the availability of electric current and were inexpensive enough so that at least wealthier members of a peasant community could afford them, so that the diffusion of political and social information increased by several orders of magnitude. These in turn partly account for the strikingly high levels of political information discovered in Egyptian and Ghanaian rural communities by Harik (1971) and Hayward (1976). Third World urbanization likewise increases at a pace many states struggle in vain to halt. Not only does this affect the swollen primary cities, particularly the national capitals, but also a host of secondary centers, especially those that are governmental outposts (Abulughod and Hay, 1977; Gugler and Flanagan, 1978).

The impact of modernization on cultural pluralism is multifold. Of particular importance are the new spheres of social competition introduced by these processes. The competition occurs on a broad front: in employment opportunity both generally and within specific enterprises; in access to education, especially at secondary and university levels where mobility payoffs are higher and places scarcer; and in command of state services (farm inputs, credit, health care) and favors (licenses, contracts). Very frequently the interface between the individual claimant and institutional resource allocator (whether a job, a permit, or a school place is involved) is by no means an impersonal and abstract bureaucracy, but a quite personalized transaction joining, for example, the job-seeker and personnel officer. Capacity to acquire competitive advantage in access to a discretionary favor of limited supply (job, school place) lies in establishing affinities with the person(s) making the decision. While this may be simply monetary, or some shared life experience (for example, school class), the transactions involved may in fact be determined by such impersonal criteria as competitive merit, but there is a high likelihood that enough will involve, at least in part, affinity criteria to foster the belief that communal groups are engaged collectively in competition for scarce goods. In an atmosphere permeated with consciousness of cultural pluralism, such perceptions intensify self-consciousness of the group and its sense of rivalry with others.

The well-known psychological process of selective perception reinforces this tendency. Be there one transaction in 10 where affinity operated, the high order of sensitization of mass cognitions of cultural cleavage will give it particular visibility. Further, the perception is not only selective but asymmetrical; award of a favor may well have been in response to a much more immediate tie of clan or village, but others observing it may impute the motivation to a broader cultural solidarity.

The peculiarities of the calculus of relative cultural advantage in social competition situations deserve mention as well. Relative social advantage has a number of dimensions: school enrollment, economic standing, state employment, political power. While advantages may be cumulative, a given group has a number of reference points from which to derive a sense of disadvantage or discrimination. A general perception of disadvantage may well become enrooted quite independently of empirical fact. Further, temporal fluctuations can play an important role; relative advantage is subject to constant recalculation. Once measured on any particular dimension, relative disadvantage takes on a scriptural quality among the aggrieved group: witness the potent role in predisposing toward the secession formula played by Bengali economists in the 1960s, who assiduously amassed evidence as to unequal benefits derived from the Ayub Khan development decade (Johan, 1972).

Modernization also relates to cultural pluralism through the mechanisms of identity formation and mobilization. Identities in the self-enclosed rural world of yore were for the most part local and diffuse. Many of the contemporary solidarity units are of historically recent origin. Cultural awareness is extended and created by those who transform related dialects into a standardized written language and equip it with a literature and a history. Communal solidarity is politicized by those who form cultural organizations, articulate collective grievances, and extend the struggle for group advantage or defense into the political realm.

The central trend has been toward enlargement and institutionalization of identities. The small-scale solidarities characterizing an earlier period tend to give way to broader groups: all Tamils, all Ibo, and so forth. As cultural segments acquire well-elaborated ideologies, their form tends to become solidified and congealed, with a smaller likelihood of further expansion or dissolution. For groups such as Bengalis or Malays, the creation of well-elaborated cultural ideologies in recent decades is very far advanced. In Africa, generally speaking, cultural ideologies are less highly articulated, and of course encounter strong effort by national governments to restrict their evolution. In cases such as Latin American Indians, or related linguistic groups labeled "Berbers" by outsiders in the Mahgreb, the absence of cultural ideology-builders or political mobilizers is part of the explanation for the very low levels of cultural self-consciousness and continued acceptability of an assimilation model of social change (becoming a Ladino or Mestizo or an Arab).

Finally, as Harold Isaacs (1975) has compellingly argued, the conditions associated with modernity give rise to psychological settings conducive to affirmation of cultural identity. Isaacs portrays this process as the retreat into a "House of Mumbi," borrowing a Kikuyu metaphor. The social insecurities of the new urban environments, the sense of aloneness engendered by city and workplace, create a powerful craving for reinforced primary ties that can give security, meaning, and mooring to the vast and marginalized populations of the primate agglomerations. This reticence of men before moral aloneness "begins to touch, it seems to me, the inwardness of the matter: insecure men who are torn loose from all moorings cling hard to whatever they can find an 'unquestionable place' where they belong, and they are finding this place more and more . . . in [cultural] affinities with their ineffable significance and their peculiarly coercive powers" (Isaacs, 1975, p. 35).

IV. POLITICAL MANAGEMENT OF CULTURAL PLURALISM

By way of conclusion, let us consider some of the state strategies devised in response to politicized communalism. At the time of independence in Africa and Asia, the potential force of cultural pluralism was widely underestimated. One may recollect the confident assertion by Sekou Toure of Guinea, at the moment of liberation, who declared, "In three or four years, no one will remember the tribal, ethnic or religious rivalries which, in the recent past, caused so much damage to our country and its population" (Toure, 1959, p. 28). Such serene confidence in the unifying power of state-centered nationalism has long disappeared. Most political leaderships have gone through the painful learning experience described by India's great premier, Jawaharlal Nehru, who confessed his mortification at hearing evidence presented to the Linguistic Provinces Commission in 1948:

> The work of sixty years of the Indian National Congress was standing before us, face to face with centuries-old India of narrow loyalties, petty jealousies and ignorant prejudices engaged in mortal conflict and we were simply horrified to see how thin was the ice upon which we were skating. Some of the ablest men in the country came before us and confidently and emphatically stated that language in the country stood for and represented culture, race, history, individuality, and finally a sub-nation [Harrison (1956, p. 621)].

A. Authoritarian Containment

A first and widespread response has been containment through authoritarian state formulas, whose common theme is what Kasfir labels "departicipation" (Kasfir, 1975). Open political competition, when it becomes structured by the cultural segments of society, can well trigger an uncontrollable dialectic of conflict, which is the functional analog of the "China syndrome" in nuclear accidents. Competitive elections, if parties are coincident with cultural pluralism, are little more than a census. Yet the peculiar melodrama and ritual of the electoral process, with its theatrical symbolization of communal division, greatly escalates tensions. The doctrine of majority rule becomes a prescription for cultural hegemony by the numerically preponderant group. The magnitude of the stakes and the intensity of the passions surrounding the competition lead all sides to pervert and manipulate the formal rules of fair electoral conduct. If we follow the argument of Rabushka and Shepsle (1972), an implacable logic of escalating conflict eventuating in crisis and decay renders competitive democracy and cultural pluralism incompatible partners. Scrutiny of the downward spiral of first republic (1960–1966) Nigeria suffices to persuade that the Rabushka–Shepsle model is a possible sequence, culminating in a meltdown of the polity core.

Military intervention and one-party regimes (or a combination of the two) are the most general formula for containing cultural challenges. The imperative of national unity is widely invoked as a justification for military takeover (Burma in 1962, Nigeria in 1966, Zaire in 1965, Burundi in 1966, to mention but a few). The ideology of single-party rule, which enjoyed particular vogue in Africa, rested heavily on a consciousness of the fragile cultural bases of the new state. We do not, of course, intend to suggest that pluralism containment is the only root of authoritarian formulas; many other factors may intervene (personal ambitions, corruption, erosion of legitimacy, threats of military corporate interests, and the like) (Decalo, 1976).

In the short run, containment and departicipation frequently appear to succeed, in the sense of lowering the temperature of intercommunal relationships. It is interesting to note that the cultural containment authoritarian state generally does not require the massive coercive and terrorist force of the social class containment state, whether their gulag archipelagos are designed to anesthetize the "popular sectors," as in Latin American bureaucratic-authoritarian states brilliantly modelled by Guillermo O'Donnell (1973), or in revolutionary states aiming to eliminate once-hegemonic social categories, as in Cambodia or Vietnam. However, the authoritarian state has its own infirmities over time. Its power-holding groups may be drawn from narrow ethnic segments, as in Idi Amin's Uganda. Containment lowers political emotions but does not necessarily win consensus. After nearly two decades of rule, Ne Win's Burma is no closer to willing acceptance of the Burmese nation-state by peripheral non-Burman groups (Shans, Karens, Arakans, Chins, Kachins, Mons) than was the preceding parliamentary democracy. Indeed, a tacitly accepted impasse appears to have emerged whereby some of the outlying minorities satisfy themselves with a twilight sovereignty within which the informal political economy of the narcotics trade can flourish, which might well be harmed by legal status as a separate sovereign state.

Autocratic containment policies do not necessarily suppress ethnicity along with dissent. Rather, they force cultural pluralism into informal channels, which may themselves become institutionalized. In a masterful synthesis of ethnic politics in Cameroon in the Ahidjo years (1960–1982), Cameroonian scholar Kofele-Kale, shows how patrimonial authoritarian rule was mediated through several tiers of "ethnic barons." By unstated yet widely recognized rules, the 200 identifiable linguistic groups were consolidated into about 15 ethnoregional groupings, accorded de facto representation in government and party posts. These ethnic conglomerates possessed "ethnic barons;" the search for favor had to be conducted through these channels. The fluidity inherent in this process created another role type, the "ethnic transvestite," able to act upon multiple ethnic identities depending upon situation and circumstance. According to Kofele-Kale:

The scramble to secure, establish and consolidate an ethnic power base has contributed to the politicization of ethnic loyalties at both the leadership and mass levels. To the extent that identification with an ethnic group was a necessary precondition for remaining in power, the need to rekindle banked ethnic feelings and to rediscover long forgotten ethnic roots became an all-consuming passion for the ethnic barons . . . at the mass level . . . is the inevitable retreat into an ethnic sanctuary since the individual peasant or worker now sees this structure as the only reliable avenue for upward mobility. For these people politics now revolves around the ethnic group and its spokesmen and women since it is they who ultimately can deliver essential services to their communities [Kofele-Kale (1984, p. 30–31)].

B. Consociationalism

A second formula, associated with Arend Lijphart (1978), is consociationalism. This model originated with the discovery by Dutch sociologists in the 1960s of the depth and persistence of "pillarization" of Netherlands society into quite separate and socially autonomous segments grounded in Catholic, Calvinist, and secular cosmologies. While Lijphart primarily uses European examples of quasi-corporatist democratic states (Belgium, Austria, Switzerland, Netherlands), he does extend his analysis to pre–civil war Lebanon.

The consociational polity seeks consensus through bargaining rather than containment through coercion. The prerequisites for its creation are political societies with distinct cleavage lines, where a broad public acceptance of the moral value of the nation-state community coexists with relatively high orders of communal solidarity. Political structure is based on a frank recognition of cultural segments as the basic structural principle of society. The polity operates through a grand coalition of leaders of the plural segments, based on proportionality in allocation of office and satisfaction of public claims, a mutual veto of the major segments, and acceptance of high internal autonomy of the cultural groups. It requires a partial depoliticization of communal issues, which are brokered through summit diplomacy, via secret bargaining, between the leaders.

A number of telling criticisms of the consociational formula have been advanced. It is reproached for elitism, susceptibility to stagnation and immobility, slowness in responding to new social forces, tendency to administrative inefficiency through the "proportionality" principle, and costs implied by multiplying jurisdictional arenas. Implicit in consociationalism is devolution of many social functions (schools, welfare) to the plural segments, and self-imposed limits on the role of the central state apparatus.

While these criticisms are cogent, it remains to be demonstrated that there is a better alternative to consociationalism than the containment–coercion state in those situations, such as Malaysia and Lebanon, where cultural pluralism permeates the entire fabric of society. In Malaysia, the 1969 explosion revealed how precarious the communal balance was; the catalyst for this momentary breakdown was a particularly heated electoral campaign. The equilibrium was restored through the alliance of communal parties; an uncertain legitimacy for the state is fostered by its competence and relative success in economic management, though fears and uncertainties, as well as dissatisfactions over relative shares, remain quite close to the surface. In Lebanon, while the consociational order had many critics within the country, especially among intellectuals from Muslim groups, its breakdown came primarily from the spillover of the Arab–Israeli conflict (Lebanon as main armed sanctuary for Palestinian forces after Black September, diverse Israeli responses to this fact). At the same time, the consociational formula is obviously limited in application to a confined set of polities where institutionalized cultural pluralism is particularly strong.

C. Ethnic Preference

A third, less comprehensive formula seeks balance by systematic ethnic preference for groups believed to be historically disadvantaged, whose consent is indispensable for the operation of the state. Malaysia is again the most obvious example. The Malay fraction of the population felt itself endangered culturally and economically by the entrenched Chinese mercantile position, and their predominance in skills relevant to leading positions in private and public sectors. Malay consent to a nation-state including Chinese and Indian resident communities within a citizenship framework was conditioned on cultural security guaranteed by an Islamic state and Malay as national language and culture, assured dominance of the bureaucratic machinery, and state promotion of Malay entry into capital-holding ranks. Chinese gained in return confirmation of their residential rights as citizens and a privately oriented economy in which their mercantile talents could flourish.

Ethnic preference policies have been pursued in a variety of circumstances. India has fixed target quotas and reserved legislative seats for harijan (untouchable) candidates, to remedy the vast inequalities of social power between the twice-born and Sudra caste groups, and the 20% of the population in the "polluted" end of the scale. Success has been ambiguous, though not insignificant; in 1976, in 14 provinces surveyed, scheduled caste (harijan) quotas range from 5 to 22.5%, while untouchable job-holders ranged from 1 (Orissa) to 6 (Punjab) percent (*India Today,* 1978, p. 55). Fiji is another state where protective policies are applied in favor of indigenous Fijians (Milne, 1981). In other countries as well, the impact of such measures, whether formal or informal, has been mixed. In Zaire, quotas on university entry were created in 1971, purportedly to equalize mobility opportunities between regions (provinces). Their discriminatory impact has been deeply resented by ethnic groups believing themselves disfavored, while enrollment data do not suggest that they have substantially benefitted those regions (Equateour, Haut-Zaire) that they were intended to serve.

Ethnic preference policies have some undoubted liabilities. They legally entrench ethnic distinction into the political process. They are likely, in practice, to benefit only a small fraction of the target group, usually at the upper end of the social spectrum. Such public goods as scholarships or preferential access to state contracts accrue to middle-class elements by definition, as Wilson (1978) and others have argued for the American case. The fluid and situational character of ethnicity may render legal definition of beneficiary groups problematic, but in such cases as Malaysia, where an unrestricted market in such distributions would almost certainly disadvantage Malays, there is no political alternative to such a policy.

D. Political Engineering

A fourth formula is the structuring of political institutions so as to foster communal accommodation by structurally inhibiting cultural mobilization. The most self-conscious experiment of this sort was the 1979 Nigerian constitution, elaborated against the backdrop of the frenzied escalation of ethnic competition in the 1960–1966 period, a bitter civil war, and 13 years of military rule. Nigerian scholars, jurists, and politicians, under the watchful supervision of the military regime, undertook the most painstaking anatomy of their society, and used as starting point an open recognition of the social forces that had overwhelmed the first republic. The overthrow of this regime at the end of 1983 would suggest the failure of the formula, in the ultimate sense that it could not persist. For those who had placed high hopes on this design for Nigerian democracy, it is perhaps small comfort to note that it was not mobilized ethnicity that undid the second republic. Cultural pluralism was, in part, tamed; corruption, alas, was not.

India, by more informal processes, has developed a rich and subtle system of governance reconciling democratic consent with what is beyond doubt the most complex and multidimensional cultural pluralism confronting any polity in the world. Colonial India was not able to resolve the Hindu–Muslim polarity that dominated the decolonization process. The founders of independent India began with a relatively unitarian nation-state ideology, which flavored the cultural premises of the early years. The secularity of the state would permit it to rise above religious conflict, which seemed in 1947 to be the most dangerous threat. An egalitarian–socialist state philosophy would gradually erode hierarchical cleavages (caste), while a regional structure, based on multilingual units and eventual implementation of Hindi as national language, would dilute the significance of language conflicts. Over the years, the dream of unitarian nationalism was dismantled, piece by piece. Linguistic states were accepted in the 1950s; in 1965, Hindi as national language was all but abandoned in the face of violent South Indian protests. In 1962, a constitutional amendment set limits to regional demands by outlawing secessionist appeals; tacitly, it made legitimate cultural claims as long as they remained within the nation-state arena. The party system, by an unperceived chemistry, transformed the highly cultural factionalism of the base into a more issue-centered national political discourse. The tensions latent in the cultural diversity of India were buffered and brokered through its complex institutional structures in such a way as to partially depoliticize them at the summit.

Finally, we may note the decartesianizing of the state as artifice for dealing with the particular claims of culturally distinct groups. Sudan was the best example of this strategy, where the nation-state entity was made acceptable—in this instance for the south, for a time—by abandoning the inarticulate major premise of symmetry as a necessary requisite of the state. The cartesian mentality has a powerful grip in constitution-making; its logic commands that hierarchies and subdivisions must be identical. Such a conception rendered a single unitary Sudan culturally intolerable to the non-Arab populations of the south, as it was a prescription for a permanent cultural domination—and, for southerners, cultural oppression and even extinction through the Arabizing impulses of a unitary, cartesian state. At the beginning of the 1980s, Sudan began to move away from the formula of a distinctive, partly autonomous southern region. As it did so, signs of renewed dissidence multiplied, and civil war seemed once again in the making.

Ethiopia is another example. The compromise imposed by the United Nations on a reluctant Eritrean population in 1952, by which the former Italian colony was awarded to Ethiopia, guaranteed a special status. Ethiopia never genuinely accepted this infringement upon the unitary self-concept of the imperial regime, and in 1962 unilaterally abolished the special provisions for Eritrea. This precipitated a guerrilla struggle for Eritrean independence, which has continued without interruption for the past two decades. No conceivable solution is available on the cartesian model of the symmetrical state; the only formula other than Eritrean independence that has even a slender chance is comprehensive autonomy and special status.

VI. CONCLUSION

The Eritrean demands for withdrawal from Ethiopia reflect the most extreme form of challenge to an existing state. As genocide represents the ultimate breakdown in civil society, so territorial dismemberment entails the final failure of a nation-state. Secessionist movements are to be found in a number of countries: Sudan, Ethiopia, India, Sri Lanka, and the Philippines, among others. Given the ubiquity of cultural pluralism in the Third World and its potential political perils, perhaps more striking than the existence of separatism is the rarity of its success. Since 1945, in the Third World, there is but a single example of state fractionalization after lasting more than 3 years: Pakistan and Bangladesh. Here the external intervention by the Indian army in support of Bangladesh independence played a decisive role. On the whole, the international system is hostile to any redrawing of state boundaries; the destabilizing risks are too great. Established states enjoy enormous advantages in access to army supplies, resources, and external support in foreclosing the secession option (Rothchild and Olorunsola, 1983). Postwar history suggests that, in most times and places—short of a major conflagration—the politics of cultural pluralism will revolve around the struggle for power and resources within extant nation-states, rather than tearing them asunder.

Conflicts defined by cultural pluralism will surely continue to play a central role in the decades ahead. The inexorable forces of modernization will mobilize and politicize ever larger fractions of our global village. Social class and cultural pluralism will provide the two most important metaphors of solidarity around which this mobilization will occur. This drama will not at all be confined to the Third World; the challenges to statesmanship posed by cultural pluralism, we believe, will be at least as great in Canada, Britain, the United States, Yugoslavia, and the Soviet Union as they are in India, Malaysia, or Nigeria. Perhaps the key issue in the balance of this century will be the nature of the nation-state itself. Its bonapartist, unitarian ideology, in the face of well-nigh universal cultural pluralism, may need to give way if the nation-state structure of the international community is to remain viable.

REFERENCES

ABU-LUGHOD, JANET, and HAY, RICHARD (eds.) (1977). *Third World urbanization.* Chicago: Maaroufa Press.
ANDERSON, PERRY (1974). *Lineages of the absolute state.* London: NLB Books.
ARMSTRONG, JOHN. (1982). *Nations before nationalism.* Chapel Hill: University of North Carolina Press.
BINDER, LEONARD ET AL. (1971). *Crises and sequences in political development.* Princeton, New Jersey: Princeton University Press.
BOURRET, F. M. (1960). *Ghana: The road to independence.* London: Oxford University Press.
CONNOR, WALKER (1978). A nation is a nation, is a state, is an ethnic group, is a . . . . *Ethnic and Racial Studies* I(4):377–400.
DECALO, SAMUEL (1976). *Coups and army rule in Africa.* New Haven, Connecticut: Yale University Press.
DESPRES, LEO A. (ed.) (1975). *Ethnicity and resource competition in plural societies.* The Hague: Mouton.
DYSON, KENNETH H. F. (1980). *The state tradition in Western Europe.* New York: Oxford University Press.
EASTON, DAVID (1965). *A systems analysis of political life.* New York: John Wiley and Sons.
EMERSON, RUPERT (1960). *From empire to nation.* Cambridge, Massachusetts. Harvard University Press.
FURNIVALL, J. S. (1948). *Colonial policy and practice.* London: Cambridge University Press.
GELLNER, ERNEST, and MICAUD, CHARLES (eds.) (1972). *Arabs and Berbers: From tribe to nation in North Africa.* Lexington, Massachusetts: Heath.
GLAZER, NATHAN, and MOYNIHAN, DANIEL (eds.) (1975). *Ethnicity: Theory and experience.* Cambridge, Massachusetts: Harvard University Press.

134   M. CRAWFORD YOUNG

GOLD, DAVID A., LO, CLARENCE Y. H., and WRIGHT, ERIC (1975). Recent developments in Marxist theories of the capitalist state. *Monthly Review* **XVII**:5–6.
GUGLER, JOSEF, and FLANAGAN, WILLIAM C. (1978). *Urbanization and social change in West Africa*. Cambridge, Massachusetts: Cambridge University Press.
HARIK, ILIYA F. (1971). Opinion leaders and mass media in rural Egypt: A reconstruction of the two-step flow hypothesis. *American Political Science Review* **LXV**:3.
HARRISON, S. (1956). The challenge to Indian nationalism. *Foreign Affairs* **XXIV**:4.
HAYWARD, FRED M. (1976). A reassessment of conventional wisdom about the informed public: National political information in Ghana. *American Political Science Review* **LXX**:2.
INDIA TODAY. 1978. 1–15 October.
ISAACS, HAROLD (1975). *Idols of the tribe*. New York: Harper and Row.
JESSOP, BOB (1982). *The capitalist state: Marxist theories and methods*. New York: New York University Press.
JOHAN, ROUNA (1972). *Pakistan: Failure in national integration*. New York: Columbia University Press.
KASFIR, NELSON (1975). *The shrinking political arena*. Berkeley: University of California Press.
KEYES, CHARLES F. (ed.) (1981). *Ethnic change*. Seattle: University of Washington Press.
KOFELE-KALE, NDIVA (1984). Ethnicity, regionalism and political power: A post-mortem of Ahidjos Cameroon. Cameroon Conference, School of Advanced International Studies, Johns Hopkins University, Washington, D.C.
KOHN, HANS (1968). Nationalism. In *International encyclopedia of the social sciences*, Vol. XI, pp. 63–70. New York: Macmillan Company and Free Press.
KUPER, LEO (1981). *Genocide*. New Haven, Connecticut: Yale University Press.
LIJPHART, AREND (1978). *Democracy in plural societies*. New Haven, Connecticut: Yale University Press.
MAGILL, JOHN (1972). *Labor unions and political socialization in Bolivia*. Doctoral dissertation, University of Wisconsin-Madison.
MILNE, R. S. (1981). *Politics in ethnically bipolar societies: Guyana, Malaysia, Fiji*. Vancouver: University of British Columbia Press.
NAGEL, JOANE, and OLZAK, SUSAN (1982). Ethnic mobilization in new and old states: An extension of the competition model. *Social Problems* **XXX**(2):127–143.
NORDLINGER, ERIC (1981). *On the autonomy of the democratic state*. Cambridge, Massachusetts: Harvard University Press.
O'DONNELL, GUILLERMO (1973). *Modernization and bureaucratic-authoritarianism*. Berkeley: Institute of International Affairs, University of California.
OSSOWSKI, STANISLAW (1963). *Class structure in the social consciousness*. New York: Free Press of Glencoe.
PASSERIN d'ENTREVES, ALEXANDER (1967). *The notion of state*. Oxford: Clarendon Press.
POGGI, GIANFRANCO (1978). *The development of the modern state*. Stanford: Stanford University Press.
PYE, LUCIAN (1966). *Aspects of political development*. Boston: Little, Brown.
RABUSHKA, ALVIN, and SHEPSLE, KENNETH (1972). *Politics in plural societies: A theory of democratic instability*. New York: Charles E. Merrill.
ROTHCHILD, DONALD, and OLORUNSOLA, VICTOR A. (eds.) (1983). *State versus ethnic claims: African policy dilemmas*. Boulder, Colorado: Westview.
ROTHSCHILD, JOSEPH (1981). *Ethnopolitics*. New York: Columbia University Press.
SETON-WATSON HUGH (1977). *States and nations*. Boulder, Colorado: Westview.
SHENNAN, J. P. (1974). *The origins of the modern European state 1450–1725*. London: Hutchison University Library.
SKOCPOL, THEDA (1979). *States and social revolutions*. Cambridge, Massachusetts: Cambridge University Press.

SMITH, CAROL (1984). Indian class and class consciousness in prerevolutionary Guatemala. Washington, D.C.: Woodrow Wilson International Center for Scholars.

STEPAN, ALFRED (1978). *The state and society*. Princeton, New Jersey: Princeton University Press.

TILLY, CHARLES (ed.) (1975). *The formation of national states in Western Europe*. Princeton, New Jersey: Princeton University Press.

TOURE, SEKOU (1959). *Towards full reafricanization*. Paris: Présence Africaine.

WALLERSTEIN, IMMANUEL (1976). *The modern world system*. New York: Academic Press.

WILSON, WILLIAM J. (1978). *The declining significance of race*. Chicago: University of Chicago Press.

YOUNG, CRAWFORD (1976). *The politics of cultural pluralism*. Madison: University of Wisconsin Press.

YOUNG, CRAWFORD, and TURNER, THOMAS (1985). *The rise and decline of the Zairian State*. Madison: University of Wisconsin Press.

6

Reinforcing Ethnic
Boundaries: South Africa
in the 1980s

WILMOT G. JAMES
Southern African Research Program
Yale University
New Haven, Connecticut 06520

I. INTRODUCTION

In 1975, South Africa's foreign minister Roelof (Pik) Botha announced to the United Nations that the government of his country was ready to depart from traditional practices of racial discrimination. In June 1979, Pieter Koornhof, minister of Co-operation and Development, declared to an American audience in Washington that "apartheid is dead." Various government spokespersons have echoed this apparent commitment to deracialization in subsequent years, and a fashioning of ideological discourse free of direct racist content has followed.[1] It has become a political norm for government to refrain from a racial legitimation of its policies.

What are we to make of government's commitment to deracialization in the historical context of a society renowned for its institutional racism? Two tentative hypotheses have been offered on this score. The one hypothesis is that the government's commitment to deracialization is mere posturing, an attempt to reshape an ideological discourse without any concomitant restructuring of racial relations. The other is that the government is genuinely interested in deracialization—albeit only in response to domestic resistance and international pressure. These hypotheses respectively represent the stance of the liberal critics of apartheid and the Reagan administration's policy of constructive engagement. What both hypotheses lack is an understanding of how the policy of deracialization as being implemented by the government actually results in a hardening of

COMPETITIVE ETHNIC RELATIONS

ethnic boundaries and the extension of the terrain of ethnic conflict over resources from civil society into the state.

I argue that deracialization actually results in the creation of ethnic conflict in the state. An examination of the record of deracialization over the past six years, i.e., 1978 to 1984, shows two things: first, that the incorporation of the two minority populations (colored and Indian) into parliament hardens ethnic boundaries and intensifies ethnic conflict over resources; second, that the incorporation of coloreds and Indians into parliament on the basis of ethnic criteria makes it even more and not less difficult to incorporate black Africans into the state. Unlike the liberal critics, I argue that deracialization has very real social consequences for racial and ethnic relations. Unlike the hypothesis of constructive engagement, I argue that current strategies of political reform make the resolution of the dilemma of black African citizenship even more problematic. I conclude the chapter with a brief analysis of the views of opposition movements on race and ethnicity.

II. THE MEANING OF DERACIALIZATION

Michael Banton has argued that racial boundaries are formed through processes that are exclusionary and ethnic boundaries through inclusionary processes (Banton, 1983.) In terms of his argument, racial boundaries tend to exclude ineligible persons from and ethnic boundaries tend to draw (or mobilize) eligible persons to group membership.

In terms of Banton's account, racial boundaries regulate group formation on the basis of color, a criterion of identification that permits the enforcibility of group boundaries. Ethnic boundaries regulate group formation on the basis of so-called cultural criteria—such as differences of language, custom, and so on—where color need not play any role at all.[2] Boundaries are formed and maintained in situations of competition over resources—such as land, employment, housing, etc.—and the intensity and meaning of the boundaries for the social actors can range from situations where soft boundaries pertain (i.e., some persons are permitted to cross a racial and/or ethnic boundary) to situations where hard boundaries pertain (i.e., no person is allowed to cross a racial and/or ethnic boundary). Moreover, the mechanisms used to maintain the boundaries can also range from voluntary instruments of enforcement to coercive ones. Finally, Banton contends that racial and ethnic group formation occurs when individuals enter markets as collectivities rather than individuals and that it is more advantageous (in material and status terms) to enter markets as a group rather than as individual class actors (Banton, 1983; pp. 104–128).

While this rendition of Banton's argument is not exhaustive, it does serve as a heuristic aid in making initial sense of dynamics of racial and ethnic boundary formation in South Africa. Racial boundaries separate the politically dominant white minority group from the subordinate black majority group. The boundaries are enforcible because of differences in skin color, and the mechanisms of enforcement are coercive and state-sanctioned. Ethnic boundaries separate Afrikaans-speaking whites from English speaking ones in the dominant racial group. The boundary is soft and voluntarily sanctioned by social mechanisms. Ethnic boundaries separate several categories of blacks—coloreds, Indians, Xhosas, Zulus, Tswanas, Sothos, Swazis, Venda, etc.—in the subordinate racial group. The boundaries are coercively imposed by the state in a number of social arenas.

Thus, in terms of Banton's argument, racial boundaries have kept all blacks out of positions of political privilege, and ethnic boundaries, by coercion and volition, have kept Afrikaners, the English, the Xhosa, Zulus, coloreds, Indians, etc. in their respective social spheres. This is a case, *par excellence,* of divide and rule.

To deracialize, in minimalist terms, is to remove coercive, and perhaps even voluntary, mechanisms of racial-boundary maintenance in the public sphere of social organization.[3] In these terms, the National Party's commitment to deracialization is self-evidently limited. It amounts to essentially two processes: first, the partial relaxation of the racial boundary in the political sphere so that coloreds and Indians, and not black Africans, are coopted into the state[4]; and second, the boundaries between white, colored, and Indian are retained and hardened by the latter's incorporation as ethnic groups. Deracialization, as implemented by the government, does not amount to the dismantling of racial boundaries but rather means the cooptation of two minority groups without desegregation in civil society.

A. Legimating Deracialization

The central component of government's commitment to deracialization and political reform has been the drafting and introduction of a new constitution. Under the previous constitution, only whites were allowed to vote, send representatives to parliament, and take up positions in the decision-making structures of the state. The new constitution enfranchises coloreds (people of mixed descent) as well as Indians (people of Asian–Indian descent). The franchise is organized on a communal-ethnic basis, which in practice means that a voter is able to choose candidates of his or her ethnic group only, who stands for election to the parliamentary chamber specified for that ethnic group only (Republic of South Africa [B91/1983]).

Colored and Indian representation in parliament is a departure from orthodox apartheid in the sense that it breaks with whites-only representation. To legitimate the extension of the franchise to its major audience, the white electorate, government has enunciated a pragmatic argument in favor of political reform. Government spokespersons contend that political stability will be promoted if the base of representation is enlarged so as to include more South Africans in the political process. The presumption of this argument is that it is clearly in the self-interest of whites to promote political stability. Stability, in turn, it is also presumed, will in the longer run promote the longevity of white domination, albeit in a new political form.

Incorporation along ethnic lines is legitimated by government's claim that coloreds and Indians constitute separable ethnic groups. The integrity of all ethnic groups as groups is assumed to be a demographic fact of the social landscape, so that the government claims all it is doing is responding in a rational manner to a social reality that is not of its own making.[5] Deborah Posel (1984, p. 2) writes on this score:

> Apparently therefore, 'multinationalism' (ethnic, political, social segregation) is not the result imposed by National Party policy: it is asserted as an objective fact. And the logical, self-evident response to this fact is allegedly a policy of segregation. Apartheid thus acquires the full weight of 'reality' behind it, being neither chosen for, nor subject to, 'ideological' (value-laden) considerations.

The incorporation of coloreds and Indians on an ethnic basis rests on government's recognition of the apparent inviolable cultural divisons in the population, divisions that have been presented as discrete, concrete, and real.

The political function of ethnic definitions and boundaries is illustrated by the changing stance of the National Party toward coloreds. In 1976, the National Party accepted the claim of the Theron commission that "the Coloured population group as a whole does not display the typical characteristics in a coherent 'nation' or 'ethnic group' in its pattern of behaviour" (Republic of South Africa [RP38/1976, pp. 463–464]. The new constitution rejects the official conclusion of 1976, in principle and in practice, for coloreds are subjected to a set of ethnic restrictions—such as residential and educational segregation in particular—that assumes that they do in fact form a coherent ethnic group. Ethnic boundaries are therefore a device by which government structures reform without surrendering white social privilege.

B. Hardening Ethnic Boundaries

The new parliament consists of three chambers, one each for whites, coloreds, and Indians. Since representation is proportional to population, there are 178, 85, and 45 seats in the white, colored, and Indian chambers of parliament, respectively. White representatives are numerically preponderant in any joint sitting of parliament. Since the National Party holds most of the seats in the dominant white chamber and since interracial political alliances are illegal under the Improper Political Interference Act of 1968, the opposition white parties cannot form alliances with the colored and Indian parties.[6] In other words, the new parliament is structured in such a way that the hegemony of the National Party cannot under present circumstances be politically circumvented.[7]

The electoral rolls for the three chambers are segregated on the basis of the 1950 Population Registration Act. This act legally defines the racial status of South Africans, and despite the ambiguity of attempts at a legislative definition of race, the legislation has had important implications for the social place of individuals in a rigidly segregated society.[8] The Population Registration Act has served as the central basis for the applicability of the Group Areas Act (legislation governing strict residential segregation), the Immorality and Mixed Marriages Acts[9] (legislation governing sexual and marital relations), the Separate Amenities Act (legislation governing separate public and recreational facilities) as well as the Acts governing segregated educational institutions. In other words, the central underpinning of the electoral basis of the chambers of parliament rests on legislation that has governed the segregation of whites, coloreds and Indians (not to mention black Africans) for the past thirty-six or so years.[10]

What this means is that deracialization actually results in representation for coloreds and Indians in parliament on the basis of the intensification, not relaxation, of ethnic boundaries. The extension of the central historical principles of segregation to parliamentary representation means that it is more, not less, crucial to be able to identify individuals in ethnic terms.

Corporate ethnic representation in parliament also means that the three chambers of parliament would stake out different and competing claims and entitlements for the communities they represent.[11] The state has historically biased the distribution of public resources in favor of whites and has been, in these terms, a racial state.[12] Under current fiscal conditions, the equalization of state spending across ethnic lines (i.e., equalizing distribution in terms of current white standards) is not possible if the parameters of the current budget are adhered to.[13] Even if the (relatively low) level of resource distribution to black Africans were to remain the same, the equalization of spending for whites, coloreds, and Indians would place severe and politically disruptive strains on government revenues. The new tricameral parliament, sitting for the first time in 1985, faced with a recession, a negative growth rate since 1983, severe balance of payments problems, would find equalization of government spending difficult, if not impossible, to achieve.

Ethnic competition over government resources and entitlements means different things for the parties in parliament. For the colored and Indian parties, a lack of sufficient returns for their participation and collaboration means that their legitimacy, already precarious since the time they declared their willingness to enter parliament in 1983, will be further undermined. In the election of colored and Indian representatives in August 1984, an average poll of less than 18% was registered. A survey conducted at the University of the Western Cape, an institution with an overwhelming colored registration, showed the colored Labor Party received less than 2% support.[14] The colored and Indian parties command only a relatively small degree of popular support among the populations they presumably represent and, unless there is an appreciable degree of returns from government, that support can even diminish. In other words, the colored and Indian parties, for reasons of legitimation, have an interest in staking out a persistent claim on government resources and entitlements.

The dominant white National Party has a different set of political concerns. The extreme right wing has, over the past 5 years, grown from a political force commanding 3% of the white vote in 1977 to a command of 22% in 1982.[15] Much of the increase in extreme right-wing support is due to the fact that white standards of living have systematically declined over the last decade. The pos- sibility that government spending on whites will remain stationary or even de- cline would result in political fall-out in favor of right-wing support among the white population. Since the National Party is desirous of carving out a support base for reformist policies in the white population, it has an interest in curtailing the growth of extreme right-wing political tendencies. In other words, the Na- tional Party would resist those colored and Indian demands that could only be satisfied at the expense of whites.[16] While competition over resources does not of necessity need to be a zero-sum game, the fact that there is competition between ethnically based parties over limited resources and entitlements means that ethnic boundaries will be reinforced and reproduced.

To conclude this argument: political reform and deracialization in relation to the two minority (colored and Indian) populations amounts to incorporation without desegregation, a hardening of ethnic boundaries, and a potential for ethnic conflict in the state over resources. In terms of Banton's argument, whites have not lost an interest in the maintenance of hard boundaries between white and colored, Indian, and black African. What they have developed is an interest in coopting only the coloreds and Indians but in a fashion that does not result in desegregation.

C. The African Majority

Since the abolition of the Cape African franchise in 1936, the disbandment of the Natives Representative Council in 1951, and the abolition of black African representation by four white parliamentarians in 1959, black Africans have had no political participation in central decision-making in parliament. Their interests have been served by the African Reserves or homelands, territories scattered throughout the rural areas of the Eastern Cape, Natal, the Orange Free State, and eastern, northern, and western Transvaal.[17]

The concept of homelands for black Africans has been a central pillar of apartheid. Essentially it is a system of divide and rule, where blacks are divided into 10 or so ethnic groups—Xhosa, Tswana, Zulu, Sotho, Venda, Swazi, and so on—and, in these designated ethnic terms, are allocated citizenship rights to be exercised in the respective homelands. Black claims to state resources and entitlements have had to be processed through the segregated ethnic channels of the various homeland governments. This has meant essentially two things: first, black African claims on entitlements and resources have been institutionally transferred from the central government to the homeland governments (with the result that when black Africans have made claims on the central government, they have been repressed); second, because the homeland governments are segregated in ethnic terms, black African claims have become institutionally fragmented. The two central functions of divide and rule—the fragmentation and displacement of black African claims on state entitlements and resources—have been served by homeland structures. However, these functions have only been partially served, since other processes—that of class formation in particular—have resulted in the persistence of black African claims on central government.

The South African economy has depended and still depends on black African labor. This has meant that black Africans have made up the larger proportion of the working class in urban areas and cities. Despite the application of influx control and population resettlement, notorious instruments of labor control, a little more than half the total black African population resides in areas outside of the homelands.[18] While government has insisted that black Africans resident in urban industrial and white agricultural areas should affiliate themselves and direct their claims to the homeland structures, in practice such claims have been directed at the central government. For example, African worker demands for trade union rights during 1973 were directed at employers and the central state, not at homeland governments. As another example, the Soweto uprisings of 1976 were directed first at central government spending patterns on black education and, more fundamentally, at the racial character of citizenship entitlements of central government. Class formation among black Africans in urban industrial areas has been a countervailing force to ethnic fragmentation to the extent that black claims on central government have persisted, not diminished.

Because government abolished all forms of black African representation in parliament, there are no institutions available to central government that can process black African claims outside of the homelands governments. Nolutshungu (1983) has argued that this is the central structural dilemma of the state. He says that by virtue of the fact that the state has systematically expelled black Africans from central governmental institutions of representation, there are no institutions nor is there a concept by which black African claims can orderly be processed outside of the homeland structures (Nolutshungu, 1983). The only means available to government in its response to black African claims are repressive ones. For example, the government responded to black African demands in 1976 (the Soweto unrest) and in 1984 (the Eastern Cape unrest) with heavy-handed violence. In other words, homeland structures have not succeeded in accommodating black African claims. Homelands, as Greenberg has argued, are implausible solutions to the dilemma of black citizenship (Greenberg, 1984).

At the time of the constitution's introduction, the minister of Constitutional

Development, Christiaan Heunis, argued that since black Africans already had rights of self-determination in the homelands ("national states," as he put it), there was no need to provide a place for blacks in the new political dispensation. However, the government has seen fit to appoint a cabinet committee charged with the brief of investigating the political status of urban black Africans, i.e., black Africans outside of the homelands. At the opening of the new parliament in January 1985, the president, Pieter Botha, publicly acknowledged that the public violence experienced on the Witwatersrand in 1984 was systematically tied up with the issue of black African citizenship rights. He added that government intended to confront this question in the near future. Two major commission reports published in 1979, one dealing with black African labor and industrial conciliation and the other with influx control, both played around with ways and means of identifying cooptable sections of the black African population (Republic of South Africa [RP47/1979], [RP32/1979]). While it is yet to be seen whether all of this probing will result in policy formation, government clearly is under pressure to construct a mechanism by which black Africans can also be incorporated into state decision-making structures.

Not only do state structures make no provision for black African incorporation, they also make future incorporation highly implausible. Consider the following two possibilities, both of which have been touted in public. Let us imagine that another (black African) chamber is added to the existing three. Such an addition would violate the ethnic principle underlying the separation of the chambers. More importantly, by virtue of the principle of proportional representation, the black African chamber would have to have about 400 seats if all black Africans were represented and about 200 seats if only urban black Africans were represented. Either way, the black African chamber would hold the majority in parliament and become the effective rulers of state. This clearly is not in the interests of the ruling National Party. Let us imagine that the ethnic principle of representation is consistently applied (in government's terms) to the black population as a whole: then 10 additional chambers of parliament need to be added to the existing three, making parliament a potentially unmanageable bureaucratic and legislative dinosaur consisting of 13 chambers. In other words, any form of black representation is implausible unless the existing nature of representation is itself transformed.

To conclude this section: minority rule based on ethnic principles has no institutional basis by which the privileges of minority rule can be retained and black African claims on entitlements and resources satisfied. In other words, any expectation that political reform, deracialization, and the tricameral parliament would set in motion a process that could possibly result in a stable incorporation of black Africans is naive. The premise of constructive engagement—i.e., that the present government's reformist program should be supported because it is more, and not less, likely that the question of black citizenship will be resolved—rests on mistaken grounds.

D. Popular Alternatives

The argument up until this point was that actors who participate in the ethnic structures of government (be they in the tricameral parliament or the homeland structures) tend to reproduce ethnic boundaries and increase ethnic competition over resources in the political sphere. Popular opposition movements of today (which, presumably, can become the regime of tomorrow) offer to transform the racial and ethnic boundaries in essentially two different ways. On the one hand, the proposition is to disentangle the state and politics from ethnic and racial group formation; on the other, the proposition is to remove both the economic-class and state underpinnings of racial and ethnic boundaries. Briefly, the stances are as follows.

(1) Non-racialism. The United Democratic Front (UDF), formed in 1983 in opposition to the new constitution, claims that ethnic and racial boundaries are primarily upheld by state policies. Currently the largest opposition social move-ment, the UDF argues that South Africa consists of one nation and it offers to reintegrate diverse groupings in a single, unitary state apparatus. In these terms, racial and ethnic boundaries are matters left entirely to the private sphere of social organization and should therefore not be upheld by the state in the public domain. The proposition is that racial and ethnic boundaries in the public sphere can be adequately transformed by a radical reordering of the state and politics, without the necessary reordering of the economy, although that might follow, it is claimed, in the course of political change. In other words, popular opposition claims to state resources and entitlements should best be channeled into a radical transformation of the state and politics. The central proposition is that racial and ethnic fragmentation will dissolve once the state is disentangled from group formation.[19]

(2) Socialism. The second strain in opposition politics (represented in part by the National Forum) claims that racial and ethnic boundaries are systemat-ically produced and upheld by class relations and capitalist development. In these terms, the abolition of racial and ethnic boundaries in the public sphere can only be transformed if the capitalist economy and its associated class structure are transformed into socialist ones. This movement, unlike the UDF, is committed to both a political and social revolution, offering the promise of a transformation of both the economic and political order. The proposition is that ethnic and racial boundaries will dissolve once the capitalist economy and its associated class structure are transformed into socialist ones.[20]

Both of these stances (to be understood as political forces giving a particular form to the expression of popular claims on current state resources and entitle-ments in civil society) deny any autonomy to racial and ethnic boundary forma-tion. In societies where universal franchise, a unitary state, and the concept of a single nation pertain (e.g., the United States and Britain), racial and ethnic

146   WILMOT G. JAMES

boundaries persist in the public sphere. In existing socialisms, racial and ethnic boundaries, underpinned by admittedly different sorts of social dynamics, also persist. In other words, in a future South Africa governed even by a democratic and socialist regime, racial and ethnic boundaries are likely to persist. It is important therefore to give an account of racial and ethnic boundary formation independent of state and class dynamics. What would such an account look like?

III. CONCLUSION

State support for racial and ethnic boundaries has been a central pillar in its persistence. I have shown in this account that state policies have upheld the racial divisions between the dominant whites and subordinate blacks as well as the divisions between ethnic groups. I have also shown that the current attempt at deracialization is a limited one and that it results in the hardening of ethnic boundaries as well as intensifying ethnic competition over resources in the state. These formulations should in part be seen as hypotheses, since the new tricameral parliament has been functioning only since January 1985.

Underpinning the centrality of the state in boundary maintenance are categories of social actors who find it difficult to participate in markets as individuals. For example, white workers have sought to engage state protection in the labor market (through job reservation and preferential state employment practices) so as to protect them from the potentially undercutting effects of the cheaper black workers. For example, white small business in the Transvaal and Natal has over the years sought to restrict Indian small business to areas where the latter's competitiveness is severely curtailed. As a final example, dominant class actors have curtailed the free movement, occupational mobility, and citizenship rights of blacks in mining and agriculture, systematically engaged in practices that restricted the labor market. In other words, various categories of social actors in the labor, capital, and property markets have engaged in what Banton calls "monopolistic forms of social organization" (Banton, 1983, p. 109).

In the South African case, it so happens that whites have been the dominant practitioners of racial and ethnic monopolies. There is, however, no reason to suppose that blacks would not also engage in monopolistic forms of social organization in a different South Africa. It is entirely plausible to imagine that in a unitary majority-rule state of tomorrow, Inkatha—a social movement in the business of mobilizing Zulu ethnicity—would make monopolistic claims on state resources and would enter markets as a group.[21] In other words, the radical transformation of apartheid is a necessary but not a sufficient condition for the removal of ethnic and racial boundaries in the public sphere. Opposition social movements have two choices. Either they regard racial and ethnic monopolies in the public sphere as legitimate—i.e., accept an ethnic pluralism in a democratic political environment—and attempt to regulate them so as to avoid the harsher inequities that flow from such social monopolies, or they regard the boundaries as illegitimate and proceed to forcibly dismantle them in the face of resistance. Either way, opposition movements must take account of ethnic and racial boundaries in addition to their preoccupation with the state and class relations.

IV. POSTSCRIPT

In the 5 months that have elapsed since this article was written, racial and ethnic conflict has intensified considerably. The actors involved in the conflict are, on the one hand, black Africans and participants in the state (African community councillors, suspected police informers, and the police), and, on the other hand, black Africans and Indians. Very few white and colored civilians have directly been in conflict with black Africans.

Conflict between black Africans and the apparatuses of state hinges around two sorts of issues. One source of conflict comes from the fact that the state is seen as an unfair landlord and a mean disbursar of resources (the immediate source of conflict tends to center around rents, housing, educational resources, and transportation, which, by the nature of things, are state-controlled and/or - owned). The other and more fundamental source of conflict is rooted in the continuing denial of citizenship entitlements to Africans. Left out of a new constitutional deal in 1984, Africans feel aggrieved and cheated, once again.

Sluggish economic performance, high levels of African unemployment (estimated at about 25% among Africans, on the average), double-digit inflation (19% on the average), and declining real wages underwrite and exacerbate the more straightforwardly political dimension of the conflict. Unable to command the resources necessary (but not sufficient) to satisfy some of the more immediate interests of Africans, the state relies almost singularly on repression. An estimated total approaching 700 Africans have already perished at the hands of the South African police since the beginning of this cycle of resistance, i.e., from September 1984 to September 1985. The state, guardian and disbursar of resources and political entitlements, stands in direct and unmediated confrontation with Africans.

The tension between Africans and Indians has a long history, with a class content. The one event that comes to mind is the clash between members of these groups in 1949, where most of the victims in the violent confrontation were the Indians. In this episode, the major grievance of the Africans was that Indians were exploiters: the traders serving African consumer wants were mostly of Indian origin and, it seems, Africans were not particularly happy with the terms of trade. The episode has left its impact and made its mark on the collective consciousness of both Indians and Africans in Natal, and the source of the conflict—a class relationship between traders and consumers in a situation where the terms of trade are viewed as exploitative in the eyes of the latter—has been reproduced over time. It cannot be argued that the participation of the two Indian parties in the tricameral parliament is a primary cause of the conflict. Colored parties are also participating, causing little conflict between African and colored civilians. The fact that Africans have been excluded from, and coloreds and Indians included in, the tricameral parliament is nevertheless seen by Africans as a statement of bad faith on the part of these two groups.

African demands for full and equal citizenship entitlements have been met by an unresponsive and repressive state. In his much heralded speech in August 1985, the president, P. W. Botha, reaffirmed his government's commitment to the basic principles and practices of apartheid. It remains the unwavering policy of this government to maintain a rigid system of ethnic segregation as well as to deny Africans citizenship entitlements in a single or unitary state structure. Conflict has been intensified as government continues to underwrite and uphold ethnic boundaries in the public sphere of social organization.

ACKNOWLEDGMENTS

My thanks to members of the Southern African Research Program Seminar, Yale University, and Micheline Tusenius for their critical comments on an earlier draft of this paper.

NOTES

[1]The dominant white National Party has formed the ruling regime since 1948. By ruling regime I mean government, consisting of the Cabinet and its secretariats. By the state I mean all of the institutions—administrative, judicial, repressive and military—of political power. For an analysis of the shifts in political discourse and legitimation, see Posel (1984) and Greenberg (1984).

[2]Frequently, skin color is also a mechanism by which ethnic boundaries are enforced. In the absence of a visible means of identification, other social mechanisms function to include some persons and exclude others [see Banton (1983)].

[3]A different but not incompatible definition of deracialization is Heribert Adam's notion of capitalism without racism. For the debate about the connection between capitalism and apartheid, see Adam (1984) and Burawoy (1981).

[4]I use the current convention in the designation of groups, i.e., blacks to refer to all nonwhites, black Africans for those of central and eastern African descent, colored for those of mixed descent, and Indian for those of Asian descent. The population of South Africa in 1980 stood at about 28 million, of whom 71% were black African, 16% white, 9% colored and 3% Indian. The estimated figures include the populations of the homelands. [see Simkins (1984)].

[5]The new language of legitimation denies the historical process by assigning no causal role to apartheid in the shaping of ethnic boundaries—see Posel (1984).

[6]In April 1985, the government advised that the Improper Political Interference Act no longer served any useful political purpose and that it would be repealed. Such a step would make interracial political alliances possible but unlikely, given that the colored and Indian parties have greater affinities with the ruling National Party than with the more liberal Progressive Federal Party.

[7]Andre du Toit has rather aptly described the tricameral parliament as a "winner-take-all system with a vengeance."

[8]By its own admission, government has acknowledged that race or ethnicity has no legal definition. See the discussion in the Theron Commission Report (Republic of South Africa [RP38/1976]).

[9]The Mixed Marriages Act and racial clauses of the Immorality Act were repealed during 1985. They are socially unnecessary (the number of people who would conclude interracial marriages is small—a range of social disincentives discourage interracial liaisons) and politically embarrassing. Most important of all, their repeal is a symbolic concession to the colored and Indian participants in the tricameral parliament, who entered parliament with the intention of pressuring the National Party into taking such a step.

[10]This is not to suggest that racial segregation did not exist prior to apartheid. It certainly did. Apartheid's contribution was to ossify social practice into legal strictures.

[11]This hypothesis should be seen as tentative, even premature. The new parliament has been functioning since January 1985. What the precise effects of the ethnic nature of parliament will be remains to be seen.

[12]See Abedien (1984).

[13]One idea advanced by economists is to use the colored level of resource allocation as the norm. Spending on whites would then be reduced and spending on black Africans increased. This is not, for quite obvious reasons, a very popular idea among whites [see Abedien (1984)].

[14]In the same survey, it was found that colored students were 85% supportive of the United Democratic Front, a multiracial front opposed to the new constitution [see van Vuuren and Louw (1984)]. The stance of the Labour Party to the political preferences of the colored student elite, the colored party in favor of participation, is best summarized by David Curry, the deputy leader: "Most intellectuals have never supported us anyway in their elitist distance from grass-roots concerns" [cited in Adam (1984, p. 282)].

[15]There are two parties to the right of the ruling National Party. These are the *Herstigde Nasionale Party* (Reconstituted National Party), formed in 1968, and the Conservative Party, formed in 1980 [see Charney (1984)].

[16]The repeal of the Mixed Marriages Act and the racial clauses of the Immorality Act is one example of such a concession. The possible repeal of the Improper Political Interference Act, as announced by government in April 1985, is another.

[17] The African Reserves or homelands take up 13% of the superficial land area. There are ten homelands—Transkei, Ciskei, Boputhatswana, Venda, Gazankulu, Kwazulu, Qwa Qwa, Lebowa, KwaNdebele, and KaNgwane. The first four have taken independence.

[18]Influx control is a system of labor regulation. Its brief is to keep unemployed and unemployable black Africans out of urban industrial areas. Pass laws give police and other officials the power to enforce influx control. Resettlement involves the (frequently forcible) removal of black Africans from areas defined as "white" ones [see Platzky and Walker (1984)].

[19]See Francis (1984).

[20]See Alexander (1983). Also cited in Adam (1984).

[21]Inkatha is a Zulu ethnic movement. Gatsha Buthelezi, paramount chief of the KwaZulu homeland, is the movement's principal sponsor. Membership of the Inkatha organization is estimated at over 1 million.

REFERENCES

ABEDIEN, IRAJ (1984). Public sector policies and income distribution in South Africa during the period 1968–1980. Conference of the Second Carnegie Inquiry into Poverty and Development in Southern Africa. Cape Town, 1984. Paper no. 127.

ADAM, HERIBERT (1984). Racist capitalism versus capitalist non-racialism in South Africa. *Ethnic and Racial Studies* 7:2.

ALEXANDER, NEVILLE (1983). Nation and ethnicity in South Africa. National Forum. Unpublished mss. Hammanskraal, South Africa.

BANTON, MICHAEL (1983). *Ethnic and racial competition.* London. Tavistock.

BURAWOY, MICHAEL (1981). The capitalist state in South Africa: Marxist and sociological perspectives on race and class. In *Political power and social theory* Vol. 2, (Maurice Zeitlin, ed.), pp. 279–335. Los Angeles, California: JAI Press.

CHARNEY, CRAIG (1984). Class conflict and the National Party split. *Journal of Southern African Studies* **10**:2.

FRANCIS, MATHEW (1984). The United Democratic Front in the Western Cape. Unpublished B. A. Honours thesis. University of the Western Cape. Bellville, South Africa.

GREENBERG, STANLEY (1984). Ideological struggles in the South African State. In *On the political economy of race,* Vol. 2. Proceedings of the Conference, Bellville, South Africa.

NOLUTSHUNGU, SAM (1983). *Changing South Africa. Political considerations.* Manchester: The University Press.

PLATZKY, LAUREEN, and WALKER, CHERYL (1984). *Surplus peoples project,* Vols. 1–5. Cape Town. SPP.

POSEL, DEBORAH (1984). Control of reform and reform of control: The South African state after 1978. In *On the political economy of race,* Vol. 2. Proceedings of the Conference, Bellville, South Africa.

REPUBLIC OF SOUTH AFRICA [RP38/1976]. Report of the commission of inquiry into matters relating to the coloured population group. Pretoria: Government Printers.

REPUBLIC OF SOUTH AFRICA [RP32/1979]. Report of the commission of inquiry into legislation affecting the utilization of manpower. Pretoria: Government Printers.

REPUBLIC OF SOUTH AFRICA [RP47/1979]. Report of the commission of inquiry into labour legislation. Pretoria: Government Printers.

REPUBLIC OF SOUTH AFRICA [B91/1983]. The Republic of South Africa constitution bill. Cape Town.

SIMKINS, CHARLES (1984). *Four essays on the past, present and future distribution of the black population of South Africa.* Cape Town: SALDRU, University of Cape Town.

VAN VUUREN, WILLEM, and LOUW, J. W. (1984). University of the Western Cape: Political Monitor. Unpublished seminar paper. Centre for Research on Africa, University of the Western Cape, Bellville, South Africa.

Part III

Competition Perspectives on Ethnic Political Movements

7

Latino Ethnicity in the City of Chicago

FELIX PADILLA
Center for Latino and Latin American Affairs
Northern Illinois University
DeKalb, Illinois 60115

I. INTRODUCTION

The concept of Latino or Hispanic (also referred to here as Latinismo or Hispanismo) is being drawn to the attention of increasing numbers of people in the United States. As Spanish-speaking people identify themselves and others in the idiom of Latino or Hispanic similarity and/or differences, several issues stand out. First, it is clear that the term Latino or Hispanic means quite different things to different people. Second, regardless of its specific meanings and connotations, the word Latino or Hispanic and its variations carry a heavy freight of emotion.

In spite of the manifestation and salience of what I shall term *a Latino or Hispanic ethnic-conscious identity and behavior,* there is little clarity on the meaning of this form of group identification. It has become common for social scientists to refer to Spanish-speaking groups, either as individual ethnics or as a wider population, as "Latinos" without an explanation of the process by which they are "Latinocized."[1] In effect, studies on Spanish-speaking groups have taken for granted the specific changes of ethnic identification among this multi-ethnic population that at times result in the manifestation of a distinct, all-embracing, wider Latino or Hispanic ethnic identity and consciousness. To date, social scientists have failed to make a conceptual distinction between behavior that is Latino- or Hispanic related and behavior that is the expression of individual and separate Spanish-speaking ethnics. In other words, there is little conceptual precision on the meaning of the concept of Latino or Hispanic when used as an expression of a particular form of group identity and behavior.

153

By using the concept of Latino synonymously with the individual experience of the separate Spanish-speaking ethnics or as an inclusive category without explaining the Latinocization process, social science research has failed to examine the empirical characteristics and boundaries of Latino group consciousness and solidarity and the important issues that an investigation of this type of multiethnic identification may raise. Further, this focus has detracted from an examination of the forces in the larger society that may encourage or influence the emergence of Latino ethnic identity and solidarity. Finally, this traditional approach has neglected to investigate and analyze the shared political histories of Mexican Americans and Puerto Ricans and other Spanish-speaking groups, and has thus obscured such innovations as Latinismo or Hispanismo that may develop in these political contexts.

In short, I argue that it is too simple to assume that behavioral phenomena relating to individual and separate Mexican American, Puerto Rican, Cuban, and Central and South American groups are necessarily expressions of Latino consciousness. In the first place, the degree of correspondence, if any, should be tested empirically and not assumed *a priori*. In the second place, the difference between behavior that is an expression of Latino consciousness and behavior that is either Mexican American, Puerto Rica, Cuban, or the like ought to be reconciled by an appropriate theory.

Toward this end, this chapter provides a way of examining the concept of Latino or Hispanic as a form of ethnic-conscious identity and behavior, using the experience of Chicago's heterogeneous Spanish-speaking population for analysis. I will provide a case study of a particular instance when Mexican Americans and Puerto Ricans crossed over the boundaries of their respective ethnic identities and formed a wider Latino unit.[2] The case will illustrate the various factors—external and internal—that have led to the ethnic change manifest in the emergence of a new Latino or Hispanic ethnic identity in an American urban setting. This chapter is part of a larger study in which I combined historical data (i.e., organization archives, accounts found in the literature, newspaper articles, and other relevant information) with interviews of community organization leaders to reconstruct the sequence of developments in American and Spanish-speaking institutions and organizations, which helps to explain the process by which the concept of Latino or Hispanic has become another form of ethnic group identity and consciousness in the city of Chicago (F. Padilla, in press).

The balance of this chapter is divided into two major parts. Section II provides an empirical definition for the concept of Latino or Hispanic. It will be shown that Latino ethnic identification represents a special form of group identity that is produced out of the intergroup relations or social interaction of at least two Spanish-speaking groups. It will be further shown that the manifestation of Latino ethnic-conscious identity is operative within *specific situational contexts* and not all of the time. The situational dimension of Latino identity implies that particular contexts determine whether the individual national/cultural identity of

Puerto Ricans, Mexican Americans, Cubans, and Central and South Americans or the all-embracing Latino identification is most appropriate or salient for social action at a point in time.

Section III presents one organizational attempt made in the city of Chicago during the early 1970s to unite people with different ethnic identities (Mexican American and Puerto Ricans) under one Latino ethnic unit. First, this case involves the examination of the process by which Mexican Americans and Puerto Ricans created a wider Latino frame in order to facilitate the acquisition of employment opportunities for Spanish-speaking workers in two American corporations, Illinois Bell and Jewel Tea. Although the two firms had received federal funds to train and hire "minorities," the Spanish-speaking population was not included in their plans. This case also includes an examination of the role played by a particular governmental policy, Affirmative Action, in contributing to mobilization of these two Spanish-speaking ethnics as one Latino unit. It will be shown that the Affirmative Action policy provided a legal sanction used by Mexican Americans and Puerto Ricans to express their grievances in concept— that is, as a Latino unit—against Illinois Bell and Jewel Tea.

II. SITUATIONAL LATINO ETHNIC CONSCIOUSNESS

At the outset of this kind of discussion, one is immediately confronted with the task of answering the following question: when is Latino identification the actual expression of a wider, all-embracing unit rather than the distinct and separate identities of Puerto Ricans or Mexican Americans? As a starting point, I will suggest, following Pitts's interpretation of "black consciousness," that Latino identity be viewed as a social product: "purposive action and interpretation of actions operating in social relationships" (1974, p. 672). From this point of view, Latino ethnic identification and consciousness may not be viewed as the product of individual Mexican American, Puerto Rican, or any Spanish-speaking groupings nor as existing independently of their intergroup social relations and behavior. Latino ethnic-conscious behavior, rather, represents a multi–group-generated behavior that transcends the boundaries of the individual national and cultural identities of the different Spanish-speaking populations and emerges as a distinct group identification and affiliation.

On the whole, Latino ethnic behavior represents another form of group consciousness among the Spanish-speaking population in the United States. It represents the tendency toward sentimental and ideological identification with a language group. It also signifies the expression, in certain circumstances, of devotion and loyalty to the wider concerns of the Spanish-speaking, while in most other instances, individual Puerto Rican and Mexican American ethnic ties and sentiments continue to share separate group affiliation and loyalties. Viewed somewhat differently, the Latino-conscious person sees himself as a Latino sometimes, and as Puerto Rican, Mexican American, Cuban, and the like at other times.

Members of the various Spanish-speaking community organizations in Chicago gave frequent and eloquent expressions to this type of sentiment. The following is a typical expression of this feeling of a situational-collective solidarity by one of the study's respondents:

> Here [in Chicago] we have a combination of different Latino population; however, in each community the majority takes care of its own first. . . . I try to use [Latino] as much as I can. When I talk to people in my community, I use Mexican, but I use Latino when the situation calls for issues that have city-wide implications.

The remarks of another respondent, who discussed the building of a new school in one of the city's Mexican American communities, also reflect the situational dimension of the Latino conscious person:

> . . . In Pilsen [a Mexican American community] you have a Latino movement when they are talking or confronting the city. But in issues such as the Benito Juarez High School, you did not find a Puerto Rican being the spokesperson for the group that was putting pressure on the city to build the new school.

Another conceptual formulation of Latinismo as a situational type of group consciousness and identity was expressed by a community organizer from one of the leading areas of Mexican settlement in the city. A strong supporter of Saul Alinsky's organizing principles, this respondent sees this form of group identity operative in those instances when the concerns and interests of both Mexican Americans and Puerto Ricans are at stake:

> When we move out of South Chicago and South Chicago is to have a relationship with the Westtown Concerned Citizens Coalition, it will have to be around issues that affect them equally. We cannot get South Chicago to get mad at Westtown if Westtown doesn't support their immigration situation [the issue of undocumented workers]. That is a Mexican problem that cannot be resolved through a Latino effort. But we can get them to come and talk to Westtown about jobs, about things that are hitting everybody.

In an interview with a newspaper reporter, one of the first Spanish-speaking members of Chicago's Board of Education gave further credence to the emergence of a distinct, situational Latino identity in this midwest metropolis. While speaking on behalf of bilingual education in the Chicago schools, this board member indicated supporting a "bicultural program which would provide the Latino child with a solid Latino identity, varying by nationality of neighborhood" (*Chicago Reporter,* 1975, p. 6).

These various ideological expressions suggest that there are at least two interdependent levels of ethnic organization that are in operation among Spanish-speaking groups: the level that is localized in certain communities of the city and the level that encompasses the city at large. Both spatially limited and spatially inclusive conceptual elements of ethnic identities are necessary ingredients for a complete understanding of the play of forces in the municipal polity that influence the expression of Latino ethnic identity and behavior among Spanish-speaking groups. A discussion of these forces follows in Section III.

These various examples also point to the shift from a traditional cultural and national population-group frame of reference between Puerto Ricans and Mexican Americans to a behavior-strategy frame, which views Latino ethnic consciousness generating out of intergroup social participation. The perception of Latino ethnic identity becomes an understanding that has meaning for the social action of the people concerned, but this meaning clearly is contained in the social situation in which the interaction is taking place. It seems from these examples that the decision of Spanish-speaking groups about when to construct an inclusive or collective group identity and come to share a consciousness-of-kind as "Latinos" is based on the groups' assessment of their goals and their options to attain those goals.

III. LATINO ETHNIC MOBILIZATION: THE SPANISH COALITION FOR JOBS

"Ethnic mobilization is," according to Olzak (1983, p. 355), "the process by which groups organize around some feature of ethnic identity (for example, skin color, language, customs) in pursuit of collective ends." From this point of view, Latino ethnic mobilization and Latino ethnic identity represent two empirically distinct processes: *Latino ethnic identity* symbolizes basic identification with a language population, while *Latino ethnic mobilization* represents the actual organization of two or more Spanish-speaking groups. Thus, while the Spanish language may serve as the characteristic symbolizing the major cultural similarity of Mexican Americans and Puerto Ricans, it is not sufficient to bring about a "Latino" response among various Spanish-speaking groups to their collective needs and wants. This language commonality can be excited into Latino ethnic mobilization by certain external stimuli, i.e., governmental and public policies that were designed to redress ethnic discrimination and inequality. Section IV of this chapter examines certain processes in the 1970s that created the conditions necessary for Latino ethnic mobilization in this Midwest metropolis. The discussion emphasizes the interplay between features of political development and expansion and sociopolitical characteristics shared by Puerto Ricans and Mexican Americans.

Before entering into this discussion, a few statements will be made on the Puerto Rican and Mexican American communities of Chicago. The latter is considered Chicago's first group of Spanish-speaking people, having arrived in the city during World War I. The larger majority of newly arrived Mexicans established settlements in three areas of the city: South Chicago, Back of the Yards, and the Near West Side. According to Ano Nuevo de Kerr, ". . . the three neighborhoods [have] persisted with one significant change. South Chicago

and Back of the Yards remained intact, while under the pressure of urban re-
newal [during the 1960s] half of the Near West Side community had moved a
few blocks south'' (1975, p. 22). This other area is called the Pilsen community.
Figure 1 shows the geographic distribution of these communities in the city.

During this period of initial immigration, the Mexican population grew very
quickly: in 1916 over 1000 newcomers lived in Chicago, and by 1930 this
number increased to surpass the 20,000 mark (Taylor, 1932). The major areas of
Mexican settlement were located nearby particular industries where the newcomers found employment: (1) South Chicago (steel), (2) Back of the Yards
(packing houses), and (3) Near West Side (railroad). The large majority of
Mexicans who comprised the first wave of immigrants to Chicago were overwhelmingly young, male, unskilled, and not prepared for the urban conditions of
the new society. Many of the immigrants came to Chicago on their own; most,
however, were recruited directly by employers and shipped to Chicago via railroad cars. Despite being hired primarily as strike-breakers and hardly ever in
permanent and steady employment, many of the Mexican newcomers did man-
age to become part of the labor force of those industries noted above, though not
on equal basis with other workers and always as the last hired and first fired. It
was primarily the labor shortage created by World War I and the industrial
expansion of the urban economy during this period that created the conditions
that allowed for the marginal integration of Mexican labor in these structures.
Although they were usually employed in the most unskilled jobs and paid the
lowest wages among the workers, the integration of Mexican newcomers in the
steel, packing houses, and railroad industries has been viewed comparable to the
experience of earlier European immigrants. Ano Nuevo de Kerr (1976) noted,
for instance, that it appeared Mexicans were following the traditional road toward assimilation in American life.

Hopes and thoughts of assimilation were shattered very quickly, however, by
the major and most obvious and devastating incident of Mexican labor exploitation in Chicago, as well as in other parts of the country where Mexicans had
established communities of settlement. The incident was the result of the Great
Depression of the early 1930s and it involved the collaboration of American
immigration officials and welfare agencies from the state of Illinois and the city
of Chicago in rounding up and returning Mexican workers and their families,
regardless of legal citizenship status, to their homeland. This process, known as
repatriation, was undertaken, according to these officials, as a relief measure. As
the 1930s came to a close the Mexicans who survived repatriation were few in
numbers; according to Taylor (1932), the number of Mexicans was reduced from
nearly 30,000 in the late 1920s to just 7000 in 1940. Ano Nuevo de Kerr
estimated the number of Mexican residents in Chicago in 1950 at 24,000, the
majority of whom were newly arrived immigrants (1975, p. 25).

Like many other ethnic groups, Mexicans responded to their conditions in
Chicago by developing voluntary social organizations and associations. The

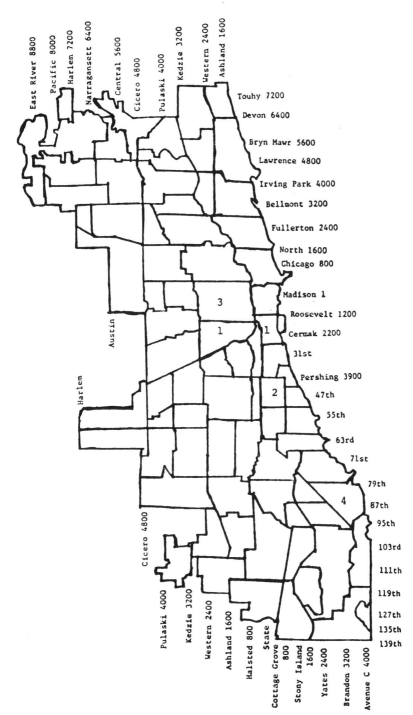

FIG. 1. Mexican communities of settlement: (1) Pilsen, (2) Back of the Yards, (3) Near West Side, and (4) South Chicago.

dispersed geographic location of Mexican settlements in the city made these social organizations develop primarily along neighborhood lines. Viewed in a different way, the early newcomers did not develop structures to deal with their collective, citywide situations. In the 1950s several groups were finally established to coalesce and politicize the different neighborhoods under one collective "Mexican ethnicity." The focus of these structures was Chicago's "Mexican American" population, and their major goal was the assimilation of this generation into the life of the larger American society. In other words, the new generation of Mexican newcomers from Mexico and the Southwest was not part of the agenda of the new "Mexican American organizations" of the period. In fact, it was not until the mid-1960s that organizational efforts were started in the Pilsen community to claim the allegiance of all of the city's Mexican and Mexican American residents.

Puerto Rican immigration to Chicago started in the late 1940s, increased substantially during the 1950s, and reached its highest proportion in the 1960s. According to the 1960s Census, the first official enumeration of Puerto Ricans in Chicago, there were 32,371 Puerto Ricans living in the city. Ten years later, this number more than doubled to a total of 78,963 residents; the Puerto Rican population increased between 1950 and 1970 was, indeed, substantial.

During this 20-year period, several sizable Puerto Rican neighborhoods, usually of a few square blocks each, sprang up in various parts of the city. Beginning with the initial group of Puerto Rican immigrants in the 1940s (E. Padilla, 1947), Puerto Rican newcomers usually settled in or near the center of the city north from the Mexican areas of settlements. In a series of articles for the *Chicago Sun Times,* Watson and Wheeler (1971) indicated that there were several major initial communities of Puerto Rican settlement in this area during the 1950s: Lakeview, Near North Side, Lincoln Park, and Uptown. The two writers also added that another group of newcomers settled in the Woodlawn community in the city's southside. Figure 2 shows the geographic location of the leading communities of Puerto Rican settlement in Chicago in the 1950s.

By 1960 the major Puerto Rican neighborhood in the city began to take shape. A large Puerto Rican enclave, located in the Westtown community on the city's near northwest side, popularly known as the "Division Street Area," was formed. Although a few of the neighborhoods that emerged as distinguishable areas of Puerto Rican settlement in the 1950s remained the core of the Chicago Puerto Rican community in the following decade, the Division Street Area served new arrivals as the leading area of first settlement throughout the 1960s and 1970s.

The massive immigration of Puerto Ricans to Chicago and other metropolitan areas began during a period of modern industrial and technological growth and expansion. During this post World War II "modern era," nationwide social and economic changes and technological developments were reducing the importance of manufacturing as a provider of new jobs in the major, older cities of the

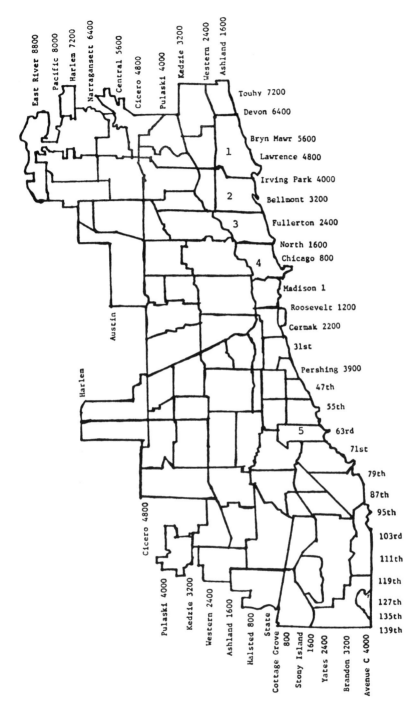

FIG. 2. Primary Puerto Rican Communities in 1960: (1) Uptown, (2) Lakeview, (3) Lincoln Park, (4) Near North Side, and (5) Woodlawn.

Midwest as well as in the Northeast. In other words, most Puerto Ricans immigrated to the United States at the same historical period when the traditional unskilled and semiskilled jobs, which had represented the initial step or phase of integration into the American institutional life for large numbers of European immigrants, were in steady decline as major economic activities in many cities and were being replaced with white-collar and professional jobs.

For Puerto Ricans in Chicago this economic and technological growth and expansion has meant concentration in nonindustrial, poorly paid, menial, and dead-end jobs. E. Padilla's (1947) study of the first group of Puerto Rican immigrants to Chicago in the late 1940s, for example, shows that many of the newcomers were employed in the restaurant business as bus boys, sweepers, kitchen help, waiters, and the like. Others were employed in the business sector as messengers and delivery men, and some in stock rooms and packaging areas of many stores. Yet another large number found jobs in the janitorial labor force of the city. According to one of the reports of the U.S. Immigration and Naturalization Service, by 1960 the majority of Puerto Rican workers were employed in three leading unskilled categories: "operatives and kindred" (45.7%), "laborers" (13.7%), and "service workers" (11.7%) (U.S. Immigration and Naturalization Service, 1968).

The employment of Puerto Ricans in noncompetitive economic sectors caused very little friction with white workers; thus, racial antagonism between the two groups became related to social, political, and community-related concerns. From the outset, housing discrimination and police injustice became the leading forces shaping group relationships between Puerto Ricans and whites in the city. As for the former, Puerto Ricans were trapped in the most deteriorated or run-down residential sections in their communities of settlement not only because of poverty but also because of a stringent pattern of housing discrimination. In terms of the latter, from the start policemen treated Puerto Ricans in Chicago with a great deal of resentment and enmity; Puerto Ricans became victims of police racist and brutal actions in Chicago.

This initial contact between Puerto Ricans and the white society during the 1950s and 1960s accelerated the growth of Puerto Rican consciousness in the city. The Puerto Ricans' ethnic identity underwent considerable evolution and growth, converting whatever residual regional/town differences may have existed between the new arrivals into a sense of peoplehood. Manifestations of Puerto Rican peoplehood and consciousness were operative in a variety of ethnic-conscious attitudes and organizations: Puerto Ricans were forced to develop and staff a parallel set of personal and social services, neighborhood businesses, and communication networks to meet the tastes and needs of a growing Puerto Rican population. The most significant organizational response among Puerto Ricans during this period was their development of community organizations. Several community organizations developed that sought principally to provide guidance and leadership for neighborhood residents.

In sum, during the immigration period individual Puerto Rican and Mexican American ethnic boundaries were clearly evident in the actions and behavior of each national and cultural group. One can suspect that while at times Puerto Ricans and Mexican Americans were in constant physical contact and were tolerant of one another, their daily life was still demarcated by individual ethnic boundaries. National and cultural ethnicity was a basis for personal trust for individual Mexican American and Puerto Rican residents, and the personal bonds promoted by ethnic consciousness-of-kind were vital to social interaction and mobilization in the individual communities, for otherwise the residents had little reason for crossing their respective ethnic lines. This began to change in the 1970s as the hardening dimensions of urban-based inequality (continued shrinking of the industrial job base in the city) gave rise to more apparent similarities among Puerto Ricans and Mexican Americans. The influence of the Affirmative Action policy, for example, contributed immensely to the organization or mobilization of these two groups as "Latinos."

IV. AFFIRMATIVE ACTION

The leading factor responsible for exciting Latino ethnic mobilization among Puerto Ricans and Mexican Americans in Chicago was the Affirmative Action policy. The Affirmative Action policy represented the instrument or mechanism used by leaders from the two communities to make claims against institutions and structures found to be discriminating against Spanish-speaking workers at the citywide level. Viewed another way, the Affirmative Action policy provided the critical base for the Mexican American and Puerto Rican leadership to advance the interests of their populations collectively, rather than as individual or separate Spanish-speaking ethnics. It enabled nonunited groups to transcend the boundaries of their individual ethnic groups and assert demands as a Latino population or group.

That the Affirmative Action policy was of great importance for the organizational development and growth of a Latino identity and agenda is clearly reflected in a memo sent by the chair of one community organization from a Puerto Rican neighborhood to social service agencies and officials in the Spanish-speaking communities of the city during the spring of 1971. In it, attention was called to the "full rights citizens from Latin America, including the protection of the government against the dehumanizing conditions of Latinos" (Spanish Coalition for Jobs, 1971, p. 1). In the same memo, the two leading priorities of the "Latino community" were specifically directed at the implementation of the Affirmative Action policy by all employers (1971, p. 1):

(1) All federal agencies, state and private, which administer federal funds, be compelled to adhere to the 1964 and 1968 Civil Rights Statutes and other federal laws to hire Latinos at all levels with direct federal criteria for enforcement;

(2) In the enforcement of full rights of American citizenship according to the U.S.
     Constitution and Federal Statutes—that all Affirmative Action plans filed by pri-
     vate companies be made public record. That a doctrine of community participation
     in the processing and implementation of the Affirmative Action plan of particular
     interest to us Latinos—be a federal requirement for compliance.

The importance of the Affirmative Action policy to the development and
growth of a Latino identity and mobilization was also expressed in an interview
by the present Executive Director of the Spanish Coalition for Jobs (a discussion
on this organization is given later):

> . . . the Spanish Coalition for Jobs started because of Affirmative Action. This was in
> the early 1970's when a group of Hispanic Manpower Service agencies throughout the
> city of Chicago became concerned mostly with the utility companies and major chain
> stores where we did not see Hispanic or our brown faces working there. The courts were
> not implementing the Affirmative Action policy as it applied to Latinos: however, the act
> was there to be used and force employer's to carry it out. So Affirmative Action gave
> birth to the Spanish Coalition.

In the same interview she added: ''We needed no longer theorize and speculate on the matter of job discrimination. We knew that equal employment opportunity could be significantly advanced via the provisions of Affirmative Action.''

Fundamentally, the Affirmative Action policy provided Puerto Rican and
Mexican American leaders the legal sanction from which to seek meaningful
responses and resolution to the various grievances of Spanish-speaking people in
general. Opening doors long closed as a necessary first step; making sure that
those who were formerly locked out had a real opportunity to compete—that is,
not only enter but also to move upward—was the thrust of the Mexican American and Puerto Rican leadership. Affirmative Action was the key to creating
organizations with a Latino boundary whose aims were to achieve these goals.

V. THE SPANISH COALITION FOR JOBS

In June 1971, a total of 23 Puerto Rican and Mexican American local community organizations, including nine employment referral agencies from the Pilsen,
South Chicago, Lakeview, and Westtown/Humboldt Park communities, formed
a coalition to enforce the implementation of Affirmative Action policy as it
applied to Spanish-speaking workers. The Spanish Coalition for Jobs (La Coali-
cion Latinoamericana de Empleos), as this coalition was named, had its roots in
issues of employment—namely, job discrimination. Several of the coalition's
member employment agencies had discovered that a large number of their Spanish-speaking referrals to certain American firms were not being hired or accepted
as trainees as stipulated by their Affirmative Action policy. This concern was
expressed in one of the Spanish Coalition's reports: ''Employers were giving two
or three token jobs to the referral agencies to satisfy them, but very few of these

companies ever considered hiring significant numbers of Latinos . . . as consumers we were welcomed, but as candidates for jobs we were being ignored" (Spanish Coalition for Jobs, unpublished). In a Proposal to the Rockefeller Foundation (1972), the same feelings are expressed: "the racist attitude of employers triggered us into utilizing our consumer power as a tool or bargaining device. . . to compete in the job market." The Spanish Coalition for Jobs was established in this context; it became the enforcer of dues owed to Spanish-speaking people in Chicago.

A. Illinois Bell

Although the Spanish Coalition for Jobs could depend on a legal statute to make claims in behalf of Mexican American and Puerto Rican workers collectively as well as on its network of existing community organizations and agencies, the organization also needed an event, issue, or threat to mobilize its mass base as a "Latino unit." The organization's support system, in other words, was simply not sufficient to excite political action or mobilization as one Latino group. The Coalition's mass-based membership had to be convinced that functioning as "Latinos" was more advantageous in some instances than working as individual Mexican American or Puerto Rican ethnics.

The event was provided during a community meeting on August 5, 1971, at the Association House in Westtown. The meeting was called by Illinois Bell officials to discuss the different services that the telephone company was offering its "Spanish-speaking customers." During the meeting, one Illinois Bell official stated that his corporation had not readily employed Spanish-speaking workers in the past. Several representatives of the Spanish Coalition for Jobs, among many in attendance, used this moment to politicize the 300 in attendance. The coalition members made the case that Illinois Bell actually had a terrible history of job discrimination against Spanish-speaking workers.

Although very few material benefits were gained from the meeting, the Spanish Coalition for Jobs won a symbolic victory. The representatives of the telephone company agreed to an initial negotiation meeting to discuss the job issue with the members of the Spanish Coalition for Jobs.

The first formal meeting between the two opposing groups was held September 15, 1971, again at the Association House. According to a *Chicago Sun-Times* report (1971, p. 13), after a list of demands was presented by the coalition, 115 jobs for Spanish-speaking workers were offered while the other demands were not recognized. The coalition refused to accept the company's offer and the following day conducted a mass demonstration as a "Latino group" at the Illinois Bell office near downtown.

This exchange of negotiations followed by protest tactics is indicative of the year-long adversary relationship between the Spanish Coalition and the Illinois Bell Telephone Company. Fundamentally, there would be negotiations, and when those broke down, picketing would begin of homes of Illinois Bell officials and executives by members of the Spanish Coalition.

Finally, on June 14, 1972, the Illinois Bell Telephone Company signed an agreement with the Spanish Coalition for Jobs. Under the terms of the agreement, according to one local newpaper, it was expected that Illinois Bell would hire at least 1323 Latinos by the end of 1976, including two top-level executives (*Booster Newspaper*, 1972, p. 2). The promise of 1323 additional Spanish-speaking workers was virtually a fulfillment of the Spanish Coalition's main demand. The *Booster* (1972, p. 3) further reported that the Spanish Coalition was pleased "with a provision in the eight-point agreement calling for regular reviews by the coalition of the company's progress toward achieving its hiring goals."

B. Jewel Tea Company

In order to sustain the Spanish Coalition for Jobs as representative of the city's "Latino" working class, it became necessary for the organization to work on several issues that affected Mexican Americans and Puerto Ricans. Fundamentally, the approach of "interrelationship of issues" is basic to the Alinsky philosophy of community organizing on which the Spanish Coalition for Jobs was founded.[3] In keeping with this approach, the Jewel Tea Company became the coalition's second target of confrontation, as it, too was found to be discriminating against Spanish-speaking workers.

By the time the Jewel issue emerged, the Spanish Coalition for Jobs seemed to have been halfway down the road from protest to negotiation. It had not yet achieved the regularized access to public and private officials necessary for a bargaining relationship; however, it was assumed that the protest tactics employed against Illinois Bell demonstrated the legitimacy of the organization's grievances, so that it was no longer necessary to dramatize an issue in order to gain a hearing from targets. As one of the coalition's organizers commented, "the coalition received the recognition that made it a respectable organization. People in government and in private business were taking a serious look at us."

In March 1972, members of the Spanish Coalition for Jobs met for the first time with representatives from Jewel. The major demands presented to Jewel officials were: "(1) a job training program for Latinos, (2) an increase of Latino workers, (3) the hiring of Latinos to administrative positions, and (4) a greater increase in participation by community residents in the supervision of how Latinos were being processed for employment" (*El Informador Newspaper*, 1973, p. 3). These negotiations broke down after several hours of bargaining when the Jewel officials rejected the Spanish Coalition for Jobs demands. In a news release, the coalition called the Jewel response to their demands a "rejection of the Latino community and a callous lack of corporate responsibility to the community."

It was not until an entire year had elapsed of bargaining negotiations with the food chain's officials that the coalition resorted to protest as a way to secure perquisites for its constituents. The coalition's first mass demonstration, in the form of a boycott against Jewell, began Saturday, April 13, 1973, at 9:00 a.m. A local community newspaper reported that "members from the Spanish Coalition for Jobs met at the front of Jewel's 14 stores for several hours distributing leaflets and urging shoppers not to buy at Jewel" (*El Informador Newspaper*, 1973, p. 3). The same source noted that the positive reaction of the shoppers could be measured by the large number who boycotted the supermarkets. It was also indicated that the real test and effect of the boycott occured the following day when the Jewel store located on Damen and North Avenues in the Puerto Rican community of Westtown closed down at 3:00 p.m. because people refused to shop at that particular store. After several months of picketing and shoppers' boycott of Jewell stores in the Spanish-speaking neighborhoods of the city, Jewel signed an agreement with the Spanish Coalition for Jobs late in the summer of 1973.

In sum, the Illinois Bell and Jewel controversies provided both material and symbolic benefits to the Spanish Coalition network of organizations and their members. The job-opening and job-training agreements secured from the two companies by the Spanish Coalition for Jobs are clearly material, for the ability to secure employment or a better-paying job improves the economic position of individual beneficiaries. The individual economic gains may contribute indirectly to community stability, in the form of increased financial support for local businesses, to cite one example.

On a more symbolic level, these successes demonstrated that adoption of a "Latino ethnic identity" can alter institutional racist practices and thus can contribute to the development of feelings of political effectiveness as one Latino group. In general, the symbolic benefit of these events demonstrated the efficacy of situational Latino ethnicity by influencing those institutions whose policies affected the wider interests of Puerto Ricans and Mexican Americans in the city of Chicago.

VI. CONCLUSION

In sum, the empirical evidence presented in this chapter indicates that the concept of Latino is an "ethnic principle of organization": it is generated out of a myth of common origin (based on language similarity) and broader social conditions not in themselves "ethnic" at all. Latino ethnicity is fabricated out of shared cultural and structural similarities and functions according to the needs of Spanish-speaking groups. The data also reveal that the organization of a larger Latino ethnic unit is, indeed, a clear case of a mobilized ethnic contender. Latino ethnic mobilization represents an attempt on the part of Spanish-speaking groups to mount a competitive front in pursuit of emerging resources and rewards. There are certain situations that Mexican Americans, Puerto Ricans, Cubans, and other Spanish-speaking groups may find a competitive edge in Latino ethnic mobilization rather than as individual ethnics. Finally, this chapter presents more than a picture of a group of aggrieved Spanish-speaking individuals banding together as a wider Latino unit to fight for their dues. It is also an examination of how the availability of a governmental policy facilitated the expression of grievances by two Spanish-speaking ethnics in the form of wider Latino unit.

Overall, this chapter showed that Latino ethnic identification is a mix both of internally generated dynamics and of pressures from the external environment. Shared structural similarities and generalized beliefs about the causes (e.g., cultural or language discrimination) and possible means of reducing these circumstances (e.g., organization of a larger Latino unit) are important preconditions for the emergence of Latino ethnic mobilization. An increase in the extent or intensity of inequality commonalities among two or more Spanish-speaking groups and the development of an ideology occur prior to Latino ethnic mobilization. This explanation holds that before Latino ethnic action is possible within a collectivity of various Spanish-speaking groups, a generalized belief (or ideological justification) is necessary concerning at least the causes of the discontent and, under certain conditions, the modes of redress. In the same way, the explanation is based on the premise that Latino ethnic mobilization cannot be perceived as occuring without certain external stimulus. In the case of Mexican Americans and Puerto Ricans in Chicago, the Affirmative Action policy represented that necessary stimulus. This policy provided nonunited, culturally distinct, resource-poor groups with clear objects for efficiently focusing their wider hostility and pressure. It supported, and, in a way encouraged, the organization of Puerto Ricans and Mexican Americans into one Latino boundary or ''community of interests.'' The presence of this legal forum, from which Puerto Ricans and Mexican Americans could make ''Latino claims and demands,'' contributed to the creation of this wider cleavage.

One final concern needs to be addressed here: why Latino and not a working class movement involving Blacks, since they, too, represent another aggrieved ''minority'' population? It is often assumed that since Spanish-speaking groups share certain commonalities with Blacks, particularly in the urban economy, a class or ''minority'' boundary would be more beneficial for the advancement of these wider interests. The advantage of a Latino boundary is that it is based on certain cultural markers and symbols that the actors are able to recognize and they imply some evaluation of the behavior of the persons so categorized in terms of what people expect of them. The set of meanings generally attached to Latino ethnic solidarity is more clear-cut than other cues; thus, overall there is less ambiguity about the relationships among individual Spanish-speaking ethnics. In other words, Latino ethnicity is construed as the set of meanings that actors attribute to certain symbols, signs or cues by means of which they are able to identify Spanish-speaking persons as members of this "cultural innovation." Once the symbols have been recognized and interpreted and the Latino ethnic identity thereby established, then the actor has available a set of expectations of the person's behavior toward him or her. The Latino ethnic boundary, therefore, has significance in that it exists as a wide representation that is not only common among a designated set of people but is also shared by them, so that the shared perceptions can become the basis of an understanding between them in their social relationships.

The "minority" cleavage, on the other hand, lacks all of these features. Interaction and solidarity between Spanish-speaking groups and Blacks, therefore, is more likely to be quite ambiguous and problematic. In the same way that the Latino boundary calls for the assessment of the appropriateness of its functions as a wider unit for two or more Spanish-speaking groups, the idea of a minority cleavage also requires the adoption of specific meanings and practices for those groups concerned. For a minority cleavage to occur, in other words, there must be, at the very least, a minimal level of adherence to a set of rules governing interaction and relationships between the members of the different groups composing the unit. These rules will constitute a deeply ungrained understanding transcending the cultural or ethnic differences that divide the groups while at the same time binding them at the level of a basic social contract.

Instead of seeking those cues or markers that can provide precision and definition to "minority-related behavior and expectations," both Spanish-speaking and Black leaders in Chicago have tended to direct most of their energies to explaining why a bond between the two groups is simply not probable. While Black leaders view Hispanics as racists, the Spanish-speaking leadership cries misunderstanding of their ethnicity as well as foul or betrayal on the part of Blacks for not distributing minority-related opportunities and rewards to all minorities. This dispute was the major focus of an article, "Competition, Cultural Differences Split Black and Latino groups in Chicago," published in 1979 by the *Chicago Reporter,* a magazine that focuses on racial issues in the city. Blacks generally claim, according to the report, that relations between the two populations are particularly "strained by cultural differences and a peculiar brand of race consciousness among Latinos, many of whom shy away from any close associations with Blacks" (1979, 1). Spanish-speaking leaders respond to these charges by maintaining that Blacks simply do not understand their ethnic needs and interests such as bilingual education. There are times when "Hispanic" interests run counter to the interests of Blacks—i.e., support for bilingual education is often perceived as a move against school desegregation (a policy strongly supported by Blacks), since the former schooling program requires the segregation of Spanish-speaking students. In addition, Spanish-speaking leaders make the claim that certain government agencies and programs controlled by Blacks receive federal funds to aid all minorities but spend them almost exclusively on Blacks. One Spanish-speaking leader is quoted as saying in the report, "The

Urban League gets all this government money to fight city problems, but the only time they remember Latinos is when they want to sell tickets to one of their banquets. The rest of the time, we don't exist'' (1979, p. 6).

It's quite obvious that these discrepant perspectives reflect differences in ethnic background and orientations; they also reflect opposed group interests related to the rights and obligations involved in minority-related behavior and action. While members of both ethnic groups agree on the relative social significance of the minority boundary, they are in disagreement as to the normative basis and interactional prerogative of this wider cleavage. Again, whatever is involved in the assessment of the salience of the minority boundary for social action, it must be carried out in the context of certain specific and meaningful markers and symbols. Behavior, attitudes, actions, and gains must be all predefined before groups can engage in minority-related activities.

NOTES

[1]A classic example is provided by Burma's (1954) study. Although it gives an impression of being a study of Latinismo or of the collective identification of Spanish-speaking groups in this country, his book is actually an accumulation of facts about several distinct groups of ''Spanish Americans,'' and about Filipinos as well. A similar approach used in the examination of a Latino or Hispanic community is evident in two more recent studies specifically about Chicago's Spanish-speaking populations: *The political organization of Chicago's Latino communities* by Walton and Salces (1977), and *Aqui estamos* by Lucas (1978). In both cases, the idea of Latinismo or Hispanismo as a singular wider identity for this population is never examined. In Walton and Salces the only mention of this concept is found in a footnote at the outset of their discussion: ''here we shall use the term 'Latino' to describe Chicago's Spanish-speaking population in the aggregate since, according to our data, it is most preferred'' (1977, p. 1). Lucas, on the other hand, says flatly: ''Popularly, the term *Latino* has been used quite often to describe this population (the Spanish-speaking), and related cultural manifestations. It will be used in this report'' (1978, p. 2).

[2]The selection of Mexican American and Puerto Rican community organizations for the study was done exclusively for methodological reasons. Primarily, there were no more than three or four Cuban community organizations and/or Central and South American organizations servicing this other component of the Spanish-speaking population in the city of Chicago. Thus, to have included these in the study would have given it a conceptually irrelevant style or sample.

[3]Alinsky's (1969, p. 60) discussion of building ''People's Organizations'' stressed the interrelationship of problems and the maintenance value of many issues:

> The conventional community council—which means practically all community councils—soon discovers that the problems of life are not wrapped up in individual cellophane packages, and because the community council cannot and does not want to get down to the roots of the problems, it retreats into a sphere of trivial, superficial ameliorations. The people judge the agency by its programs and soon define the agency as insignificant.
>
> The program of a real People's Organization calmly accepts the overwhelming fact that all problems are related and that they are all progeny of certain fundamental causes, that ultimate success in conquering these evils can be achieved only by victory over all evils.

REFERENCES

ALINSKY, SAUL (1969). *Reveille for radicals.* New York: Vintage.

ANO NUEVO DE KERR, LOUISE (1975). Chicano settlements in Chicago: A brief history. *Journal of Ethnic Studies* **2** (4, Winter):22–32.

ANO NUEVO DE KERR, LOUISE (1976). The Chicano experience in Chicago, 1920–1970. Unpublished Ph.D. dissertation, University of Illinois, Chicago Circle Campus.

BOOSTER NEWSPAPER (1972). Bell Telephone Co. increases its number of Latin employees. June 17. Chicago, Illinois.

BURMA, JOHN H. (1954). Spanish-speaking groups in the United States. Durham, North Carolina: Duke University Press.

CHICAGO REPORTER (1975). Reporter survey identifies 18 Chicago Latino leaders considered most influential in their community. Vol. 4(7, July):6–9.

CHICAGO SUN-TIMES (1971). Latinos beset Bell aides with job demands. September 15. Chicago, Illinois.

EL INFORMADOR NEWSPAPER (1973). Boicott a la Jewel por tiempo indefinado. May 13. Chicago, Illinois.

ENLOE, CYNTHIA H. (1980). *Police, military and ethnicity: Foundations of state power.* New Brunswick, New Jersey: Transactions.

LUCAS, ISIDRO (1978). Aqui estamos: An overview of Latino communities in Greater Chicago. Report to Chicago United.

OLZAK, SUSAN (1983). Contemporary ethnic mobilization. In *Annual Review of Sociology* (Ralph H. Turner and James F. Short, eds.), Vol. 9, pp. 355–374.

PADILLA, ELENA (1947). Puerto Rican immigrants in New York and Chicago: A study in comparative assimilation. Unpublished Ph.D. dissertation. Chicago: University of Chicago.

PADILLA, FELIX M. (In press). *Latino ethnic consciousness: The case of Mexican American and Puerto Rican in Chicago.*

PITTS, JAMES (1974). The study of race consciousness: Comments on new directions. *American Journal of Sociology* **80** (November):665–687.

PROPOSAL TO THE ROCKEFELLER FOUNDATION (1972). Submitted by the Spanish Coalition for Jobs, Fall 1972.

SPANISH COALITION FOR JOBS (1971). Acute depression in the Latin American community. Memo, Spring 1971.

SPANISH COALITION FOR JOBS (Unpublished). History of the Spanish Coalition for Jobs.

TAYLOR, PAUL S. (1932). *Mexican labor in the United States: Chicago and Calumet region.* Berkeley: University of California Press.

U.S. IMMIGRATION AND NATURALIZATION SERVICE (1968). Annual report of the U.S. Immigration and Naturalization Service.

WALTON, JOHN, and SALCES, LUIS M. (1977). *The political organization of Chicago's Latino communities.* Evanston, Illinois: Northwestern University Center for Urban Affairs.

WATSON, J., and WHEELER, C. N. (1971). The Latins. *Chicago Sun-Times,* September 12–20. Chicago, Illinois.

8

Structural Conduciveness
and Ethnic Mobilization:
The Flemish Movement
in Belgium

FRANÇOIS NIELSEN
Department of Sociology
University of North Carolina
Chapel Hill, North Carolina 27514

I. INTRODUCTION

Resurgences of ethnicity in a number of advanced industrial societies have recently come under the scrutiny of social scientists, largely because of their paradoxical nature with respect to long-established currents of social thought [e.g., Glazer and Moynihan (1975), Rothschild (1981), Smith (1981), Banton (1983); Tiryakian and Rogowski (1985), and see Olzak (1983) for a review].[1] One of the most straightforward and empirically accessible indicators of ethnic mobilization is the rise of ethnic parties, groups that formulate claims defined on the membership of an ethnic group in opposition to, or in contradistinction with, other groups in society and that seek electoral support to implement these claims. The use of ethnic voting as an indicator of mobilization is illustrated by the work of Hechter (1975), Beer (1980), Nielsen (1980), and Olzak (1982) in the cases of Britain, France, Belgium, and Canada, respectively.

Studies of ethnic voting usually assume that the success of the party in the environment, such as an electoral district, in which it competes for votes is a good indicator of mobilization and is affected by social structural characteristics of the environment such as the occupational distribution, urbanization, the income level, and the degree of cultural assimilation of the population. With this assumption, it is possible to test various structural theories concerning social

COMPETITIVE ETHNIC RELATIONS

structural factors associated with ethnic mobilization. [See Hechter, Friedman, and Applebaum (1982) and Nagel (1984) for the use of "structural theories" in that sense.] These assumptions, however, are problematic. For example, Ragin and Davies (1981) argue that the success of the Plaid Cymru (the Welsh party) in Wales between 1959 and 1974 does not represent so much a substantive choice of the subnational alternative on the part of voters as it reflects the growing dissatisfaction with the class-based party system (Labour and Conservative) that characterized the whole of Britain during the period.[2] If this is the case, Plaid Cymru vote is an ambiguous indicator of ethnic mobilization, since it represents in part negative voting, and purely political mechanisms should be taken into account in addition to social structural factors.

The case of Wales studied by Ragin and Davies (1981) is but one instance of a situation common in industrial societies, in which an ethnic party starts its mobilization drive in an outsider position, with a small number of adherents, and confronts a political environment dominated by older parties associated with different cleavages, such as class.[3] The purpose of this chapter is to analyze the way in which the structure of political alignments in the environment prior to the creation of the ethnic party affects its success. Following Smelser (1962) and Pinard (1971, 1975), I use the term *structural conduciveness* to denote the degree to which the alignment structure facilitates or inhibits ethnic electoral mobilization. I will argue that conduciveness mechanisms are better understood within the framework of an ecological model of electoral competition based on the concept of the *variable niche* of a party in an environment. The central theme is that, given certain social structural conditions, success of the new ethnic party should be greater in environments characterized by a low degree of political competition (or diversity). In such environments, the niche of existing parties is likely to be expanded to include a weakly identified fringe membership that can be more easily recruited by the new competitor. The ecological model is discussed in Section III. The model is later used to analyze the rise of the Flemish movement in Belgium after World War II. In Section II, I discuss first some of the theoretical underpinnings of the general model.

II. OUTSIDER PARTIES, CONDUCIVENESS, AND SECTIONALISM

The focus of the discussion is on the political, as opposed to the social, factors that affect ethnic mobilization in a bounded environment such as a district. It is useful to distinguish two aspects of the environment in which a party competes for votes.[4]

(1) The *social environment* is the population of the district together with the social structural characteristics that describe it. Structural characteristics such as literacy, median income, and occupational distribution are aggregated from indi-

vidual values of an attribute, but this need not be the case. For example, the existence of large oil reserves is an attribute of the social environment that has no direct individual counterpart.

(2) The *political environment* consists of all the political factors that affect the distribution of electoral support in the district. Electoral laws and the relative organizational strengths of various parties are examples of such factors. Of particular interest here is the structure of political alignments prior to mobilization by the ethnic party.

A. Structural Conduciveness and Outsider Parties

Pinard's (1971) analysis of the emergence of third parties (which I will call outsider parties in what follows, to take into account the possibility of a multiparty system) is purely political-environmental in that it involves only political factors. He argues that one-party dominance makes the political environment conducive to the rise of outsider parties. Outsider success is facilitated by one-party dominance because the electorate perceives the opposition as a weak alternative to the dominant party. In the presence of strains, the dissatisfied electorate turns to the new party as the only plausible alternative, since the traditional opposition is demonstrably unable to satisfy the dissident claims. In a revised version of the theory, Pinard (1975, postscript) recognizes that the one-party dominance effect is a special case of a more general mechanism of structural conduciveness. The key factor of conduciveness is the nonrepresentation of social groups through the electoral process. Thus, even in a balanced system with a strong opposition, the political environment may be conducive for outsider parties if a group cannot accommodate its claims through the existing parties.[5]

An interesting implication of Pinard's generalized model is that a conducive situation in which a social group is not, or is unsatisfactorily, represented in the party system corresponds to a situation in which the support for some existing party (or parties) is inflated by individuals who cannot vote for a party with the ideal program and are forced to settle for a second-best alternative. Then, support for the second-best party may consist in part of a half-hearted membership of negative voters.[6] For example, Pinard (1975, p. 288) argues that in a situation of one-party dominance, identification for all parties tends to be weak and, in particular, "among those supporting the dominant party . . . there will be many doing it simply for lack of any other alternative rather than out of any positive identification." I will interpret such mechanisms in the context of the variable niche model in the next section.

B. Peripheral Sectionalism

In a seemingly unrelated discussion, Hechter (1975) points to specific mechanisms that can make the political environment conducive (in Pinard's sense) to the success of an ethnic party. In his study of the Celtic fringe of Britain, he defines *peripheral sectionalism* as the failure of national political integration (Hechter, 1975, pp. 218–219):

> A society is nationally integrated to the extent that individual, or group, orientations towards political action are made on the basis of class, or social structure, rather than status, or non-structural considerations . . . a group is malintegrated to the extent that the voting behavior of its members cannot be explained by reference to its social structural composition.

Peripheral sectionalism is one possible expression of ethnic solidarity. Some individuals vote for the party that seems to represent their interests better, as members of an ethnic group, rather than as members of a particular occupational, educational or other category within the social structure. These individuals would rather support ethnic issues explicitly but are forced to vote for a substitute. Therefore, the degree to which the social environment *does not* account for variations in party support in culturally distinct subsets of the population is an indicator of solidarity.[7] This argument implies that, in the absence of an ethnic party, support for one or more of the existing (nonethnic) parties will be inflated relative to their natural support determined ideally by social structural criteria. Peripheral sectionalism clearly makes the political environment conducive to the rise of outsider parties.

C. Structural Conduciveness and Ethnic Parties

Mechanisms of structural conduciveness and peripheral sectionalism have theoretical implications in historical instances in which a new ethnic party starts mobilizing electoral support. The success of the ethnic party in an environment may depend on two categories of factors pertaining to the social and political environment.

First, the new party may be successful because of social structural factors in the environment that facilitate ethnic mobilization. Such considerations pertain to the category of structural theories, and opinions differ. The social environment may facilitate ethnic mobilization because of a cultural division of labor (Hechter, 1975), a split labor market (Bonacich, 1972), or intergroup competition (Hannan, 1979) [see also Nielsen (1980, 1985), Olzak (1983), Nagel and Olzak (1982), and Portes (1984)]. In all these theories, despite their differences, social structural variables are deemed to explain variations in party success across environments. Second, the new party may be successful for purely political environmental reasons, because the existing structure of alignments is conducive to the rise of *any* outsider party. Peripheral sectionalism, for example, can induce part of the electorate to vote half-heartedly for one of the existing parties. These voters are likely to defect quickly when any alternative to the existing system is proposed.

A major methodological problem in such historical instances is that peripheral sectionalism and voting for a party with explicit ethnic claims are alternative indicators of ethnic mobilization. Therefore, as the ethnic party mobilizes, one would expect it to be more successful in social environments that, because of social structural conditions, were prone to a sectionalist response. The same conditions should facilitate mobilization by the new party. However, sectionalism may also have made the political environment more conducive to the success of any outsider party, net of social structural considerations. If there are systematic relationships between the conduciveness of the political environment and characteristics of the social environment, as is probably the case, social structural correlates of ethnic party success are difficult to interpret. Party success may be due to underlying social conditions, or it may be an epiphenomenon resulting from the greater conduciveness brought about by these conditions. Distinguishing the two types of mechanisms is particularly important where social environmental and political environmental effects on ethnic mobilization are in opposite directions, as seems to be the case for the Flemish movement in Belgium to be discussed later. Section III attempts to clarify these issues.

III. POLITICAL DIVERSITY AND OUTSIDER PARTIES

In this section, I will first attempt to reformulate Pinard's (1971, 1975) model of structural conduciveness from an organizational ecological perspective. Then I will introduce a measure of the diversity of the political environment arising out of this reformulation.

A. The Variable Niche Model

Political parties are organizations, and as such they need to draw resources from their environment (McCarthy and Zald, 1977). In a democratic system of political representation, a main resource of parties is the individual vote. Thus parties, as organizations, attempt to capture individual votes by adjusting their program to relevant individual interests. Obviously, no single party usually succeeds in capturing support from the entire electorate, since constituent interests are heterogeneous and often conflicting. Therefore, parties must restrict their mobilization efforts to a subset of the population with relatively homogeneous interests (Przeworski, 1975). This subset of the social environment is the one that the party can exploit most efficiently given its program, in that it can generate stronger commitment among the individuals in this subset and capture their votes. The subset of the population to which a party directs its appeal may be thought of as its natural basis of support. Members of the subset presumably tend to share a number of socioeconomic, cultural, and demographic characteristics.

In the population ecology perspective of organizations articulated by Hannan and Freeman (1977), central concepts are organizational forms, environments, and dimensions of the environment that determine the success of particular organizational forms.[8] In the present context, parties with different structures and programs are the organizational forms; electoral districts are the environments; and the dimensions of the environment are the social structural variables that characterize the population of a district. This is equivalent to the concept of social environment introduced earlier. The idea of a natural basis of support for a party corresponds to the concept of the *niche* of an organizational form in an environment. The concept of a niche is crucial in the following discussion. Bioecologists distinguish between the fundamental and realized niches of a species. In the current application, the *fundamental niche* of a political organization corresponds to that subset of the electorate from which it could extract votes in the absence of competition by other parties. The *realized niche* is the support the political organization actually obtains given the presence of competing parties in the political environment. When competing parties are present, the fundamental niche of the party normally contracts, as some voters find the program of a competitor more attractive. However, when a competitor (real or potential) fails to penetrate the political arena, the niche expands to include voters who would have supported the competitor but are unable to do so.[9]

The variable niche model can be applied to Pinard's (1971, 1975) discussion of mechanisms of structural conduciveness. First, parties with expanded niches (i.e., where competitors are absent), everything else constant, are likely to be more affected by a redefinition of political alignments, such as the emergence of an outsider party, than are parties with compressed niches. This is because voters are likely to be only weakly attached to the party: they support it only because there is no better alternative. In ecological terminology, parties with expanded niches exploit inefficiently (generate weak identification in) part of their environment. When an alternative becomes available, the half-hearted membership is likely to defect quickly. The above discussion can be summarized in the following proposition.

PROPOSITION 1. *Parties in environments in which their niches are expanded should loose more support with the rise of an outsider party than should parties with contracted niches. This proposition may be viewed as the converse of Pinard's central thesis on outsider parties.*

Second, an outsider party is a new competitor invading the social environment. When the outsider party faces other parties with expanded niches, it should be able to attract their weakly identified fringe memberships quickly. Therefore:

PROPOSITION 2. *Environments in which existing parties have expanded niches should be conducive to the success of an outsider party. This is the ecological analog of Pinard's main argument.*

The variable niche model thus yields two theoretical expectations: one with respect to the traditional parties (Proposition 1) one with respect to outsider parties (Proposition 2). I now turn to the problem of measuring the key concept of niche expansion.

B. Niche Compression and Political Diversity

Empirical measurement and testing of political environmental mechanisms of structural conduciveness are complicated by the need to control for characteristics of the social environment. A large proportion of votes for a party in a district does not necessarily indicate that the niche of this party is expanded. Support can be large because social structural conditions are such that the natural basis of support for the party in the district is large. The concept of niche expansion rests on the possibility of distinguishing between this natural following and the fraction of support generated by the lack of a better alternative.

However, I will first use an uncontrolled indicator of niche contraction, *political diversity*, to test the conduciveness propositions in their raw form, to see if there is any superficial merit to them. If one were to assume that the natural bases of support for parties are equal, and social structural characteristics are similar across districts (these are *ceteris paribus* conditions), political diversity would be an indicator of pure niche contraction. Later, I will introduce controls for social structural factors.

Political diversity is calculated by the Shannon–Wiener formula

$$H = \sum_i P_i \ln (1/P_i)$$

where H is the diversity index, P_i is the proportion of votes for party i, and ln is the natural logarithm. The measure, derived from information theory, has been extensively studied by ecologists (Pielou, 1969, pp. 221–235, 1975) and economists (Theil, 1971, pp. 636–644).[10] Given N parties in the political environment, the maximum value of H, reached when each party receives a fraction $1/N$ of the vote, is $\ln N$. Therefore, the index captures both the notions of the number of competitors and the evenness of their successes. For example, in a two-party system, H has its maximum value when each party receives 50% of the votes and is small when one party has a large majority. In such a system, diversity is always negatively related to one-party dominance. However, in a multiparty system the relationship between diversity and one-party dominance as measured by Pinard (1971), as the weakness of the main opposition, is less straightforward. Given a majority, diversity is higher when the rest of the votes are equally split between the other competitors, while the main opposition is obviously weaker in that case. The diversity index, justified by the variable niche model, is more akin to Pinard's (1975) extension of his model in terms of the nonrepresentation of groups.[11]

In the next section I examine the relationships between political diversity and both the success of the Flemish movement and the decline of the Catholic party in Flanders after World War II.

IV. POLITICAL DIVERSITY AND THE RISE OF THE FLEMISH MOVEMENT AFTER WORLD WAR II

As argued earlier, it is important to consider mechanisms of structural conduciveness in connection with the emergence of parties defined along ethnic lines because the political system may have been previously characterized by a situation of peripheral sectionalism, with a high degree of niche expansion for a party that is not explicitly ethnic but agrees best with ethnic feelings of the electorate. This inflated support for one party, relative to its natural membership determined by social structural variables, should correspond *ceteris paribus* to lower political diversity and a situation conducive to outsider party success.

In the following subsections, I investigate the rise of the Flemish movement in Flanders after World War II, using as an indicator the proportion of votes for the Flemish movement (mostly the Volksunie). I use electoral and census indicators at the canton (district) level, which are fully described elsewhere (Nielsen, 1978a, 1980). The sample consists of 96 cantons in the Flemish region selected for cultural homogeneity (an overwhelming majority of Flemish speakers) and a reasonable degree of geographical continuity over time.

A. The Rise of the Flemish Movement

The evolution of support for the four major parties during the eight elections from 1950 to 1974 is described in Table 1. Salient features of the table are continued dominance, but steady decline, of the Catholic party during the period (from 65.70% in 1950 to 42.91% in 1974, unweighted canton averages) and the corresponding electoral gain of the Flemish movement (from 0% in 1950 to 16.12% in 1974). Support for the Socialists remain relativement constant during the period, while Liberal support increases somewhat. Average political diversity, computed for each election by the Shannon–Wiener formula, is presented in the last column of Table 1. The political system exhibits a steady increase in average diversity, from 0.844 in 1950 to 1.328 in 1974. This increase in diversity is largely related to the decline in Catholic support and the growth in Flemish support. However, the increase in average diversity is paralleled by a steady decline in the coefficient of variation (the standard deviation divided by the mean), from 0.263 in 1950 to 0.081 in 1974. This trend indicates that cantons are becoming more similar during the period in the diversity of their political alignment.[12]

The general evolution of the political system summarized in Table 1 can be interpreted as representing a shift from a sectionalist to an explicitly ethnic

TABLE 1. Evolution of support for the four major parties in Flemish cantons, 1950–1974,[a] with average political diversity (Shannon–Wiener)[b]

Election year	Socialists	Liberals	Catholics	Flemish	Political diversity
1950	22.41	9.91	65.70	0	0.844
Standard deviation	9.15	6.34	12.75	—	0.222
Skewness	0.25	0.54	0.05	—	−0.522
Coefficient of variation	0.41	0.64	0.19	—	0.263
1954	25.48	11.38	57.52	4.06	1.017
Standard deviation	9.55	7.32	12.81	2.73	0.203
Skewness	0.13	0.58	0.18	2.38	−0.566
Coefficient of variation	0.37	0.64	0.22	0.67	0.200
1958	24.18	10.52	61.92	3.20	0.917
Standard deviation	9.59	6.97	12.50	1.86	0.190
Skewness	0.37	0.62	−0.01	2.80	−0.580
Coefficient of variation	0.40	0.66	0.20	0.58	0.207
1961	25.34	11.73	56.31	5.39	1.074
Standard deviation	8.88	6.68	12.04	2.70	0.166
Skewness	0.21	0.72	0.12	1.12	−0.600
Coefficient of variation	0.35	0.57	0.21	0.50	0.155
1965	21.41	16.20	48.97	11.16	1.234
Standard deviation	7.94	7.93	11.90	4.82	0.157
Skewness	0.37	0.41	0.21	1.17	−0.384
Coefficient of variation	0.37	0.49	0.24	0.43	0.127
1968	23.04	15.51	44.14	16.09	1.276
Standard deviation	7.86	7.36	10.64	5.31	0.119
Skewness	0.23	0.37	0.17	0.66	−0.485
Coefficient of variation	0.34	0.47	0.24	0.33	0.093
1971	22.00	16.90	41.14	18.20	1.319
Standard deviation	8.30	7.74	9.00	6.07	0.097
Skewness	0.33	0.58	0.23	0.26	−0.234
Coefficient of variation	0.38	0.46	0.22	0.33	0.074
1974	20.09	18.12	42.91	16.12	1.328
Standard deviation	7.40	7.98	8.86	5.23	0.107
Skewness	0.18	0.69	0.23	0.06	−0.157
Coefficient of variation	0.37	0.44	0.21	0.32	0.081

[a] Averages (unweighted) of cantons percentages ($N = 102$). The figures *do not* correspond to the total percentages of votes in Flemish cantons. The coefficient of variation is an indicator of territorial heterogeneity obtained by dividing the standard deviation by the mean.
[b] See text for computation formula of Shannon–Wiener index of diversity.

expression of ethnic solidarity in Flanders. First, most political observers (e.g., Roy, 1968; Hill, 1974) agree that Catholic support included much that was generated by ethnic and regional feelings rather than the purely religious appeal of the party. Second, there is the traditional dominance of the Catholics in Flanders as contrasted with the Socialist dominance in the French-speaking parts of the country. While this is not, in itself, a proof of the sectionalist appeal of the Catholic party in Flanders, it strongly suggests a regional-ethnic coloration of its support. Finally, analyses of survey data on political preferences of Belgian voters (Delruelle, Evalenko, and Fraeys, 1970; Hill, 1974) show that the basis of support for the Catholic party is heterogeneous with respect to occupational status. This suggests a low salience of the class factor among Catholic voters. Therefore, one can speculate that the Flemish movement, particularly after the creation of the Volksunie in 1954, provided a *specialized alternative,* in terms of a program focusing on ethnic and regional issues, to ethnic feelings previously expressed through a sectionalist Catholic vote. This makes the historical episode similar to the rise of the Plaid Cymru in Wales studied by Ragin and Davies (1981). [See also Hechter (1975) and Ragin (1979, 1980)].

B. Diversity and Electoral Trends

The two propositions derived from the variable niche model suggest that:

(1) Catholic party losses should be greater in environments with low political diversity.
(2) Flemish party success should be greater in those environments.

To examine the two hypotheses, I use as a dependent variable the trend in percentage party support during the elections from 1954 to 1974 in each canton. This amounts to a temporally aggregated measure of success.[13] Testing hypotheses involving the effect of political diversity on the evolution of support for one party or another can easily become tautological, since diversity is computed precisely from the relative proportions of votes. To avoid this problem, I measure the diversity of the political environment in 1950, an election in which the Flemish movement did not participate. The temporal ordering guarantees one-directional causality.

The trend for Catholic support for each of the 96 cantons is plotted against diversity in 1950 in Figure 1. The range of values on the vertical axis (from −9.26 to −64.20, measured as the percent gain in 10 elections) indicates that the Catholic party has lost on the average in every canton in the sample. Keeping in mind that a smaller absolute value of the trend indicates a higher degree of success (or resistance) over the 20-year period considered, Figure 1 shows that Catholic success is strongly, and positively, associated with the diversity of the political environment. This party, presumably the most vulnerable to niche expansion, has maintained its support better in more diverse environments, a result consistent with Proposition 1. The correlation between diversity and trend is 0.757 and is significant at the 0.001 level. The relationship is also strikingly linear, which is remarkable given that the Shannon–Wiener formula involves the percentages of the votes in a nonlinear way. Linearity makes it legitimate to estimate the simple regression of Catholic trend on diversity. The slope of the

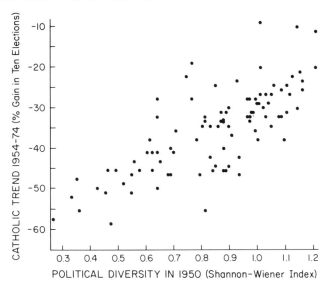

FIG. 1.   Relationship between maintenance of Catholic support in 96 Flemish cantons during 1954–1974 period and political diversity in 1950 (Shannon–Wiener index). See text for discussion of the political diversity index. Catholic trend represents the average gain in percent support for the party in a canton over the seven elections held between 1954 and 1974, measured as percent gain in 10 elections. A negative trend indicates that the party has been losing support over the period. Correlation = 0.757. Estimated regression line, $Y = -65.99 + 36.588X$. Standard error $b = 7.1$; $N = 96$ ($p < 0.001$).

regression is 36.588, so that an increase of one unit of diversity in 1950 prevents a loss of more than 3.6% per election for the party. This result is consistent with the variable niche model: low-diversity environments were those in which the Catholic party had an expanded niche and was therefore more vulnerable in competition with the Flemish movement.

The second hypotheses derived from the variable niche model is closer to the original conduciveness model of Pinard (1971, 1975): Flemish success, insofar as the party starts as an outsider, should be greater in political environments with low political diversity. The Flemish trend is plotted against diversity in Figure 2, using the same technique as for Figure 1.

The variable niche model predicts a negative relationship. Overall, the correlation associated with the plot of Figure 2 is negative (-0.142), which is in the expected direction. However, the relationship is not at all as sharp as the one exhibited in Figure 1. The significance level for the correlation is only 0.083 and, more important, the relationship appears curvilinear, with a negative slope in the rightmost two-thirds of the plot and a positive one in the leftmost third.

A comparison of Figure 1 and Figure 2 points to an interesting inconsistency. The political environmental model of niche expansion seems more appropriate,

184

FRANÇOIS NIELSEN

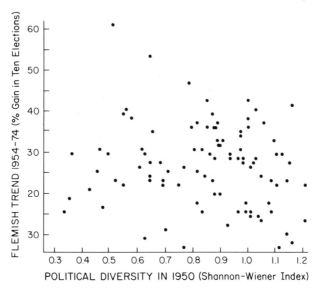

FIG. 2. Relationship between Flemish success in 96 Flemish cantons during 1954–1974 period and political diversity in 1950. See text and Figure 1 for details. Correlation = -0.142. Estimated regression line, $Y = 32.84 - 6.442X$. Standard error $b = 10.029$; $N = 96$.

at least in the simple form in which it is implemented here, to the loss of the dominant party than to the success of the new competitor. In a politically diverse environment, the Catholic party maintains its position much better, as if its support had already been shaven by competition to yield the core membership of the party: the voters most seriously committed to party organization, with the strongest identifications, and least likely to be recruited by competing mobiliza-tion drives. By contrast, Flemish success is weakly related to diversity. This finding also casts doubt on the simple argument in terms of Catholic defectors that could be construed on the basis of the historical trends in aggregate evolu-tions of support that were evident in Table 1. If most of the support for the Flemish movement had been recruited among Catholic defectors, the Catholic and Flemish trends would tend to offset each other at the canton level, and one would expect the relationships between trends of the two parties and political diversity to be mirror images of each other. A comparison of Figures 1 and 2 shows this is not the case. The data are inconsistent with the simple individual model of the shift in membership from the Catholic to the Flemish party.[14]

V. POLITICAL DIVERSITY AND THE SOCIAL STRUCTURE

The bivariate analyses of the previous section involved only political environ-mental variables: political diversity and electoral trends. The absence of a strong effect of political diversity on Flemish success (Figure 2) may be due to the lack of control for the social environment. It may be that social structural characteristics, insofar as they determine both political diversity and the size of the natural basis of support for the new ethnic party, have conflicting effects on party success. On the one hand, low diversity may be conducive to penetration by the new party. On the other, low political diversity may be characteristic of a social environment in which the new party has a low natural basis of support. In that case, political environments and social environmental effects are in opposite directions, which would explain the weak or inconsistent relationship between diversity and success observed for the Flemish movement. In the present context, effects in opposite directions may occur if the social structural conditions of ethnic mobilization expressed as a specialized movement (such as the Volksunie) are different from those associated with the sectionalist response.

A. Social Correlates of Political Diversity

To investigate this possibility, a first task is to examine social structural correlates of political diversity. As before, I use political diversity measured on the 1950 returns, so that the measure cannot be influenced by Flemish success. The social structural variables (S_1 to S_6) are six indicators of development from the 1961 census, standardized per capita: the number of housing units in one-family houses, a negative measure of urbanization [see Jouret (1972)]; the male labor force in agriculture and fishing; the floor area (in 100 square meters) used for industrial activities; the male and female labor force employed in commercial activities; the active population working outside the commune of residence; and total income, in millions of Belgian francs. [See Nielsen (1978a, 1980) for a more complete discussion of the nature and sources of these data.]

Correlations between political diversity and the six social structural indicators are presented in Table 2. Salient features of the table are the negative correlation of political diversity with employment in agricultural activities (-0.294) and the positive correlations with industrialization (0.170), employment in the tertiary sector (commerce) (0.539), and income (0.501). (These correlations are all significant at the 0.05 level.) Taken together, these results suggest that there was in 1950 a positive relationship between development and political diversity: those cantons that were most developed, in terms of low employment in the primary sector, high employment in the secondary and tertiary sectors, and higher income, were also more diverse politically.

B. Social Correlates of Ethnic Mobilization

The second part of the argument made at the beginning of this section concerns the effects of social structural characteristics of the environment on ethnic mobilization. Here, the literature on ethnic resurgences provides clues as to the nature of these effects. The ethnic competition perspective (e.g., Hannan, 1979; Ragin, 1979; Nielsen, 1980, 1985; Olzak, 1982; Banton, 1983; Portes, 1984) postulates

TABLE 2. Correlations between political diversity 1950 (Shannon–Wiener index) and selected social structural indicators (1961)[a]

	Political diversity	Structural indicator					
		S_1	S_2	S_3	S_4	S_5	S_6
Political	—	0.335	−0.294	0.170	0.539	0.151	0.501
diversity		(0.000)	(0.002)	(0.049)	(0.000)	(0.072)	(0.000)
S_1		—	0.266	0.069	0.152	−0.218	−0.165
			(0.004)	(0.252)	(0.070)	(0.017)	(0.054)
S_2			—	−0.389	−0.262	−0.299	−0.690
				(0.001)	(0.005)	(0.002)	(0.001)
S_3				—	0.181	−0.070	0.365
					(0.039)	(0.251)	(0.001)
S_4					—	−0.115	0.600
						(0.132)	(0.001)
S_5						—	0.185
							(0.035)
S_6							—

[a]Social structural variables S_1 to S_6 standardized per capita. Levels of significance in parentheses. Definitions of variables are as follows: S_1, housing units in one-family houses; S_2, male labor force in agriculture and fishing; S_3, industrial floor area (in 100 square meters); S_4, male and female labor force in commercial activities; S_5, actives working outside the commune of residence; S_6, income (millions of Belgian francs).

that as development affects different ethnic groups more homogeneously, assignments of individuals to occupations and the distribution of societal rewards tend to be made increasingly on the basis of rational and achieved criteria that crosscut ethnic boundaries. In such a situation, members of different groups find themselves increasingly in a position to compete for the same occupations and rewards. The competitive tensions are manifested by ethnic mobilization and conflict.

The competition perspective implies that ethnic mobilization should be more successful in more developed environments. The positive association between development and mobilization has been demonstrated empirically in the case of the Flemish movement in Belgium (Nielsen, 1980). Social structural characteristics associated with development, then, can affect ethnic mobilization in two conflicting ways through social environmental and political environmental processes. Figure 3 depicts symbolically such a situation and summarizes the previous discussion.

The horizontal dotted line in Figure 3 separates the social and political environments. Development, a characteristic of the social environment, is associated with greater diversity of the political environment. The negative sign associated with the arrow from diversity to Flemish success corresponds to the inhibiting effect of diversity on the success of the movement because of the lower

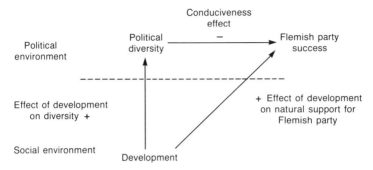

FIG. 3.   Direct and indirect effects of social environment on Flemish party success.

conduciveness of the political environment (Proposition 2). Therefore, the indirect effect of development on Flemish mobilization is negative. On the other hand, development has a direct positive effect on the natural basis of support for the movement, denoted by the plus sign on the corresponding arrow. When the level of development is not taken into account in a bivariate analysis such as the one in Figure 2, the negative direct effect of political diversity on Flemish success may be suppressed and the relationship spuriously appear to be absent. The analytical problem associated with the model of Figure 3 is that it is not easy to differentiate between the direct and indirect effects of the social environment on Flemish success. Since political diversity is itself a function of support for the movement, usual regression techniques applied directly to the model would be meaningless. Section VI discusses a method to disentangle these two categories of effects.

VI. DYNAMICS OF ETHNIC MOBILIZATION

The discussion in previous sections suggests that while the variable niche model alone seems appropriate to explain the decline of the Catholic party after World War II, it fails to explain the rise of the Flemish movement. I argued that confounding effects of social structural characteristics are responsible for this ambiguity. The purpose of this section is to reformulate the variable niche model in a dynamic framework, discuss various mathematical and statistical aspects of the reformulation, and present empirical results.

A. Protest and Radical Voting

In the elaboration of his model of political conduciveness, Pinard (1975, pp. 280–284) proposes distinguishing between two types of outsider parties: protest movements and radical movements. Protest movements tend to be based on "weakly articulated generalized beliefs of discontent" (p. 281) and recruitment for these movements is relatively independent from social structural factors. The success of protest movements is a symptom of the temporary dissatisfaction of the electorate with existing parties and the relationship between the movement's ideology and the social structure is of lesser importance. By contrast, "in a radical movement, . . . one is more likely to have been recruited on the basis of an ideology shared by the members of a specific social class or communal group" (pp. 281–282). Therefore, success of radical movements should be more dependent on the correspondence between their ideology and social structural conditions.[15] Pinard also explicitly introduces dynamic considerations in comparing the two types of movements. He argues that "protest movements should have an advantage, compared to radical movements, in rapidly recruiting a large following. Conversely, . . . the decline (of a protest movment) could be quite swift once the grievances have disappeared" (pp. 283–284). This discussion implies a distinction between what was called earlier the natural basis of support for a party and the speed of mobilization of support for this party.

It is useful in the present context to elaborate Pinard's distinction between types of movements even further. It may happen that a given movement appears for different subsets of the electorate either as a protest or a radical movement. Voting for the outsider party may be an act of "protest" for some and a "radical" choice for others. Therefore, some social environments may have a low natural basis of support for the party but the latter may be able to mobilize quickly the fringe memberships of other parties, and vice versa. If this is the case, it is possible to distinguish between social enviornmental and political environmental effects on outsider party success by modeling the dynamics of the mobilization process in such a way as to obtain separate estimates of the natural basis of support (a function of social structural characteristics) and the speed of mobilization.

Pinard's discussion implies that the political environment may affect only the speed of mobilization for the outsider party, not its eventual success, which depends on social environmental factors. In the terminology of the variable niche model, voters in the low-diversity environments in which parties have expanded niches should be more prone to a protest, rather than radical, response to the outsider party, and mobilization should proceed more quickly. This view leads to a dynamic reformulation of Proposition 2:

PROPOSITION 3.   *Mobilization for an outsider party should be faster, controlling for its natural basis of support, in environments characterized by a low degree of political diversity.*

B. A Dynamic Model of Mobilization

Empirical tests of Proposition 3 necessitate estimating the speed of mobilization net of the effects of social structural variables on the natural basis of support.

To do this I use a linear differential equation model of a type that has been extensively studied (Coleman, 1968; Doreian and Hummon, 1976; Nielsen and Rosenfeld, 1981; Rosenfeld and Nielsen, 1984). The model used for estimation is a regression equation with support at election t as the dependent variable, and support at the preceding election and the six social structural indicators introduced above, measured at the time of the preceding election, as the independent variables. In equation form, the model is

$$P_t = b'P_{t-1} + c_0' + c_1'S_{1,t-1} + c_2'S_{2,t-1} + \cdots + c_6'S_{6,t-1} + W_t \qquad (1)$$

where P_t denotes party support at election t, c_0' is a constant term, and S_1 to S_6 are the six social structural indicators of development introduced earlier (see Table 2). W_t denotes a random disturbance.

Equation (1) can be interpreted as the integral equation corresponding to a continuous model of political mobilization represented by a differential equation of the form

$$dP/dt = -b(P^* - P) \qquad (2)$$

In Eq. (2), P denotes the current level of support and P^* represents the natural basis of support for the party in the social environment. Since the exact form of the functional relationship between the natural basis of support for the party and characteristics of the social environment is not known, I assume a linear one, which is the simplest possible:

$$P^* = C_0 + c_1S_1 + c_2S_2 + \cdots + c_6S_6 \qquad (3)$$

where the S symbols have the same meaning as in Eq. (1).

The dynamic model of mobilization, represented by Eqs. (2) and (3) combined, assumes that there is a natural basis of support P^* for a party given characteristics of the social environment. However, a party does not mobilize its natural electorate instantaneously. Equation (2), in which dP/dt denotes the instantaneous rate of mobilization, describes the way in which support is assumed to grow or decline. The growth in support is proportional to the discrepancy between the natural basis of support and current participation. The model assumes that b is negative. Then $-b$ is positive and support for the party increases (dP/dt is positive) when current support is smaller than its natural one in the social environment. When current support P is larger than P^*, participation declines. In both cases, P reaches its equilibrium value P^* as time elapses.

The absolute value of the parameter b determines the speed at which the process of mobilization (or demobilization) takes place. A large absolute value of b means that the party recruits its potential membership quickly; a small absolute value of b indicates slow mobilization. Pinard's (1975) discussion of the differences in speed of mobilization between protest and radical movements implies that protest movements, insofar as they are able to recruit a sizable membership quickly, should have their mobilization equations characterized by a larger absolute value of b compared to radical movements.

Coleman (1968) has shown that it is possible to manipulate the coefficients of the regression equation [Eq. (1)] in a straightforward way to obtain estimates of the dynamic model represented by Eqs. (2) and (3). I will not reproduce these mathematical derivations here [see, e.g., Nielsen and Rosenfeld (1981)]. The important point is that explicit dynamic modeling, using differential equations, provides a methodology to distinguish between social environmental and political environmental (conduciveness) effects on outsider party success. To investigate Proposition 3, I estimate the coefficients of Eq. (1) separately for cantons that were below or above the median value of political diversity in 1950. If mechanisms of structural conduciveness operate for the rise of ihe Flemish movement, the speed of mobilization, measured as the absolute value of the coefficient b in (2), should be greater in cantons characterized by a low degree of political diversity in 1950, since this situation should correspond to a higher degree of niche expansion and a greater likelihood of a protest response by voters. Before presenting the results, I discuss statistical aspects of the model briefly.

C. Statistical Considerations

Equation (1) has the form of a linear equation with lagged dependent variable. Given the data available, Eq. (1) could be estimated using electoral results, and the corresponding values of the socioeconomic variables, for any one of the six pairs of election years from 1954 to 1974.[16] Rather than estimating Eq. (1) in six different ways, I pooled all the data into a single model. This technique of pooling time series and cross-section data has been discussed extensively by Hannan and Young (1977) [see also Rosenfeld and Nielsen (1984)]. It permits dealing with an estimation problem that plagues most analyses of panel data in sociology: the autocorrelation of disturbances. Disturbances are correlated when stable characteristics of a canton, such as the distance from the capital, have been omitted from Eq. (1). These unmeasured features of the social environment are forced into the disturbance term W_t in Eq. (1) and, since they presumably operate at every point in time, disturbances are correlated over time and with the lagged value of the dependent variable. Consequently, ordinary least-squares estimators applied to Eq. (1) are biased and inconsistent.

Autocorrelation of disturbances is not the only estimation problem in this case. Preliminary analyses indicated that the absolute values of the residuals increase sharply with the size of the canton, as measured by the total number of valid votes. This finding suggests that the distribution of disturbances is heteroscedastic (the variance of disturbances is not constant). Heteroscedasticity implies that ordinary least-squares estimators of Eq. (1) are also inefficient. To control for both autocorrelation of the disturbances and heteroscedasticity, I used a generalized least-squares estimator labeled WGLS ("weighted generalized least-squares"). The derivation of the WGLS procedure is quite technical. A detailed discussion may be found in Nielsen (1978a, Chapter 6, Appendices A and B).

D. Results

Results of the estimation of the model represented by Eq. (1) are presented in Table 3. The two columns on the left of the table contain the raw regression coefficients of the model of Eq. (1), estimated by the WGLS method. The numbers in the two columns on the right of the table are computed from the regression coefficients and constitute the parameters of substantive interest in the present context, since they correspond to the parameters b of Eq. (2) and c_1, c_2,

TABLE 3. Regression of Flemish vote on support at preceding election (FLE_t, dependent variable) and socioeconomic indicators: comparison of cantons according to political diversity in 1950, with regression coefficients (WGLS estimates) and coefficients of differential equations model[a]

Independent variables	Regression coefficients for political diversity 1950		Coefficients of differential equations for political diversity 1950	
	Low	High	Low	High
Lagged party support	0.549[b]	0.608[b]	−0.600[b]	−0.498[b]
	(0.052)	(0.049)		
S_1, Housing units in one-family houses	0.024	−0.007	0.053	−0.018
	(0.050)	(0.017)		
S_2, Male labor force in agriculture and fishing	0.078	−0.099	0.173	−0.253
	(0.136)	(0.108)		
S_3, Industrial floor area (100 square meters)	−0.058	−0.044[b]	−0.129	−0.112[b]
	(0.054)	(0.016)		
S_4, Male and female labor force in commerce	0.260	0.549[b]	0.576	1.401[b]
	(0.238)	(0.120)		
S_5, Actives working outside commune of residence	−0.001	0.054[b]	−0.002	0.138[b]
	(0.051)	(0.019)		
S_6, Income (millions of Belgian francs)	0.986[b]	0.253	2.186[b]	0.645
	(0.301)	(0.172)		
Constant	−25.221	−45.395	−55.922	−115.804
	(153.44)	(107.59)		
R^2	0.902	0.944		

[a]Cantons assigned to the low or high political diversity set according to their position below or above median value of Shannon–Wiener political diversity index computed on 1950. Number of cases in each set, 48. Number of time periods, 6. Total number of cases in each pooled regression, 288. Weighting variables, number of valid votes at time t.

[b]Regression coefficient significant at 0.05 level.

..., c_6 of Eq. (3). The coefficient b for the low-diversity sample (-0.600) is larger in absolute value than the one estimated for the high-diversity sample (-0.498).[17] This finding lends support to Proposition 3, the dynamic version of the political conduciveness hypotheses: controlling for the natural basis of support for the Flemish movement, a function of social structural variables, the mobilization process is quicker in less diverse environments. There is, therefore, an autonomous effect of the political environment on Flemish success, manifested as a greater speed of mobilization.

The effects of social structural variables on P^*, the natural basis of support for the Flemish movement, provide additional indirect evidence for the variable niche model. These effects, the parameters of Eq. (3), are estimated in the two columns on the right side of Table 3. These coefficients can be meaningfully compared across samples because they are corrected for differences in the dynamics of mobilization in the two types of environments. An interesting difference between the two subsets of cantons emerges. For the subset of cantons characterized by a low degree of political diversity in 1950, there are no significant coefficients (see the leftmost column of Table 3), except for income, which is more than three times as large as the corresponding standard error of estimate. In low-diversity environments, therefore, support for the ethnic party is positively associated with a generalized indicator of development, income, but does not seem to depend on variations in the occupational structure (measured by such indicators as the employment in agriculture, commercial activities, and the degree of industrialization).

In the high-diversity subset, by contrast, the regression coefficient associated with income is insignificant, but the coefficients of industrialization (-0.112), employment in commercial activities (1.401), and employment outside the commune of residence (0.138) are significant. Such results are consistent with the variable niche model. In high-diversity environments, the ethnic party competes with groups that have had their membership reduced by competition to the hard core determined by the social structure. Therefore, the bases of support for different parties, including the Flemish party, are more sharply differentiated with respect to occupational cleavages. For example, the negative coefficient associated with the indicator of industrialization must be interpreted in light of the fact that the working class in Flanders has traditionally been strongly organized through the network of grass-roots organizations (such as trade unions) of both the Socialist party and the liberal wing of the Catholic party. Intense competition from both entrenched groups, with their specialized institutions, makes penetration difficult for an outsider party, such as the Flemish movement, with a less specialized definition on class lines.

To summarize the argument above, it is normal to expect that success of an outsider party will be more strongly determined by the social structure in environments with high political diversity, because the political environment has already been invaded by groups that specialize in the recruitment of electoral resources from particular categories of voters defined by occupational criteria. To use Hechter's (1975) terminology, politically diverse environments are characterized by a low degree of sectionalism and a high degree of political integration. In low political diversity environments, outsider party success should depend less on the occupational distribution, since the existing composition of supports corresponds to a less perfect mapping of occupational sectors.

A final remark to be made concerning the effects of social structural indicators on Flemish support is that, in both samples, the results support the competition model of ethnic mobilization: the movement has a larger natural basis of support in more developed environments [see also Nielsen (1980)]. I will return to this topic in the next section.

VII. CONCLUSION

The central purpose of this chapter was to investigate circumstances surrounding the emergence of ethnic parties in peripheries characterized by a tradition of sectionalism. Two distinct categories of factors affect the success of the new ethnic party in a local environment such as an electoral district: the structure of the social environment and the conduciveness of the political environment. An ecological reformulation of Pinard's (1971, 1975) model of structural conduciveness yielded predictions concerning conditions conducive to both the success of the new party and the loss of the older dominant party. Crude bivariate analyses revealed that the conduciveness model could explain the loss of the dominant Catholic party but not the success of the Flemish movement in Flanders: political diversity and Flemish success are only weakly related.

I argued that this inconsistency is due to the way development affects ethnic mobilization in opposite directions through social-environmental and political-environmental processes. On the one hand, development is associated with greater political diversity, which lowers the conduciveness of the political environment for outsider parties. On the other, development creates a larger basis of support for the ethnic party in the social environment. A comparison of the dynamics of mobilization in environments with high or low political diversity yielded results consistent with this interpretation.

Other clues gathered in the course of the analysis shed additional light on the meaning of this historical episode. These clues point to mechanisms that might be of general relevance in other instances of the phenomenon, such as the rise of the Plaid Cymru in Wales (Ragin and Davies, 1981) or the Parti Québecois in Canada (Olzak, 1982). First, the asymmetrical relationships of the Catholic and Flemish trends with a third variable, political diversity (Figures 1 and 2), exclude a massive switch of Catholic voters to the Volksunie as a major factor in the rise of the new party. This suggests that the meanings of ethnic solidarity expressed as sectionalism (support for the Catholic party) and expressed as explicit ethnic voting (support for the Volksunie) are different, in the sense that the two responses are typical of different groups of voters. Furthermore, votes lost by the Catholic party during this period of 24 years must have been allocated elsewhere, largely to the Socialists (a working-class party) or the Liberals (in Belgium, a party representing laical-conservative interests).[18] This implies that the evolution of political alignments during the period has incorporated a trend toward greater national political integration in Hechter's (1975) sense, and away from sectionalism.

Second, the previous conclusion is consistent with the observed increase in the average political diversity of cantons, together with the decrease in the variation of diversity across cantons. As pointed out earlier, this trend is likely to be associated with the industrialization of Flanders during the period and the spread to outlying areas of a standard system of political alignments typical of a developed society. This again points to an increased importance of structural characteristics in the determination of electoral behavior in a local setting.

Finally, the results of Section VI show that support for the Flemish movement is more strongly determined by social structural features (such as the occupational distribution) in environments characterized by a high degree of political diversity. Specifically, Flemish support is positively associated with employment in the tertiary sector, and negatively associated with employment in industry and agriculture. This pattern indicates a degree of specialization of the party in catering to the more economically advanced occupational categories.

Taken together with the main results of the analysis, these clues suggest that ethnic parties have a natural, stable niche in developed polyethnic societies. The rather strong association between ethnic mobilization and the shift from the primary and secondary to the tertiary sector indicates a definite structural basis of the movement. !n that sense, ethnic voting may well be an integral part of national political integration, as defined by Hechter (1975). Ethnic mobilization may be the most rewarding form of expression of the interests of the new middle-class, white-collar strata in the culturally heterogeneous populations (Tiryakian and Rogowski, 1985, p. 376). The ethnic competition perspective discussed above agrees with this conclusion. The important question of why mobilization of the middle class should succeed on the basis of ethnicity, rather than on the seemingly more straightforward basis of occupational position, is beyond the scope of this chapter, although attempts at an answer may be found in Nagel and Olzak (1982) and Nielsen (1985).

ACKNOWLEDGMENTS

I wish to thank Rachel Rosenfeld and the editors of this collection for comments on an earlier version presented at the annual meetings of the American Sociological Association, San Francisco, September 1978.

NOTES

[1]The paradox arises from the difficulty in reconciling such resurgences with the functionalist, Marxist, and even ecological traditions [e.g., Lipset and Rokkan (1967, p. 1–64), Marx (1964), and Park (1950)]. See Ragin (1979), Nielsen (1980, 1985), and Olzak (1983) for discussions.

[2]Hechter (1975) argued that Welsh subnationalism had been traditionally expressed through anti-Conservatism, and that Plaid Cymru success resulted from a disillusionment of the electorate with Labour. See, however, Ragin (1977).

[3]In several European countries, another basis of political affiliation important historically is religion. West Germany and Italy, with their Christian-Democratic parties, are examples. The case of Belgium will be discussed specifically below.

[4]The distinction between social and political environments is akin to the one proposed by Przeworski (1974, p. 34) between social and political contexts.

[5]The revised model of structural conduciveness discussed by Pinard (1975) is no longer purely political environmental, since success of the outsider party depends on the size of the nonrepresented group. The substance of the program set forth by the new party must reflect the preference of that group. It is no longer the case that *any* outsider party succeeds better in conducive environments.

[6]An obvious alternative for the voter is to refrain from voting. In the case of Belgium, which I will discuss later, voting is compulsory. However, voters do have the possibility of protesting the existing party system by deliberately invalidating their ballot, by scribbling obscenities on it, for example. A small but consistent percentage of voters do this at each election.

[7]Hechter (1975) uses this definition directly in his empirical analyses of the Celtic fringe of Britain, in which solidarity is measured as the county residual of conservative voting regressed on a set of social structural variables [see also Ragin (1977)].

[8]See also Lloyd *et al.* (1975) for a similar approach to the ecology of economic organizations and Nielsen (1978b) for an elaboration with respect to collective action in general.

[9]The variable niche model is central in explaining species diversity in biological communities (McArthur and Wilson, 1967, pp. 94–122; McArthur, 1972).

[10]The Gibbs–Martin (1962) index of diversity (or competition, fragmentation, differentiation) is more commonly used in sociology. However, it is less completely theoretically motivated than the Shannon–Wiener index (Pielou, 1969, 1975). The Shannon–Wiener index and the Gibbs–Martin index are strongly correlated in this empirical context, so that the findings presented later would probably be similar if the latter indicator were used.

[11]Despite this theoretical difference, the diversity index is strongly related in practice with two straightforward measures of one-party dominance. Using data to be described later, I found that for the 1950 Belgian election returns, the correlation between diversity and the strength of the main opposition was 0.781. Diversity was also correlated at -0.952 with support for the Catholic party, the dominant party in Flanders at the time. (All but two of the 96 cantons used in that analysis had a Catholic majority.) Both correlations have significance levels smaller than 0.0001. However the strength of the main opposition, which is the negative indicator of political conduciveness proposed by Pinard (1971), performs less well in predicting the success of the Flemish movement and the loss of the Catholic party than political diversity in analyses similar to the ones presented in Figures 1 and 2 in the next section. The correlation between main opposition in 1950 and the 1954–1974 trend for the Catholic party is only 0.729, as opposed to a correlation of 0.757 with diversity; the correlation between Flemish trend and main opposition is only -0.028 (significance 0.392), as opposed to a correlation of -0.142 between the trend and political diversity (significance level 0.083). The main opposition variable, interpreted as a negative measure of the perceived weakness of the opposition by the voter, could have been discounted as of little significance *a priori* given the proportional representation system used in Belgium, by virtue of which an individual vote can have an effect at the level of electoral units (arrondissements and provinces) that are much larger than the local canton. [see Hill (1974)].

[12]This trend is almost certainly associated with the spread of development in Flanders during this period of 24 years, with the resulting spread of a typical "modern" distribution of political alignments. I will return to this topic in the last section.

[13]The trend for each canton is computed as the slope of the regression line of party support on time, assuming that the time interval between elections is constant. This assumption is justified by the fact that the mobilization efforts by parties are likely to be concentrated within a short period before each election. Therefore, with respect to political mobilization, calendar time is likely to be a less useful concept than "political" time, in which the time unit is represented as the interval between two elections.

[14]This reasoning shows that there are situations in which a particular type of individual-level hypothesis (in this case, the individual shift in membership from the Catholic to the Flemish party) can be disconfirmed using only aggregate data at the canton level. The underlying logic of the argument is akin to the instrumental variable method in quantitative methodology, with the instrumental variable being in this case political diversity.

[15]A similar distinction is made by Ragin and Davies (1981, p. 225) with respect to Plaid Cymru in Wales. They distinguish between ethnic voting as a "positive act" reflecting a substantive choice and voting as indicator of "dissatisfaction" with existing alternatives.

[16]Census data are available only for 1961 and 1970, and at the level of the commune, which are subsets of cantons. I obtained values of the social structural variables for each canton at each election year by first aggregating 1961 and 1970 commune data at the canton level and then using linear interpolation and extrapolation from the 1961 and 1970 figures.

[17]A t-test of the difference between the two regression coefficients of lagged party support, from which the b values are calculated, shows that it is not significant at the 0.05 level. However, since the standard errors of the b coefficients of theoretical interest are not known, the significance of their difference cannot be assessed.

[18]Although this reasoning is cast in terms of individual voters switching allegiances, it should be kept in mind that an electorate undergoes considerable turnover during such a long period because of mortality and younger cohorts reaching voting age. In reality, the issue has to do with the relative success of older voters in reproducing their own voting pattern among younger cohorts (Przeworski, 1975).

REFERENCES

BANTON, MICHAEL (1983). *Racial and ethnic competition.* Cambridge, England: Cambridge University Press.

BEER, WILLIAM R. (1980). *The unexpected rebellion: Ethnic activism in contemporary France.* New York: New York University Press.

BONACICH, EDNA (1972). A theory of ethnic antagonism: The split labor market. *American Sociological Review* 37(October):547–559.

COLEMAN, JAMES S. (1968). The mathematical study of change. In *Methodology in Social Research* (H. M. Blalock and A. B. Blalock, eds.), pp. 428–478. New York: McGraw-Hill.

DELRUELLE, NICOLE, EVALENKO, RENÉ, and FRAEYS, WILLIAM (1970). *Le comportement politique des électeurs belges.* Brussels: Institut de Sociologie, University of Brussels.

DOREIAN, PATRICK, and HUMMON, NORMAN P. (1976). *Modeling social processes.* New York: Elsevier.

GIBBS, JACK P., and MARTIN, WALTER T. (1962). Urbanization, technology and the division of labor: International patterns. *American Sociological Review* 27(5, October):667–677.

GLAZER, NATHAN, and MOYNIHAN, DANIEL P. (eds.) (1975). *Ethnicity: theory and experience.* Cambridge, Massachusetts: Harvard University Press.

HANNAN, MICHAEL T. (1979). The dynamics of ethnic boundaries in modern states. In *National development and the world system* (John W. Meyer and Michael T. Hannan, eds.), pp. 253–275. Chicago: University of Chicago Press.

HANNAN, MICHAEL T. and FREEMAN, JOHN (1977). The population ecology of organizations. *American Journal of Sociology* **82**:929–964.

HANNAN, MICHAEL T., and YOUNG, ALICE A. (1977). Estimation in panel models: Results on pooling cross-sections and time series. *Sociological Methodology* **1977**:52–83.

HECHTER, MICHAEL (1975). *Internal colonialism: The Celtic fringe in British national development*. Berkeley: University of California Press.

HECHTER, MICHAEL, FRIEDMAN, DEBRA, and APPLEBAUM, MALKA (1982). A theory of ethnic collective action. *International Migration Review* **16**(2):413–434.

HILL, KEITH (1974). Belgium: Political change in a segmented society. In *Electoral behavior: A comparative handbook* (Richard Rose, ed.), pp. 29–107. New York: Free Press.

JOURET, BERNARD (1972). *Définition spatiale du phénomène urbain bruxellois*. Brussels: Editions de l'Université Libre de Bruxelles.

LIPSET, SEYMOUR H., and ROKKAN, STEIN (1967). *Party systems and voter alignments*. New York: Free Press.

LLOYD, CLIFF, RAPPORT, DAVID, and TURNER, JAMES (1975). The market adaptation of the firm. In *Adaptive Economic Models* (Richard H. Day and Theodore Groves, eds.), pp. 119–135. New York: Academic Press.

MARX, KARL (1964). *Precapitalist economic formations*. Translated by Jack Cohen, edited by E. J. Hobsbawm. New York: International Publishers.

MCARTHUR, ROBERT H. (1972). *Geographical ecology*. New York: Harper and Row.

MCARTHUR, ROBERT H., and WILSON, EDWARD O. (1967). *The theory of island biogeography*. Princeton, New Jersey: Princeton University Press.

MCCARTHY, JOHN D., and ZALD, MAYER N. (1977). Resource mobilization and social movements: A partial theory. *American Journal of Sociology* **82**(6):1212–1241.

NAGEL, JOANE (1984). A structural theory of ethnicity. Paper presented at the annual meeting of the American Sociological Association, San Antonio, Texas, August.

NAGEL, JOANE, and OLZAK, SUSAN (1982). Ethnic mobilization in new and old states: An extension of the competition model. *Social Problems* **30**(2):127–143.

NIELSEN, FRANÇOIS (1978a). *Linguistic conflict in Belgium: An ecological approach*. Ph.D. dissertation, Stanford University, Stanford, California.

NIELSEN, FRANÇOIS (1978b). A competition model of collective action. Paper presented at the 1978 annual meeting of the Southern Sociological Society, New Orleans.

NIELSEN, FRANÇOIS (1980). The Flemish Movement in Belgium after World War II: A dynamic analysis. *American Sociological Review* **45**(February):76–94.

NIELSEN, FRANÇOIS (1985). Toward a theory of ethnic solidarity in modern societies. *American Sociological Review* **50**(April):133–149.

NIELSEN, FRANÇOIS, and ROSENFELD, RACHEL A. (1981). Substantive interpretations of differential equation models. *American Sociological Review* **46**(April):159–174.

OLZAK, SUSAN (1982). Ethnic mobilization in Quebec. *Ethnic and Racial Studies* **5**:253–275.

OLZAK, SUSAN (1983). Contemporary and ethnic mobilization. *Annual Review of Sociology* **9**:355–374.

PARK, ROBERT E. (1950). *Race and culture*. Glencoe, Illinois: Free Press.

PIELOU, E. C. (1969). *An introduction to mathematical ecology*. New York: Wiley.

PIELOU, E. C. (1975). *Ecological diversity*. New York: Wiley.

PINARD, MAURICE (1971, 1975). *The rise of a third party: A study in crisis politics*. First edition. Englewood Cliffs, New Jersey: Prentice-Hall. Second edition (enlarged). Montreal, P. Q.: McGill–Queen's University Press, 1975.

PORTES, ALEJANDRO (1984). The rise of ethnicity: Determinants of ethnic perceptions among Cuban exiles in Miami. *American Sociological Review* **49**(3, June):383–397.

PRZEWORSKI, ADAM (1974). Contextual models of political behavior. *Political Methodology* **1**(1):27–61.

PRZEWORSKI, ADAM (1975). Institutionalization of voting patterns, or is mobilization the source of decay? *American Political Science Review* **69**(1, March):49–67.

RAGIN, CHARLES (1977). Class, status and "reactive ethnic cleavages": The social bases of political regionalism. *American Sociological Review* **42**:438–450.

RAGIN, CHARLES (1979). Ethnic political mobilization: The Welsh case. *American Sociological Review* **44**(August):619–635.

RAGIN, CHARLES (1980). Celtic nationalism in Britain: Political and structural bases. In *Processes of the world-system* (Terence Hopkins and Immanuel Wallerstein, eds.), pp. 249–265. Beverly Hills, California: Sage.

RAGIN, CHARLES, and DAVIES, TED (1981). Welsh nationalism in context. In *Research in social movements, conflict and change,* Vol. 4, (Louis Kriesberg, ed.), pp. 215–233. Greenwich, Connecticut: JAI Press.

ROSENFELD, RACHEL A., and NIELSEN, FRANCOIS (1984). Inequality and careers: A dynamic model of socioeconomic achievement. *Sociological Methods and Research* **12**(3, February):279–321.

ROTHSCHILD, JOSEPH (1981). *Ethnopolitics: A conceptual framework.* New York: Columbia University Press.

ROY, ALBERT DU (1968). *La guerre des Belges.* Paris: Seuil.

SMELSER, NEIL J. (1962). *Theory of collective behavior.* New York: Free Press of Glencoe.

SMITH, ANTHONY D. (1981). *The ethnic revival.* Cambridge, England: Cambridge University Press.

THEIL, HENRI (1971). *Principles of econometrics.* New York: Wiley.

TIRYAKIAN, EDWARD A., and ROGOWSKI, RONALD (1985). *New nationalisms of the developed west.* Boston, Massachusetts: Allen & Unwin.

9

The Impact of Celtic Nationalism on Class Politics in Scotland and Wales

CHARLES C. RAGIN

Department of Sociology
Center for Urban Affairs and Policy Research
Northwestern University
Evanston, Illinois 60201

I. INTRODUCTION

Social scientists usually think of ethnic political mobilization as a challenge to class-based politics. The basic idea is simple: political actors—voters, for example—are influenced by a wide range of possible affiliations, such as class and ethnic memberships, when they engage in political action. When these affiliations are reflected in a nation's system of political cleavages, they channel the behavior of political actors. Some of the many possible bases for affiliation and cleavage are compatible; many are not. By most accounts, class and ethnicity are among the most incompatible affiliations. This is because classes are economically defined and often contain a variety of ethnic groups, while ethnic divisions usually cross-cut class divisions. Thus, a political actor may have difficulty supporting his or her class and ethnic group simultaneously. The former affirms the importance of occupationally based economic divisions; the latter denies them. Furthermore, political mobilization on the basis of class often carries with it an ideological commitment to an end to ethnic divisions. In fact, class mobilization often is successful only when ethnic antagonisms within classes can be disregarded or, better yet, forgotten altogether. Similarly, ethnic mobilization may require a submergence of class antagonisms within an ethnically defined collectivity.

This chapter examines the relationship between class and ethnic affinity in the

COMPETITIVE ETHNIC RELATIONS

Copyright © 1986 by Academic Press, Inc.
All rights of reproduction in any form reserved.

political arena by assessing the impact of ethnic political mobilization on class politics in Great Britain. Britain is an ideal setting for this study for several reasons. First, the country has been highly mobilized along class lines since the early decades of the twentieth century (Pelling, 1968, 1972). Britain is often cited as the (almost) ideal typic class-mobilized polity: there are two dominant parties, each with a clear class constituency and identity. Second, despite the dominance of class politics in all regions of the country, Great Britain is a truly multinational polity (Rose, 1974, p. 20–23). Scotland and Wales were both once independent of England, and they remain culturally distinct. According to some scholars (e.g., Blondel, 1963, p. 26; Alford, 1963, p. 151), Great Britain is a thoroughly modern polity because class thrives as a basis for political mobilization in the face of regionally based ethnic diversity. Third, there was a strong resurgence of support for ethnic parties—the Scottish and Welsh nationalist parties—in Britain during the late 1960s and early 1970s, an outbreak of ethnic political mobilization that has received considerable scholarly attention. In contrast to many previous examinations, this study focuses exclusively on the late 1960s—the period of rapid ethnic mobilization. Fourth, there is a simple and straightforward way to assess the strength of the relationship between class and party support that holds across Celtic and English regions. Thus, it is possible to examine the political tendencies of Celtic regions within the context of polity-wide patterns. [The merits of this strategy are discussed in Ragin and Davies (1981).]

Section II of this chapter presents a brief overview of four perspectives on ethnic political mobilization and extends them by contrasting their different approaches to ethnic political mobilization in class-mobilized polities. Section III examines the British case and then derives specific hypotheses about Celtic nationalism in Britain. Subsequent sections present the results of statistical analyses of data on British constituencies and link the results to the discussion of theoretical perspectives. The basic issues addressed in the analysis are fundamentally descriptive questions with considerable theoretical importance:

(1) What was the fate of class support for the major parties in Scotland and Wales during the period of rapid ethnic mobilization?

(2) Was there a systematic relationship between the degree of support for the nationalist parties and emerging differences in class support?

II. FOUR PERSPECTIVES ON ETHNIC POLITICAL MOBILIZATION

Three of the four perspectives—the developmental perspective, the reactive ethnicity perspective, and the ethnic competition perspective—are well known to most social scientists and require only brief discussion. A fourth, the ethnic subnationalism perspective, is not as formalized as the others, but is important to arguments presented later in the chapter and will be developed in greater detail. None of the four perspectives has been used specifically to address the effect of ethnic political mobilization on class support, although all four have been used to guide examinations of ethnic mobilization in advanced polities such as Great Britain, Belgium, and Canada [see, e.g., Hechter (1975), Ragin (1977, 1979), Nielsen (1980), and Olzak (1982)].

In the developmental perspective, ethnicity is viewed as a primordial sentiment (Geertz, 1963) and is predicted to decline in importance in modern societies once they have experienced significant social structural differentiation (Bell, 1975; Parsons, 1975). In a modern setting, therefore, ethnic mobilization is viewed simply as an historical residue (e.g., of separate administrative institutions established during an earlier period). Furthermore, ethnic mobilization is likely only if there has been some failure to draw culturally distinct, peripheral regions into the developing national economy. This view of ethnic mobilization has been applied to the analysis of political cleavages in Western European countries by Libset and Rokkan (1967, pp. 1–64). They argue that in these countries, culturally based political cleavages tended to be superseded by functional cleavages reflecting economic interests.

According to developmental logic, the ideal typic ethnic minority is a culturally distinct, geographically remote collectivity that has remained outside of the national economic mainstream. Members of the ethnic minority are poorer than members of the dominant cultural group, and they may inhabit a resource-poor region of the nation. In this perspective, ethnic political mobilization occurs because of the growing economic, cultural, and political divergence of the peripheral region from the rest of the nation. Because of their poverty and relative backwardness, minority members may lack an appropriate outlet among the major national parties for the expression of their grievances. (National, as opposed to nationalist, is used in this chapter to refer to parties that are polity-wide.) Regional, ethnic, or populist-agrarian parties should flourish in minority areas until the area is integrated economically with the rest of the nation. Political alignment along class lines, especially of the minority working class with the party of the left, should follow economic advancement and integration. In the developmental perspective, ethnic mobilization in a polity that is already uniformly mobilized along class lines is unlikely.

The second view, the reactive ethnicity perspective, argues that a particularistic allocation of valued roles and resources to members of the dominant cultural group is the primary cause of the persistence of ethnicity and, by implication, minority ethnic political mobilization. In contrast to the developmental perspective, which argues that a particularistic allocation of scarce goods is incompatible with structural differentiation, the reactive ethnicity perspective argues that it can occur in societies at any level of structural differentiation. Thus, ethnic identity is preserved in modern societies by a coincidence of ethnicity and social class [see Gellner (1969)]. This "cultural division of labor," Hechter (1975, p. 38) argues, can exist even in an advanced industrial society. He asserts that urbanization and industrialization intensify the link between social class and ethnicity by concentrating members of the minority in low-status positions and neighborhoods (Hechter, 1975, p. 42).

In common with the developmental perspective, the reactive ethnicity perspective sees the ideal typic ethnic minority as a relatively disadvantaged cultural minority residing in the periphery of an advanced nation-state. However, in this perspective the ethnic region has been infiltrated and exploited by members of the dominant cultural group. The minority region is developed as an appendage of the national economy, and its interests are subordinated to national interests. Furthermore, peripheral social structure is distorted by the cultural division of labor that is instituted. The dominant strata come to be seen as alien by the lower strata, and the culture of the lower strata becomes steroryped as inferior by members of the dominant culture. The minority may become bound to the larger nation through national working class organizations because the cultural division of labor reinforces class divisions and enhances the potential for mobilization along class lines. However, persistent economic problems in the periphery may erode ties to these organizations and promote mobilization of the minority as an ethnic, as opposed to class, collectivity (Hechter, 1975, p. 309).

The ethnic competition perspective (Deutsch, 1953; Van den Berghe, 1967; Barth, 1969; Hannan, 1979; Nagel and Olzak, 1982; Nagel, 1982; Olzak, 1983; Nielsen, 1985), the third major view, argues that social structural modernization affects nations and their component regions in two ways.

(1) Modernization reduces ethnic diversity within regions and within the dominant culture by eroding small-scale or local cultural identities.

(2) Modernization increases the importance of large-scale ethnic identities by altering the conditions of competition between politically definable collectivities [see especially Hannan (1979)].

Specifically, because the size of the most powerful competitor (i.e., the core in a modern nation-state) increases with modernization, organized resistance to the core succeeds only when it is organized around large-scale identities, such as class and ethnicity. Thus, modernization acutally increases the political viability of broadly defined ethnic identities [see Nielsen (1985)]. Ethnic political mobilization is likely when the level of economic competition between ethnic groups (dominant and subordinate) increases and they are forced to compete more directly for the same rewards and resources, especially in the labor market. A competitive situation is likely when a stable cultural division of labor is disrupted [see Ragin (1979), Nielsen (1980)].

In the ethnic competition perspective, the ideal typic ethnic minority may or may not be peripheral. The primary requirement is one of size—it must be big enough in potential membership to muster a significant challenge to the core.

The second major requirement is for some form of structurally based provocation that might increase competition. Many different contexts might provide a basis for ethnic mobilization. Typically, however, this provocation takes the form of new roles, rewards, and resources that draw ethnically defined collectivities into heightened competition. Thus, ethnic mobilization is unlikely to occur in backward regions or in declining regions. It is most likely in areas where positive economic changes create competition between ethnic groups in the labor markets.

Elements of a fourth view, the ethnic subnationalism perspective, exist in the literature on ethnic political mobilization; however, it has been used only in an *ad hoc* manner by a few researchers (e.g., Linz, 1973; Ragin, 1977, 1980; Rothschild, 1981). This fourth perspective is a variation of the ethnic competition perspective but draws special inspiration from theories of nationalism (e.g., Smith, 1971; Nairn, 1977). It applies to regionally concentrated minorities with cultural institutions and internal class differentiation. These cultural and economic resources are often the result of successful prior mobilization against the core cultural group. In such cases, prior mobilization, regionalism, and cultural and economic resources are confounded because they are all mutually reinforcing. However, these special cultural and economic resources also may exist as a consequence of particular historical forces (e.g., the restructuring of national boundaries following a war).

The ethnic subnationalism perspective is primarily concerned with the use of ethnicity in political struggles between established minority and majority populations and emphasizes the choices confronting the dominant strata of the ethnic minority. These strata face two main opponents; the lower strata of the minority population and the dominant strata of the culturally dominant or core population. The first cleavage is a class cleavage within the minority population. The second is an ethnic or cultural cleavage involving culturally distinct class fractions. Ethnic political mobilization may emerge out of this dual conflict because it is an especially attractive option for the dominant strata of the minority population. By sponsoring or at least encouraging ethnic political mobilization, these strata can defuse class conflict within the minority population and, at the same time, gain leverage in their struggles with national and other external elites, especially the dominant strata of the core cultural group. The exercise of this ethnic option by minority dominant strata seems likely in the face of external pressure of some sort (e.g., ethnic competition, threatening economic changes, or the imposition of national policies that discriminate against or disadvantage the minority population in some way). Thus, this perspective emphasizes many of the same causal conditions emphasized by the ethnic competition perspective. The primary difference between the two is the ethnic subnationalism perspective's emphasis on the dominant strata of the minority population.

In the ethnic subnationalism perspective, the ideal typic ethnic minority is a more or less territorially intact and culturally integrated collectivity. It does not suffer from an externally imposed cultural division of labor, at least not a severe one, because it possesses its own dominant strata and an identifiable minority culture. Nor is it likely to be an economic backwater area. Class conflict within the minority population is an enduring threat, indicating a commensurate level of social structural differentiation—probably in line with larger national trends. In short, this perspective sees the minority as a nation within a nation. This is what makes the ethnic option politically viable and attractive to the dominant strata of the minority population. In this perspective, ethnic political mobilization is most likely when class conflict within the nation as a whole or within the minority population is relatively low. While the minority dominant strata may play an important part in stimulating ethnic mobilization, the success of the movement ultimately depends on winning lower strata support.

The next section presents an overview of ethnic political mobilization in Scotland and Wales and lays a foundation for developing specific propositions from the general perspectives just outlined.

III. HYPOTHESES SPECIFIC TO WELSH AND
   SCOTTISH NATIONALISM

Prior to the eruption of Celtic nationalism in the late 1960s, both Scotland and Wales were solidly in the Labour camp. Their strong support for Labour was due in part to their social structural composition (Ragin, 1977). Historically, both regions have had high levels of employment in mining and heavy manufacturing and unemployment rates exceeding those of England. These conditions have been shown to produce strong support for Labour throughout Britain. The Conservative Party traditionally has been weak in Celtic Britain (Hechter, 1975; Ragin, 1977), and both the Liberal Party and the Labour Party have benefitted from this weakness. After World War I when the Labour Party became the major challenge to the Conservatives, the Liberal Party remained stronger in Scotland and Wales than in England.

Alford (1963) examined differences between England, Scotland, and Wales in class voting using survey data from the 1950s and early 1960s. He found that the differences between Wales and Scotland, on the one hand, and England, on the other, were relatively minor. Generally, both manual and nonmanual support for Labour tended to be slightly higher in Celtic Britain (Wales, especially) than in England, and manual and nonmanual support for the Conservative Party tended to be lower. Regional differences in class voting (the percent of manual workers supporting Labour minus the percent of nonmanual workers supporting Labour) were negligible. Alford's findings thus support the idea that the Labour Party, in the 1950s and early 1960s at least, served as an outlet for the expression of Celtic "peripheral sectionalism" (disproportionate regional support for a national party; see Nielsen, this volume).

The higher relative levels of manual and nonmanual support for the Labour Party in Scotland and Wales observed by Alford should not be construed as definitive proof of sectionalism, however. Butler and Stokes (1969) present data that suggest that Labour is strong in these regions because of their social structural composition, not because Labour serves as a regional party. Using data on hundreds of British constituencies, they showed that the greater the percentage of manual workers in a constituency, the higher the level of manual and nonmanual support for Labour. It follows that because Wales and Scotland both contain a disproportionate percentage of manual workers, the Labour Party should receive relatively higher levels of support from both manual and nonmanual workers. However, Butler and Stokes did not attempt an explicit statistical assessment of Celtic peripheral sectionalism. It is impossible to tell from their results whether or not Celtic regions depart from national patterns of class support. This question is addressed directly in the analyses that follow.

What effect did the resurgence of Celtic nationalism in the late 1960s have on patterns of class support in Scotland and Wales? Three of the four perspectives outlined above—the reactive ethnicity perspective, the ethnic competition perspective, and the ethnic subnationalism perspective—can be used to frame specific hypotheses concerning patterns of class support for national parties in Scotland and Wales during this period. The developmental perspective is not applicable to ethnic mobilization in class-mobilized polities. This perspective indicates that once class becomes dominant, ethnic mobilization is unlikely. The evidence from Great Britain and other advanced countries clearly contradicts these expectations [see Nielsen (1985)].

The reactive ethnicity perspective is clearly more useful than the developmental. It treats ethnic mobilization as a mass defection of minority lower strata from the national-level party representing their class interests. Because the ethnic minority can mobilize as either a class collectivity or an ethnic collectivity, the possibility of ethnic mobilization is an enduring threat, even when the minority is thoroughly mobilized as a class collectivity. Thus, this perspective predicts that a relatively lower level of minority manual support for the national working class party should accompany ethnic mobilization. Specifically, the areas of greatest support for the Celtic nationalist parties should have lower levels of manual support for the Labour Party.

The predictions of the ethnic subnationalism perspective are opposite those of the reactive ethnicity perspective. According to this perspective, ethnic mobilization begins in earnest among minority dominant strata. Thus, ethnic mobilization is at first a defection of minority dominant strata from the national-level party most supportive of dominant strata interests. When national levels of class politics decline (as they did in Britain in the late 1960s), these strata sieze the opportunity to generate cross-class opposition to the core and thereby gain leverage in their struggles with the dominant strata of the dominant cultural group. Thus, according to the ethnic subnationalism perspective, areas of greatest support for the Celtic nationalist parties should witness low levels of nonmanual support for the Conservative Party.

The ecological emphases of the ethnic competition perspective provide a basis for making general predictions concerning the impact of ethnic political mobilization on class politics. In the absence of a viable ethnic party, ethnic minority areas, regardless of their class or occupational composition, may exhibit inflated levels of support for certain national parties (i.e., they may exhibit peripheral sectionalism). The national party most sympathetic with the minority's plight, for example, might attract the disproportionate support of minority dominant and subordinant strata. From an ecological perspective, the emergence of a viable ethnic party should deflate patterns of peripheral sectionalism. Thus, patterns of minority support for national parties should conform to national patterns once an appropriate outlet for the expression of ethnic sentiment exists. Thus, this perspective predicts that areas of greatest support for the Celtic nationalist parties should display the least peripheral sectionalism. In short, these areas should exhibit levels of manual and nonmanual support for Labour (the class party that, according to some authors, has served as an outlet for peripheral sectionalism) consistent with national patterns of class support (see Nielsen, this volume).

These different hypotheses are examined next in statistical analyses of regional variation in the relation between class and party support in England, Scotland, and Wales in the late 1960s, the period of rapid growth in the support for the Celtic nationalist parties.

IV. DATA, MEASURES, AND MODEL

While the primary data unit used in this study is the British Parliamentary Constituency, and is therefore aggregate, the study also uses data on the relationship between class and party preference at the individual level. Specifically, National Opinion Polls conducted in Great Britain during the peak of nationalist mobilization in the late 1960s were aggregated into a single file and then sorted into constituencies ($N = 199$). With 200–500 individuals per constituency, it was possible to compute measures of the strength of the relationship between class and party preference specific to each constituency, a technique also used by Butler and Stokes (1969). (Note that these calculations do not use actual voting data, but data on party preferences stated by individual citizens in interviews.) Respondents in each constituency were grouped into manual and nonmanual occupational categories, as delineated by Butler and Stokes (1969), and the support for each major party within each of the two major occupational categories was assessed. Basic descriptive statistics on the different measures of class support used as dependent variables in the statistical analyses are presented in Table 1.

TABLE 1. Descriptive data on British constituencies

Variable	Mean for Welsh constituencies	Mean for Scottish constituencies	Mean for English constituencies
Percent manual support for Labour	58.7	48.7	45.1
Percent nonmanual support for Conservatives	52.3	54.5	68.7
Alford's index of class voting	29.3	25.3	24.8
Percent nonmanual support for Labour	29.4	23.4	20.3
Percent manual support for Conservatives	26.7	26.9	43.4
Percent in mining and manufacturing	58.7	55.3	54.3
Percent in manual occupations	73.9	69.5	64.7
Rate of unemployment	1.8	2.2	0.9
Nationalist support	4.8	17.0	0.0

The aggregated National Opinion Polls were combined with data from the 1966 Census of British Parliamentary Constituencies to create a merged file containing data on aggregate-level social structural variables (e.g., percent of the population employed in mining and manufacturing, percent unemployed, etc.) and data on the individual-level relationship between class and party preference, specific to each constituency (e.g., the percent of manual workers in each constituency supporting the Labour Party). Structured in this way, the data set offered a unique opportunity to assess the independent effects of ethnic political mobilization and social structural variables on regional variation in the strength of the individual-level relationship between class and party preference. In contrast to previous studies that use support for ethnic parties as dependent variables, this study uses support for ethnic parties as an independent variable because the goal is to assess the impact of ethnic mobilization on class politics.

The first set of statistical analyses examines broad differences in class support across England, Scotland, and Wales. To assess these differences properly, it is necessary to take into account known causes of regional variation in class support. For example, it is well known that coal miners and workers in heavy manufacturing industries are stronger Labour supporters than other workers, and it is also well known that a disproportionate percentage of Wales's labor force is employed in these industries (see descriptive data in Table 1). To assess differences between Wales and England in percentage of manual workers supporting the Labour Party without also correcting for differences in the percentage of the labor force employed in mining and manufacturing would distort the estimation of the gap between the two regions. The effects of industrial composition and of other social structural variables on levels of class support must be taken into account. The form of the basic model used to correct for the effects of social structural variables is

$$CS = a + c_1(W) + c_2(S) + b_i(X_i) + e \qquad (1)$$

where CS is the measure of class support, a is the constant, W is a dummy-coded variable indicating Welsh constituencies, c_1 is an estimate of the difference between Welsh and English constituencies in class support, S is a dummy-coded variable indicating Scottish constituencies, c_2 is an estimate of the difference between Scottish and English constituencies in class support, X_i are measures of social structural variables known to affect class support, b_i are regression coefficients for social structural variables, and e is the error term.

In this type of model the coefficients for the dummy-coded variables are of key interest because they show the regression-adjusted differences in class support between Scottish and Welsh constituencies, on the one hand, and English constituencies, on the other. This model assesses patterns of class support in Celtic areas relative to national patterns of class support. The coefficients for the relationship between social structural variables and class support are estimated from data on all constituencies, not just Celtic constituencies. Thus, the coefficients for the dummy-coded variables are adjusted according to national patterns of class support.

The regression analyses include four constituency-level social structural control variables: percentage of the labor force employed in manual occupations, this same variable squared (and then residualized; see below), percentage of the labor force employed in mining and manufacturing, and the rate of unemployment. All social structural variables were taken from the census of Parliamentary Constituencies mentioned above.

The percentage of the labor force employed in manual occupations is included because Butler and Stokes (1969) have shown a powerful contextual effect of the percentage of manual workers on class voting in British constituencies. Specifically, they have shown that the greater the percentage of manual workers, the greater the support of manual workers for the Labour Party. Conversely, the greater the percentage of nonmanual workers, the greater the support of nonmanual workers for the Conservative Party. Both relationships are moderately nonlinear. Therefore, both the percentage of manual workers and the percentage of manual workers squared are included as predictors. (To reduce multicollinearity and simplify interpretation of regression coefficients, the percentage of manual workers squared was residualized on the percentage of manual workers and then converted to standardized scores.) Percentage employed in mining and manufacturing is included as an independent variable because, as noted, support for the Labour Party tends to be very strong among workers in mining and manufacturing. Unemployment rate is included as an independent variable because the Labour Party wins strong support from manual workers in economically depressed areas.

Five separate measures of the individual-level relationship between class and party support are used as dependent variables. Three are measures of class voting: the percentage of manual workers supporting the Labour Party, the percentage of nonmanual workers supporing the Conservative Party, and Alford's (1963) index of class voting. Alford's index is the simple difference between the percentage of manual workers supporting the Labour Party (the party of the left) and the percentage of nonmanual workers supporting the Labour Party. The index potentially varies between -100 and $+100$, but all British constituencies register scores greater than zero on Alford's index. Two measures of cross-class support were also examined: the percentage of manual workers supporting the Conservative Party and the percentage of nonmanual workers supporing the Labour Party. The first is important because the Conservative Party, as the party of the right, presents itself as the party of the whole (British) nation, and it is important to assess the success of this appeal among Celtic manual workers. The second measure of cross-class support, the percentage of nonmanual workers supporting the Labour Party, is important because the Labour Party, as the party of the left, presents itself as a muscular national party, capable of tackling the economic problems of depressed Celtic regions. Class support for the Liberal Party is not examined because this party does not make a specific class appeal.

The second set of analyses below examines the relationship between ethnic political mobilization and class support. These analyses add a single independent variable to the analysis of aggregate regional differences in class support: the percentage of respondents in Welsh and Scottish constituencies supporing Celtic nationalist parties—the Plaid Cymru in Wales and the Scottish Nationalist Party in Scotland. (Party preference data from the NOP surveys were used to construct the measure of nationalist support.) This measure is used to assess the relationship between ethnic political mobilization and class support, and was added to the equation described above in separate analyses. This second equation has the general form

$$CS = a + c_1(W) + c_2(S) + c_3(N) + b_i(X_i) + e \qquad (2)$$

where N is the percentage of the population supporting the Celtic nationalist parties and c_3 is the regression coefficient showing change in class support resulting from a unit change in support for a nationalist party; the remaining symbols in the equation follow the pattern established in Equation (1).

In this model the coefficients for Wales and Scotland (c_1 and c_2) show the level of class support in Celtic constituencies offering no support to the Celtic nationalist parties, a hypothetical value. There was considerable variation among Welsh and Scottish constituencies in support for the nationalist parties during this period. In Wales the percentage supporting the nationalist party ranged from less than 1 to 10%; in Scotland it ranged from 11 to 24%. Note that the inclusion of the measure of the support for the Celtic nationalist parties has little, if any, effect on the predicted values for English constituencies because popular support for the Celtic nationalist parties was virtually nonexistent outside of Scotland and Wales.

V. ANALYSIS OF REGIONAL DIFFERENCES IN CLASS SUPPORT

The first set of analyses below examines broad regional differences in the relationship between class and party support. Specifically, five dependent variables (percentage of manual workers supporting Labour, percentage of nonmanual workers supporting the Conservative Party, Alford's index of class voting, percentage of manual workers supporting the Conservative Party, and percentage of nonmanual workers supporting Labour) are regressed on the dummy-coded variables for Wales and Scotland and on the interval-scale social structural variables: the percentage of manual workers, this same variable squared (and residualized), the rate of unemployment, and the percent employed in mining and manufacturing. These equations show the difference between Welsh and Scottish constituencies, on the one hand, and English constituencies, on the other, in the relation between class and party preference, net of the effects of important social structural causes of regional variation in class support. Table 2 reports these results.

The first column of Table 2 shows the results of the analysis of regional variation in the percentage of manual workers supporting Labour. The coefficients for the percentage of manual workers and the percentage of manual workers squared show the curvilinear relationship first documented by Butler and Stokes (1969). The coefficients for rate of unemployment and for percent employed in mining and manufacturing are also significant and in the expected direction. Of more interest are the coefficients for the dummy-coded variables indicating Welsh and Scottish constituences. The coefficient for Scotland (-2.160) is not significant, indicating no important difference between Scottish and English constituencies in percent of manual workers supporting Labour, net of the effects of social structural variables. The coefficient for Wales, however, is strongly positive (7.482) and significant at the 0.01 level, indicating a higher level of support by manual workers for the Labour Party in Wales than in England. During the period of ethnic mobilization, therefore, the level of support of Celtic manual workers for the Labour Party was strong.

The second column of Table 2 shows the results of the analysis of nonmanual support for the Conservative Party. As might be expected, the effects of the social structural variables on nonmanual support for the Conservatives are opposite their effects on manual support for the Labour Party. High unemployment, a high percentage of manual workers, and a high percentage of employment in

TABLE 2. Regression analysis of regional variation in measures of class support[a]

	Dependent variables				
	Percent manual for Labour	Percent nonmanual for Conservatives	Alford's index	Percent manual for Conservatives	Percent nonmanual for Labour
Constant	15.190** (4.010)	88.236** (4.142)	16.632** (3.810)	61.818** (3.702)	-1.442 (3.847)
Welsh dummy variable	7.482** (2.802)	-12.105** (2.894)	2.728 (2.662)	-12.209** (2.586)	4.754 (2.688)
Scottish dummy variable	-2.160 (2.341)	-10.179** (2.418)	-1.556 (2.224)	-11.864** (2.161)	-0.603 (2.245)
Percent manual workers	0.216* (0.091)	-0.223* (0.094)	0.013 (0.087)	-0.178* (0.084)	0.203* (0.088)
Percent manual workers squared	1.605** (0.634)	-1.956** (0.655)	-0.299 (0.603)	-1.529** (0.586)	1.904** (0.609)
Percent in mining and manufacturing	0.245** (0.064)	-0.067 (0.066)	0.108 (0.060)	-0.090 (0.059)	0.136* (0.061)
Unemployment rate	3.031** (0.847)	-1.658* (0.875)	1.545* (0.805)	-2.349** (0.782)	1.486 (0.813)
Adjusted R-squared	0.413**	0.364**	0.047*	0.449**	0.273**

[a]Unstandardized regression coefficients are reported; standard errors are in parentheses; * significant at 0.05 level; ** significant at 0.01 level.

mining and manufacturing all depress nonmanual support for the Conservative Party. More dramatic are the coefficients for the regional dummy-coded variables. The coefficients for Scottish and Welsh constituencies are both strongly negative and highly significant. On the average, Scotland's nonmanual support for the Conservative Party is 10.179 percentage points lower than England's, and Wales's support is 12.105 points lower. During the period of rapid ethnic mobilization, therefore, nonmanual support for the Conservative Party was remarkably low in Celtic areas.

The third column of Table 2 reports the results of the analysis of Alford's index of class voting. Only one variable is significant in this analysis, rate of unemployment, which has a positive effect on class voting. Neither dummy-coded regional variable has a significant effect on Alford's index. This indicates that the general political salience of class was remarkably uniform throughout Britain during the period of Celtic mobilization. Thus, even during a period of rapid ethnic mobilization the level of class voting in Wales and Scotland remained comparable to England's. This finding is consistent with the argument of Ragin and Davies (1981) concerning polity-wide causes of minority ethnic mobilization. Specifically, they argue that polity-wide fluctuation in the political salience of class is reflected in support for third parties, including ethnic parties, in minority and majority regions. During the period of ethnic mobilization in Celtic areas in the 1960s, the Liberal Party in England experienced a modest revival, signaling a parallel decline in the importance of class politics.

The fourth column of Table 2 reports the results of the analysis of manual support for the Conservative Party, the first measure of cross-class support. This analysis is important because the Conservative Party presents itself as the party of the whole British nation. The coefficients for the social structural variables in this equation are remarkably similar to those reported in the analysis of nonmanual support for the Conservative Party. The coefficients for the dummy-coded regional variables also show a strikingly similar pattern. Relative to England and polity-wide patterns of class support, manual support for the Conservative Party was low in Scotland (11.864 points lower) and Wales (12.209 point lower) during the period of ethnic mobilization. Both coefficients are significant at the 0.01 level. This indicates that Conservative efforts among Celtic manual workers during this period were largely unrewarded. Ethnic mobilization probably depressed manual support for the Conservative Party to a level lower than premobilization levels.

The last column of Table 2 reports the results of the analysis of nonmanual support for the Labour Party. This equation was computed to examine Labour's appeal among Celtic nonmanual workers. The coefficients attached to the social structural variables show a pattern very similar to those reported in the analysis of manual support for the Labour Party. However, the coefficients for the dummy-coded regional variables are not significant. This indicates that net of the effects of social structural variables, there were no statistically significant differences between Wales and Scotland, on the one hand, and England, on the other, in the overall level of nonmanual support for the Labour Party.

To summarize: during the period of rapid ethnic mobilization, the Conservative Party suffered most. Including controls for the effects of social structural variables that influence levels of class support (and that also distinguish Celtic Britain from England; see Table 1) does not alter this conclusion. The dummy-coded variables for Wales and Scotland show considerable disaffection with the Conservative Party during this period. The analyses of class support for the Labour Party, however, show that manual and nonmanual support for Labour was strong, equal to or greater than English levels. In Wales, manual support for the Labour Party was significantly above England's level. The analysis of Alford's index of class voting shows that the level of class voting in Scotland and Wales did not drop below England's level, despite the resurgence of Celtic nationalism.

VI. ANALYSIS OF ETHNIC MOBILIZATION AND CLASS SUPPORT

It is possible to go beyond an examination of average, adjusted differences between Celtic and English constituencies in class support, for the impact of ethnic mobilization on class support across Celtic constituencies also can be assessed. To analyze this relationship it is necessary simply to reestimate the equations in Table 2 with an indicator of ethnic mobilization, percent supporting the Celtic nationalist parties in Welsh and Scottish constituencies, added to each equation. Note that the addition of this variable alters the interpretation of the dummy-coded regional variables. Originally (in Table 2), they assessed the average gap between Celtic and English constituencies in class support. In the second set of equations, they estimate (hypothetical) levels of class support in Celtic constituencies exhibiting no ethnic mobilization (i.e., no support for the Celtic nationalist parties). The coefficients for Celtic nationalist support show the differences in class support between Celtic constituencies with high levels of ethnic mobilization and those with low levels of ethnic mobilization.

Consider, for example, the first column of Table 3, which reports the results of the analysis of percent of manual workers supporting the Labour Party. In this equation, the coefficient for nationalist support is not significant, indicating that there is no significant difference in manual support for Labour between Celtic constituencies with high levels of nationalist support and those with low levels of nationalist support. This shows that ethnic mobilization had relatively little impact on manual support for the Labour Party in Celtic Britain; Labour remained strong among manual workers even in areas of high ethnic mobilization. Conversely, Labour did not serve as an outlet for peripheral sectionalism in areas where the nationalists were not strong. The other coefficients in this equation do not differ markedly from their Table 2 values.

TABLE 3. Regression analysis of impact of nationalist mobilization on class support[a]

	Dependent variables				
	Percent manual for Labour	Percent nonmanual for Conservatives	Alford's index	Percent manual for Conservatives	Percent nonmanual for Labour
Constant	15.155**	87.890**	16.483**	61.688**	-1.329
	(4.024)	(4.115)	(3.815)	(3.708)	(3.856)
Welsh dummy variable	7.906*	-7.955*	4.511	-10.641**	3.395
	(3.475)	(3.553)	(3.294)	(3.202)	(3.329)
Scottish dummy variable	-0.586	5.209	5.054	-6.050	-5.639
	(7.937)	(8.115)	(7.524)	(7.314)	(7.605)
Percent nationalist	-0.095	-0.927*	-0.398	-0.350	0.303
	(0.457)	(0.467)	(0.433)	(0.421)	(0.438)
Percent manual workers	0.217*	-0.211*	0.018	-0.174*	0.199*
	(0.092)	(0.094)	(0.087)	(0.085)	(0.088)
Percent manual workers squared	1.605**	-1.958**	-0.299	-1.530**	1.904**
	(0.636)	(0.650)	(0.603)	(0.609)	(0.609)
Percent in mining and manufacturing	0.244**	-0.079	0.103	-0.095	0.140*
	(0.064)	(0.066)	(0.061)	(0.059)	(0.061)
Unemployment rate	3.057**	-1.399	1.656*	-2.251**	1.401
	(0.859)	(0.878)	(0.814)	(0.791)	(0.823)
Adjusted R-squared	0.410**	0.374**	0.047*	0.448**	0.271**

[a]Unstandardized regression coefficients are reported; standard errors are in parentheses; * significant at 0.05 level; ** significant at 0.01 level.

However, the analysis of nonmanual support for the Conservative Party, reported in the second column of Table 3, sharply contrasts with the analysis of manual support for Labour. This equation shows that there is a substantial difference between Celtic constituencies with high levels of nationalist support and those with low levels of nationalist support. In constituencies with a high level of nationalist support, nonmanual workers almost completely deserted the Conservative Party. The Conservatives maintained their nonmanual support only in constituencies with very low levels of nationalist support. The coefficients for the dummy variables show that even when nationalist supporting is nil, the percent of nonmanuals supporting the Conservative Party in Wales is lower than the level in England. In Scotland, when nationalist support is nil, manual support for the Conservatives is not significantly different from the English level. Note, however, that this is a purely hypothetical value, for all Scottish constituencies registered support for the Scottish Nationalist Party. The other coefficients in this column are close to their Table 2 values.

The third column of Table 3 shows the results of the analysis of the impact of nationalist support on class voting. The equation shows that there is no significant difference between constituencies with high nationalist support and those with low nationalist support in class voting. Thus, a relatively lower level of class voting did not accompany ethnic mobilization in the most strongly nationalist of Celtic constituencies.

The fourth column shows the impact of nationalist support on an indicator of cross-class support, percent of manual workers supporting the Conservative Party. The results show no significant difference between Celtic constituencies with strong nationalist support and constituencies with weak nationalist support; the coefficient for nationalist support is small and not significant at the 0.05 level. The other coefficients in this equation are similar to their Table 2 values. This finding shows that ethnic mobilization in Celtic Britain was not associated with lower levels of manual support for the Conservative Party. Thus, the support of Celtic manual workers for the Conservative Party was relatively low throughout Celtic Britain during the period of nationalist mobilization (see Tables 1 and 2).

The last column of Table 3 shows the relation between ethnic mobilization and nonmanual support for Labour in Celtic Britain. The coefficient estimating the effect of nationalist support on nonmanual support for Labour is not significant at the 0.05 level. This shows that ethnic mobilization in Celtic Britain did not stimulate a defection of nonmanual workers from Labour Party. As noted, the Labour Party is much stronger in the periphery of Britain (and of England) because these areas are economically depressed, and the Labour Party presents itself as the party most capable of redressing regional imbalances and inequalities. This appeal apparently was successful, for the most strongly nationalist areas of Celtic Britain did not experience relatively lower levels of nonmanual support for the Labour Party during the period of rapid ethnic mobilization.

To summarize: ethnic mobilization in Celtic Britain was linked to a mass disillusionment, particularly of nonmanual workers, with the Conservative Party. Many of these former Conservatives apparently supported the Celtic nationalists, for the areas of nationalist strength are the same areas that exhibited lowest levels of nonmanual support for the Conservatives. Nationalist mobilization appears to have had relatively little, if any, impact on the patterns of class support manifested by manual workers. There were not strong differences between Celtic areas with strong nationalist support and areas with weak nationalist support in percent of manual workers supporting either the Conservative or the Labour Party.

VII. DISCUSSION

The results for Great Britain during the late 1960s indicate that ethnic mobilization in class-mobilized polities occurs at the expense of the party of the right, especially its nonmanual support. The Conservative Party fared poorly in Scotland and Wales, relative to England and the national pattern of major party support, during the period of rapid nationalist mobilization. This outcome should be seen as an intensification of historical patterns of anti-Conservativism. With the emergence of viable ethnic parties, Celtic anti-Conservative sentiment found an outlet and intensified. Support for the Labour Party, by contrast, followed national patterns. No Scottish or Welsh deficits were detected, and nationalist support did not depress Labour support within Celtic Britain.

These results offer little support for the reactive ethnicity perspective, at least in its most popularized form. This perspective emphasizes minority subordinate strata, especially the disillusionment of these strata with the party of the left. Because this perspective views the minority as both an ethnic group and an exploited economic class (the product of a cultural division of labor), ethnic mobilization is treated as an alternative to lower strata mobilization along class lines. Consequently, ethnic mobilization should entail depressed levels of manual support for the working class party. This view is rejected on the evidence presented in this chapter. Welsh manual workers remained disproportionately supportive of the Labour Party, and Scottish manual workers were as supportive of Labour as were English manual workers. These findings follow patterns observed by Alford (1963) for the 1950s and early 1960s.

The results offer strongest support for the ethnic subnationalism perspective. According to this perspective, ethnic mobilization primarily is a response of minority dominant strata. The ethnic alternative is launched when members of these strata repudiate their class party, in this case the Conservative Party, and attempt to generate cross-class opposition to the core cultural group. Consistent with these expectations, the analyses demonstrate that the areas of greatest support for the Celtic nationalists were areas of Conservative weakness, and nationalist mobilization was clearly linked to nonmanual rejection of the Conservative Party. Furthermore, this attempt to stimulate cross-class, ethnic opposition to the core coincided with a polity-wide decline in the importance of class, for the levels of class support found for the late 1960s were lower than those reported for the 1950s and early 1960s (Alford, 1963). This crack in the walls of class politics gave the nationalists their foothold and increased the likelihood of a successful ethnic appeal.

As noted, the ethnic subnationalism perspective is best understood as a variation of the ethnic competition perspective because the two perspectives emphasize the same causal variables. The main difference between the two is the former's emphasis on the dominant strata of the minority group. In its more general form, the ethnic competition perspective predicts that the emergence of variable ethnic parties should depress the disproportionate support of ethnic manual and nonmanual strata for national parties (i.e., disproportionate relative to the social structural composition of ethnic areas). In short, patterns of peripheral sectionalism expressed through such national parties as the Labour Party should disappear.

The analyses presented in this study do not address premobilization patterns—specifically, the possibility of Celtic peripheral sectionalism expressed through disproportionate Labour support. The results of Alford (1963) and Hechter (1975) suggest that Labour may have served as an outlet for peripheral sectionalism. However, the results of Ragin (1977) challenge this interpretation. In any event, this study finds no direct link between nationalist mobilization and either manual or nonmanual support for Labour. Manual and nonmanual support for Labour was relatively strong (equal to or greater than England's level) in areas of strong and weak nationalist mobilization. If the premobilization pattern was one of disproportionate Labour support, however, then the effect of nationalist mobilization was to decrease Labour support to levels consistent with national patterns (with the exception of support for Labour among Welsh manual workers). This general pattern is consistent with the predictions of the ethnic competition perspective.

The ethnic subnationalism perspective argues that for ethnic mobilization to be successful, minority dominant strata must generate cross-class support for ethnic mobilization. The data for the late 1960s indicate that they were not successful. Manual support for Labour remained strong in Celtic Britain, especially in Wales, even in the areas where the Celtic nationalists were most successful. Despite the polity-wide decline in the success of the class appeal, the nationalists were not able to gain strong manual support and mount an effective challenge to the dominant parties.

Support for the Celtic nationalists peaked in late 1960s and early 1970s and then declined as class-related issues returned to the forefront. If the nationalists had successfully generated lower strata support for Celtic nationalism before class issues regained prominence, the movement would probably remain strong

CHARLES C. RAGIN

today. The cultivation of a mass base among manual workers who support the Labour Party remains a major task facing the Plaid Cymru (Philip, 1975) and the Scottish Nationalist Party.

ACKNOWLEDGMENTS

Arthur Stinchcombe and Susan Olzak provided many useful comments on early drafts of this chapter.

REFERENCES

ALFORD, ROBERT (1963). *Party and society: The Anglo-American democracies.* Chicago: Rand-McNally.
BARTH, FREDERICK (1969). *Ethnic groups and boundaries.* Boston: Little, Brown.
BELL, DANIEL (1975). Ethnicity and social change. In *Ethnicity: Theory and experience* (N. Glazer and D. Moynihan, eds.), pp. 141–174. Cambridge, Massachusetts: Harvard University Press.
BLONDEL, JEAN (1963). *Voters, parties, and leaders.* London: Cox and Wyman.
BUTLER, DAVID, AND STOKES, DONALD (1969). *Political change in Britain.* New York: Saint Martin's Press.
DEUTSCH, KARL (1953). *Nationalism and social communication.* Cambridge, Massachusetts: MIT Press.
GEERTZ, CLIFFORD (1963). The integrative revolution: Primordial sentiments and civic politics in the new states. In *Mass politics* (E. Allardt and S. Rokkan, eds.), pp. 105–157. New York: Free Press.
GELLNER, ERNEST (1969). *Thought and change.* Chicago: University of Chicago Press.
HANNAN, MICHAEL (1979). The dymancs of ethnic boundaries in modern states. In *National development and the world system: Educational, economic and political change, 1950–1970* (M. Hannan and J. Meyer, eds.), pp. 253–275. Chicago: University of Chicago Press.
HECHTER, MICHAEL (1975). *Internal colonialism: The Celtic fringe in British national development.* London: Routledge and Regan Paul.
LINZ, JUAN (1973). Early state building and late peripheral nationalism against the state: The case of Spain. In *Building states and nations.* Vol. II, (S. E. Eisenstadt and S. Rokkan, eds.), pp. 32–116. Beverly Hills, California: Sage.
LIPSET, SEYMOUR, AND ROKKAN, STEIN (1967). *Party system and voter alignments.* New York: Free Press.
NAGEL, JOANE (1982). Collective action and public policy: American Indian mobilization. *Social Science Journal* 19(July):37–45.
NAGEL, JOANE, AND OLZAK, SUSAN (1982). Ethnic mobilization in new and old states: An extension of the competition model. *Social Problems* 30(2):127–143.
NAIRN, TOM (1977). The twilight of the British state. *New Left Review* 101(2):3–61.
NIELSEN, FRANCOIS (1980). The Flemish movement in Belgium after World War II: A dynamic analysis. *American Sociological Review* 45(February):76–94.
NIELSEN, FRANCOIS (1985). Toward a theory of ethnic solidarity in modern societies. *American Sociological Review* 50(April):133–149.
OLZAK, SUSAN (1982). Ethnic mobilization in Quebec. *Ethnic and Racial Studies* 5:253–275.

OLZAK, SUSAN (1983). Contemporary ethnic mobilization. *Annual Review of Sociology* **9**:355–374.

PARSONS, TALCOTT (1975). Some theoretical considerations on the nature and trends of change in ethnicity. In *Ethnicity: Theory and experience* (N. Glazer and D. Moynihan, eds.), N. pp. 56–71. Cambridge, Massachusetts: Harvard University Press.

PELLING, HENRY (1968). *Popular politics and society in late victorian Britain*. New York: Saint Martin's Press.

PELLING, HENRY (1972). *A history of British trade unions*. London: Macmillan.

PHILIP, ALAN B. (1975). *The Welsh question: Nationalism in Welsh politics, 1945–1970*. Cardiff: University of Wales Press.

RAGIN, CHARLES (1977). Class, status and "reactive ethnic cleavages": The social bases of political regionalism. *American Socioligical Review* **42**(June):438–450.

RAGIN, CHARLES (1979). Ethnic political mobilization: The Welsh case. *American Sociological Review* **44**(August):619–635.

RAGIN, CHARLES (1980). Celtic nationalism in Britain: Political and structural bases. In *Processes of the world system* (T. Hopkins and I. Wallerstein, eds.), pp. 249–265. Beverly Hills, California: Sage.

RAGIN, CHARLES, AND DAVIES, TED (1981). Welsh nationalism in context. In *Research and social movements, conflicts and change* (L. Driesberg, ed.), pp. 215–233. Greenwich, Connecticut: JAI Press.

ROSE, RICHARD (1974). *Politics in England*. Boston: Little, Brown and Company.

ROTHSCHILD, JOSEPH (1981). *Ethnopolitics: A conceptual framework*. New York: Columbia University Press.

SMITH, ANTHONY (1971). *Theories of nationalism*. New York: Harper and Row.

VAN DEN BERGHE, PIERRE (1967). *Race and racism: A comparative perspective*. New York: Wiley.

10

For God and Crown: Class, Ethnicity, and Protestant Politics in Northern Ireland

KATHERINE O'SULLIVAN SEE
James Madison College
Michigan State University
East Lansing, Michigan 48824

I. INTRODUCTION

> Against the altar and the throne
> The democrat may prate.
> But while I am an Orangeman
> I'll stand for Church and State.
> Let not the poor man hate the rich
> Nor rich on poor look down.
> But each join each true Protestant
> For God and for the Crown.

This traditional Orange song provides one explanation for the seemingly intractable sectarian suspicion and animosity that divide Northern Ireland today. For centuries, God and Crown have been firmly wedded in the ideology of loyalist ascendancy that has historically characterized Protestant politics there. Such an inference of historical inevitability assumes an immutability to ethnic conflicts. This chapter counters that inference and focuses on critical periods of conflict in Ulster in order to evaluate four important models of ethnoregional mobilization: internal colonial, uneven development, split labor market, and resource competition theories. In contrast to most works on Northern Ireland, which concentrate on the Catholic/Protestant polarity, the emphasis here is on class relations *within* the Protestant populace, to examine how these have shaped the patterning of ethnic politics.

COMPETITIVE ETHNIC RELATIONS

A. Internal Colonialism

Among the most prominant interpretations of ethnoregional movements, the internal colonial model has been most elegantly spelled out in the work of Michael Hechter. In his early work *Internal Colonialism,* Hechter proposed that uneven economic development and political dominance by a core state sets the ground for quasi-national solidarity in a dependent periphery. Internal colonies create a hierarchical ethnic division of labor, a material basis for mobilization on the part of the subordinated ethnic group. Efforts to integrate the periphery into the metropole are likely to trigger such mobilization, especially where a relative economic deprivation coincides with a high degree of cultural difference. And this is most characteristic of developing regions, with low levels of industrialization. Sharp ethnic differences can be more easily preserved in preindustrial societies, where the populace is less mobile, the ethnic division of labor is unchallenged, and communal associations are stronger (Hechter, 1975; Hechter and Levi, 1979; MacDonald, 1982; Stone, 1979). The following claim can be culled from this interpretation.

PROPOSITION 1. *Reactive ethnic mobilization is most likely where the metropole seeks to integrate a peripheral region into the metropolitan state system (P1a); where there is a low level of industrialization (P1b); where ethnic groups are segregated in the labor market (P1c); and where ethnic societies provide internal organizations for ethnic mobilization (P1d).*

B. Uneven Development Models

Unlike internal colonialism, which views the ethnic division of labor in a more undifferentiated way, uneven development theorists emphasize the crucial role of the elites in the periphery and the important relations among capitalists in shaping ethnic relations. Most evident in the work of Tom Nairn, *The Break Up Of Britain,* this perspective argues that uneven economic development may provide a core state with the resources to respond flexibly to the interests of peripheral elites, providing benefits from imperial expansion, tolerating or encouraging an ethnically exclusive labor aristocracy. Reactive mobilization is likely in a period of significant economic change, when traditional patrimonial relations between the elites of the center and the periphery are destabilized. The dominant classes are unable to differentially reward a fragment of the peripheral working class and sustain their paternalist relation with them (Nairn, 1977, p. 42).[1] The following proposition can be derived from this analysis.

PROPOSITION 2. *Reactive ethnoregional mobilization in a peripheral region is most likely when the elites of the two regions seek to deflect class conflict through fostering an ethnically exclusive labor aristocracy (P2a) and when economic development erodes the alliance and patrimonial relations between economic elites (P2b).*

C. Split Labor Market Analysis

Split labor market theory is an influential variant of uneven development analyses, but it disputes the central proposition that roots ethnic antagonisms in *capitalist* efforts to deflect class conflict. According to Edna Bonacich, the architect of this theory, capital is essentially unconcerned with ethnic difference: left to its principles of efficiency, impersonal labor market rules and accumulation, capitalist growth would erode such distinctions. However, capitalists are not unconstrained. An indigenous labor force may already monopolize a market and seek to protect its incremental advantages through political actions: exclusionary movements, job segregation, protectionist policies that block access to cheap labor. If it has greater political resources than its cheap competitors, high-priced labor is likely to limit capital's ability to use workers interchangeably. In short, it is labor, rather than capital, that instigates reactive mobilization (Bonacich, 1972, 1979).

PROPOSITION 3. *Reactive ethnoregional mobilization in a peripheral area is most likely when the privileges of ethnically distinct, high-priced labor are threatened by the introduction of cheaper labor into the same labor market.*

D. Resource Competition Models

Resource competition models constitute the last of the models to be examined. The basic presupposition here is that individuals align with groups whenever this will maximize their perceived economic and political interests (Banton, 1983; D. Bell, 1975; Enloe, 1973; Fox, Aull, and Cimino, 1981; Nagel and Olzak, 1983; Olzak, 1983; Rothschild, 1981). In contrast to the internal colonial model, these theorists argue that industrialization and the concomitant expansion of secondary and tertiary economic sectors will enhance the likelihood of ethnic mobilization. When the labor market is relatively fluid, the level of direct contact between previously segregated groups and intergroup job competition increases. Ethnic associational networking is also more easily accomplished in urban areas where groups may be residentially segregated. Urban ethnic leaders can utilize developing neighborhood and urban networks to mobilize the populace, to persuade others that solidary mobilization is in their collective interest. In contrast to the uneven development and split labor market models, these theorists emphasize the varying *kinds* of interests that can generate conflict. Expansion of the state sector, massive state–private planning, welfare states, and multinational corporations foster the development of large-scale ethnic affiliations and generate new forms of competition. In propositional form:

PROPOSITION 4. *Reactive ethnoregional mobilization is most likely in a changing economy, where shifts in labor market composition and job opportunity generate greater intergroup competition (P4a); in urban areas where there is increased intergroup contact and competition for control of urban territory (P4b); where bureaucratization and centralization of the state erodes the competitive advantages of the dominant ethnic group in the peripheral area (P4c);*

and where prior ethnic organization formations exist as a base for mobilization (P4d).

Despite variations in their arguments, there is a common core to these four models. Each emphasizes the importance of class factors and economic development in shaping ethnic interests. All agree, as Crawford Young has remarked of recent scholarship in the field, that the salience of ethnic identity is situationally determined, shaped in large part by the ways a particular economic system supports group images and social solidarity and by "the intrusion of the political process in the form of perceived domination, competition, threats or advantage" (Young, 1983, p. 656).

Beyond those shared presuppositions, however, these models differ in the ways in which they examine the intersection of class and ethnic processes in state systems. Internal colonialism assumes a coincidence of these structures and interests in preindustrial societies and hence predicts a higher degree of regional mobilization along ethnic lines in periods before the expansion of secondary and tertiary sectors. It expects ethnic mobilization to peak under conditions of a highly segregated division of labor. In contrast, uneven development, split labor market, and resource mobilization and competition analysts are wary of an ethclass approach for its failure to consider internal differentials within ethnic groups. They place a particular emphasis on the conditions under which competition and competitive resources within and between ethnic groups are altered. However, there are differences among these last three models as well. Uneven development theorists focus on the decline of particular economic sectors and hence the relations between capitalists as crucial to the contours of ethnic conflict; it is the diminishing political and economic power of indigenous capital that precipitates reactive ethnic mobilization, when they can no longer provide support for a "labor aristocracy," or when their own privileged position is undermined by multinational corporations. Split labor market focuses largely on labor market interests within particular firms, views the efforts to rationalize a market as the primary precipitant to reactive ethnic mobilization, and sees this mobilization as largely by high-priced workers. Resource competition approaches view ethnic antagonism as rooted both in labor market and in broader economic and political interests (e.g., control of housing markets, public sector jobs). Thus, it is shaped by a shifting constellation of economic and political interests in both the core and the peripheral areas.

The remainder of this chapter assesses the applicability of the several models through an analysis of the major instances of ethnic mobilization in Ulster during three historic periods.

II. COLONIZATION AND THE DEVELOPMENT OF ETHNIC ANTAGONISM IN NORTH IRELAND

The colonization of Ireland from the reign of Elizabeth I onward was an integral part of the efforts to centralize the English state, to prevent alliances with

Catholic continental powers, and to provide a base for imperial expansion. Throughout the Elizabethan reign, the Irish succeeded in limiting the power of the Crown to an area on the eastern coast of southern Ireland. Beyond "the Pale," colonization was unsuccessful. The subsequent Jamesian settlement scheme was more successful, although it worked only in the easily protected coastal areas of the northeast; there, four-fifths of the land was expropriated from the natives and set aside for English landlords, then granted to settler tenants: "masterless men," Protestants from lowland Scotland and England (Quinn, 1966, pp. 106–122). In the rest of the country, an exploitative pattern of colonization was adopted, in which land was expropriated, granted to absentee English lords, and managed by a complex system of middlemen and native overseer. The Catholic natives were granted leases only on sufferance, and their development of the land was constantly undermined by shifts in metropolitan demands for specialized agricultural produce (Kee, 1972).

The Protestants constituted a classic frontier society, surrounded by a native populace that had been displaced from its land and that challenged their property and religion. They depended on the metropole for protection from periodic Catholic raids, and in turn they served the Crown as a foothold for capital growth and as a bastion of Protestant support. With military and state protection, the new settlers had a stable basis for the growth of cottage industries and agricultural products. The "Ulster Custom" based on the settlement compact (long fixed leases, no rent increases on the land even when improvements had been made) guaranteed the ethnic, as well as the regional, uneven development of Ireland (Beckett, 1969; Cullen, 1969, 1972; de Paor, 1970; Gibbon, 1975; Moody and Martin, 1967; Robinson, 1982; Rose, 1971). However, the economic privileges of Presbyterian settlers were not designed to establish a labor aristocracy. The purpose was to attract settlers who would form an outpost of British control; concessions were necessary, simply to encourage and sustain the needed immigrants. That the Crown did not see a particular affinity for or obligation to the economic interests of the settlers was evident in the protectionist measures that were adopted from plantation forward in the interests of imperial capital.[2]

However, for Scots Presbyterians settlers, economic privilege was considered part of their settlement compact. Doctrinally anti-Catholic, they defined their relation to the Crown as a *religious covenant* in which loyalty was conditional, predicated on *de facto* protection of Protestant property and custom. The covenant of reciprocal rights—the Ulster Custom—had both religious and economic dimensions. The linguistic notation that incorporated all aspects of this covenant was "Protestant liberty." Catholics were seen by the settlers as disloyal subjects, and any rights or resources ceded to them were interpreted as a threat to Protestant liberty and a violation of the "covenanted" rights. In short, the relation between Presbyterian tenants and Anglican landlords was a patrimonial one, but the principle of obligation was a shared *Protestant* loyalty to the Crown (Gibbon, 1975, p. 33; Miller, 1978).

Having established an ethnically split labor market through the Ulster Custom, neither the Crown nor capital could easily undo it. The forms that ethnic conflict took and the outcomes of these in the late eighteenth century illustrate this well. During that period, both agricultural and industrial capitalists challenged this patrimonial relation, as they sought more efficient use of land and labor. Landed interests in England without great holdings in Ireland consistently sought to impose high trade restriction on Irish agricultural commodities so as to protect their own market advantage. Their success in Parliament in the 1740s forced Anglo-Irish landlords to reduce agricultural acreage and shift to grazing. The inevitable and awful effect was massive displacement of tenants and escalating competition for land. In Ulster, owners sought to raise rents and replace Protestant tenants with Catholics who were willing to pay the higher rents and to farm on smaller plots. This abandonment of the Ulster Custom and the religious covenant embittered the Presbyterian tenants. Paramilitary organizations sprang up throughout the rural areas, attacking both landlords and Catholics, demanding a return to the covenant of Protestant loyalism.[3]

Industrial ethnic mobilization followed a similar pattern. The weaving industry, based on the extensive cottage industries which Scots settlers had been able to develop, was until the late 1770s almost exclusively Protestant. However, if ethnic exclusivity was largely the result of traditional craftwork, "to the weavers of Armagh . . . [it] constituted a recognition by manufacturers of the traditional obligations to loyalties which many landlords had recognized before" (Gibbon, 1975, p. 33). However, with the introduction of power spinning in Belfast in 1780, many manufacturers began to abandon the Ulster craft custom and to employ Catholics in their shops. Presbyterian weavers responded to this threat of displacement, organized the Society of Orangemen, smashed the looms of Catholic families, and attacked the mill owners and manufacturers who employed them. Both on the land in the 1740s and in the craft shops in the 1780s, the dominant classes capitulated to Protestant labor's demand. In short, ethnic conflicts of eighteenth century Ulster were responses by Protestant laborers to the actions of landed and manufacturing capital that would have undermined their privileged position. The elite classes were forced to concede because their own struggles with Irish peasants and the emerging Protestant bourgeoisie made it necessary that they retain the loyalty of the lower-class settlers. However, these concessions and the sustenance of a split labor market ensured that the patrimonial relations forged by the Crown and its landed lords would be shaped as well by Protestant tenants and industrial labor.

The United Irishmen rebellion of 1798 failed because the Belfast leadership was not able to undermine (or to appreciate) the strength of this patrimonial sectarian relationship. The metropolitan government and Anglican landlords, on the other hand, exploited it well. Anglican gentry now joined the Orange Society and used it as a base for organizing loyalist associations in the country. They armed Protestant Orangemen, warning them that separation from the Crown would ensure a loss of religious liberty and economic privilege (Ellis, 1972; Kee, 1972; de Paor, 1970; Edwards, 1970). However, if the metropole sought to "play the Orange hand," it was a hand that had been developed by peasants and craftsmen in conjunction with imperial capitalists.

From this survey, several conclusions can be drawn about the *origins* of ethnic conflict in colonial Ireland and the explanatory power of the various propositions. The material difference of interests between Catholics and Protestants was evidently rooted in uneven economic development that fostered Protestant advantage. However, our review does not support the claims of Nairn that the metropole sought to develop an ethnic labor aristocracy in order to prevent secular politics in Ireland (P2a). It was only toward the end of the eighteenth century as the republican nationalist movement developed that Anglican leaders explicitly argued the need for economic discrimination along ethnic lines. Nor is there much support for Hechter's claim about the association of industrialization and sectarian outbursts (P1c), since reactive mobilization occurred in both Belfast and the countryside. On the other hand, there is significant support for the propositions of split labor market and competition theorists (P3, P4a). The efforts of landlords to ignore the Ulster Custom and displace Protestant tenants precipitated the first wave of agrarian ethnic violence; the effort of manufacturers to hire Catholic workers precipitated the second. In both cases, as well as in the reaction to the United Irishmen, the mobilization of Protestants was grounded in ethnic associations, which provided the solidarity, numbers, and organization for the political action (P1d, P4d).

III. UNEVEN DEVELOPMENT, CLASS RELATIONS, AND THE ORANGE ORDER: THE STRUCTURING OF LOYALISM UNDER THE UNION, 1800–1922

During the period of the Union, the economy of Ireland was inextricably welded to the development of English capital, as a market for British manufactured goods, a source of labor for industrial development, and a supplier of food for the English market. The Union abolished even the minimal protective tariffs that had existed during the colonial period. Free trade meant Irish subordination, since most underdeveloped Irish industry could not withstand British competition. However, as a dependent internal colony, Ireland developed unevenly along the differential lines established by the colonial pattern. Commerce and peasant agriculture remained the mainstays of the southern economy. Industrial policies that favored the English market so disadvantaged southern Ireland that by 1825, most southern-based industry had been driven out of business. And land policies shifted regularly in accord with English market needs.[4] An utterly different situation evolved in the North where industries flourished. There, successful cottage industries and maintenance of tenant rights had facilitated the growth of a capital base. The farm-based cottage industries organized on a factory basis: iron shipbuilding and subsidiary spinoffs grew up in Belfast's harbor area. These firms served the expanding trade of the British empire and supplied an essential part of her naval power (Wilson, 1950, p. xviii; Beckett and Glassock, 1967). Moreover, this was the only area that was able to resist the introduction of ranching—in Ulster, oats and flax remained the cash crops.[5]

Inevitably, these regional differences entailed variations in social relations, political infrastructures, and reactions to imperial dominance. In the South and West, politics were rooted in rural and commercial issues, particularly land reform and the franchise. In the North, rural politics were gradually subordinated to those in urban centers and focused on industrial concerns. Since the South could not provide a market for Ulster's expanding industrial goods, Belfast's bourgeoisie was increasingly drawn into British markets and credit structures and wedded to imperial policies. In short, regional differences in the mode of production constituted a powerful obstacle to national unity. However, uneven development does not sufficiently explain the basis or structure of an ethnically defined loyalist politics, which opposed secular nationalism and left it a virtually Catholic movement. Not all Protestants benefitted equally from the fruits of imperialism—nor was the language of loyalty always identical with the interests of the Empire. To understand the nature of loyalism under the Union, we need to examine carefully the economic and social changes in this era and the role of ethnic organizations in political mobilization.

As we have seen in the previous section, Protestant tenant farmers constituted something approximating a high-wage labor force prior to the Union. However, the mere fact of the Union did not insure that their economic privileges would be sustained. It is true that the Ulster Custom protected Protestant tenants from the worst effects of imperial agricultural policies, but the famine and the gradual consolidation of lands produced a significant decline in the number of small farms in Ulster, produced a proletarianization of the countryside, and eroded the base for ethnic patrimonialism.[6] Moreover, the Catholic Emancipation movement and developing nonsectarian land reform movements confronted Anglican landlords with the possibility of continuous unrest, particularly as the economic base of their clientilist relations with the rural Presbyterians began to erode. To ward off the possibility of land war and to restore their patrimonial relation to Protestant tenants, the landlords turned to organizing an evangelistic, anti-Catholic crusade out of the rural Orange lodges (Gibbon, 1975, pp. 44–66). Under the cry "Home Rule Means Rome Rule," they organized Orange lodges in the countryside and recruited enthusiastic Presbyterian ministers into their ranks. Each member of the higher gentry who formed the Grand Lodge of the Orange Order was required to join a "private," local lodge so as to "mingle with their humbler brethren" (Miller, 1978, p. 56). Secret meetings in local lodges emphasized the shared symbols of Protestant history. When Westminister banned secret societies as provocative in 1835, the Tory gentry provided their estates for alternative meetings. "This aspect of Orangeism was particularly attractive to the 'lower orders,' who were pleased with the idea of sharing the same sphere with so many of those moving in the higher spheres of society." But it was not simply status honor that Orange lodges provided: they also served as a base for recruiting and arming Protestant rural laborers to collect tithes and rents from the Catholics (Miller, 1978, pp. 56–78). In this way, Orangeism became the symbol of Protestant dominance and an institutional encapsulation of the traditional patrimonial relationship between Protestant gentry and peasants.[7]

During the first half of the century, the major locus of ethnic violence and antagonism was in the countryside. In nearly every case, conflicts were precipitated by provocative processions and parades, sponsored by the Orange Order and by Catholic nationalist counter responses. During the second half of the century, however, the major sites of conflict shifted, as eastern Ulster industrialized and as the famine forced migration from the agricultural areas to Belfast. As I have already pointed out, Ulster's industrial bourgeoisie, were strong supporters of the Union, as their economic fortunes were interwined with British economic growth and policies, but what of the laboring classes?

In response to industrialization and to the famine, Catholic and Protestant labor began to migrate from the agricultural West to the coastal North.[8] Prior to the massive famine migration, trade associations had developed in Belfast to regulate jobs in the industrializing crafts. Frequently based in Orange Lodges, these were marked by an intricate system of recruitment, a combination of nepotism, localistic politics, and patronage. By the time of the famine-induced population influx, the system was quite strong, and craft exclusiveness was easily transformed into ethnic exclusivity. However, given the interests of capital and the supply of low-wage labor during the famine period, the threat of displacement was strong. Whenever industrialists adopted nonsectarian policies, Protestant skilled laborers disrupted production, intimidated the new hirees, initiated riots on the shop floor, and insisted on job segregation and hiring discrimination. Their success was significant. Catholics were excluded from the skilled and semiskilled jobs in shipyards, engineering, and the linen mills and were restricted larely to menial jobs on the docks (Gibbon, 1975, pp. 95–97; Fitzgibbon, 1972, p. 245). This period provides clear evidence of the role of high-wage labor in sustaining an ethnically split labor market. Nonetheless, to view Protestant workers' loyalism as always precipitated by the protectionist efforts of a high-wage labor force would be to oversimplify the structure of the Protestant labor force.

To the Anglican landlords and to Ulster's bourgeoisie, loyalism implied explicit support for the British connection. However, the same slogan meant different things to different sectors of the working class. As I shall demonstrate, the data on ethnic conflicts in nineteenth-century Belfast indicate that different sectors of the Protestant labor force engaged in loyalist ethnic politics for different reasons. The skilled Protestant workers in the shipbuilding, ironworkers, and engineering firms easily perceived the correlation between success of British imperialism and fluctuations in their industrial jobs. This was a high-wage sector that served readily as a political linkage between the industrial bourgeoisie and unskilled labor. Studies of this period indicate that these workers constituted a leadership cadre among Protestant workers, strongly opposed to Home Rule, active in Orange Lodges and in the Ulster Protestant Association working to protect their ethnic compatriots from unemployment (Gibbon, 1975, pp. 69–77). In contrast, unskilled workers, especially recent migrants from rural areas, experienced few of these economic advantages, and recognized shared interethnic class interests in temporary situations (e.g., the Dock Strike of 1907). For this group, ethnic conflicts during the Union can be traced more to challenges to the ethnic boundaries, forged by residential segregation and reinforced by the Orange Lodges and by the significant cultural differences between Catholic and Protestant unskilled labor.[9] By 1850, Belfast was a totally segregated city: Catholics resident in the Falls and Ardoyne areas and Protestants clustered in Sandy Row and Shankill. Segregation reinforced localism and a laager mentality in both communities, one that was reinforced by the different religious and social institutions characteristic of each neighborhood. Thus, for Ulster's unskilled Protestants, loyalism was disconnected from imperialism or the rewards of a labor aristocracy; rather, it constituted the personalistic bonds of working people in ghetto communities and reflected the threat of Catholic encroachment on assumed territorial and communal rights (Gibbon, 1975, p. 80). It was this laager mentality that labor organizers and socialist leaders failed to penetrate in their labor organizing in Belfast.

A careful analysis of the sectarian outbreaks in this period supports my argument that other kinds of competition, particularly political and territorial were the major precipitants to ethnic mobilization. As Table 1 shows, the major conflicts in nineteenth-century Belfast were most frequently precipitated by provocative parades organized by the Orange lodges to celebrate the Protestant Ascendancy on ritual dates or in reaction to nationalist activity in Parliamentary elections. Nor is there any connection between the riots and industrial economic discontent. In 1857, severe unemployment occurred in the linen industry, but the riots preceded this recession. The year 1864 was prosperous, with high employment and wages in every industry; 1872 was a normal year; and although agricultural depression occurred in 1886, the shipyards and docks where the leaders of the riot were employed, were kept extremely busy. Moreover, none of these riots was preceded by efforts on the part of industry to displace Protestant workers with Catholics. There was no use of Catholics as strikebreakers.[10] During the struggle for Home Rule, the important role of the Orange Order in pulling together these varied forms of loyalism became quite apparent.[11] Now the threat of job displacement mounted. Warnings abounded that Home Rule would dismantle factories, eliminate the shipbuilding industry, destroy working-class reforms such as the 8-hour day, and lead to papist tyranny. The story of dominant

TABLE 1.   Religious riots in Belfast, 1813-1912[a]

Date	Year	Precipitating event	Duration
12 July	1813	Orange procession	1 Evening
12 July	1832	Parliamentary election	1 Day
12 July	1835	Orange meeting	1 Day
8 July	1841	Parliamentary election	2 Days
12 July	1843	Protestant procession	5-7 Days
12 July	1854	Parliamentary election	5-7 Days
12 July	1857	Orange procession	56 Days (sporadic)
8 August	1864	Unveiling of O'Connell statue in Dublin	18 Days
15 August	1872	Nationalist procession	9 Days
15 August	1880	Catholic procession	4 Days
13 July	1884	Orange procession	1 Day
3 June	1886	Defeat of Home Rule	4 Months (sporadic)
7 June	1898	Nationalist procession	2 Days
11 August	1907	Undetermined	4 Days
13 June	1909	Orange procession	2 Days

[a]From Budge and O'Leary (1973, p. 89).

class efforts to "play the Orange hand" has been told frequently. Local Orange lodges were used for recruiting support for Unionism and later for training members of the illegal Ulster Volunteer Force. In Unionism, the modern loyalist convenant was developed, calling on the tradition of Protestant reciprocity and fraternity to fight "Catholic tyranny."[12]

In summary, under the Union, the nature and source of Protestant loyalty to the Crown was class differentiated. For the conservative Anglican landlords, it constituted a defense against land reform agitation; to rural workers, it was a way to protect their coveted Ulster Custom and to accommodate to the proletarianization of the countryside. For the industrial bourgeoisie, loyalism derived from the knowledge that capital growth would be stunted were Ulster to be separated from British credit markets. And among the urban working class, loyalism implied both a fidelity to the local community and a protection of the ethnic division of labor. These different economic interests were mediated through the agency of the Orange Order and spoken through the language of religious fraternity.

We can place this period in a more coherent theoretical perspective by returning to the four propositions and considering their adequacy in explaining Protestant ethnic mobilization against Irish nationalism. The evidence on the *rural* mobilization against land reform in the first half of the century provides significant support for Nairn's claim that the capitalist elites of Ulster and England sought to reward Protestant labor for their loyalty and that the patrimonial relations between capital and labor played a major role in fostering a sectarian politics during the Home Rule Movement (P2a). However, it also supports the resource competition claim that reactive ethnic politics are most likely when the resources of a formerly dominant group are challenged by economic changes (P4a). For this period, the existence of *prior* ethnic organizations together with an increased sense of competition for land may best explain how easily Anglican landlords accomplished their efforts. The evidence about *urban* ethnic conflict again supports the claims of resource competition theorists. And although in some general sense an effort to protect labor advantages motivated Protestant working-class politics, especially as Catholics migrated to Belfast, this was only partially precipitated by introduction of cheaper labor into the same labor market (P3). It was also enhanced by warnings by capital that secular labor politics and Home Rule would erode ethnic segregation in industry and the differential economic advantages of Ulster over the rest of Ireland (P2A). Finally, I have indicated that Protestant politics cannot be reduced to economic competition. Fidelity to local community, territorial competition, and a sense of a prior right to political resources sparked urban Protestant mobilization against Catholics. The ethnically exclusive trade unions, the spatial segregation of neighborhoods, and the Orange Order all provided an institutional infrastructure for reactive ethnic mobilization (P4d).

IV. THE STATE, THE ORANGE ORDER, AND LOYALISM FROM PARTITION TO DIRECT RULE, 1920–1972

Under the Government of Ireland Act of 1920, the country was partitioned and the six counties of the northeast remained within the United Kingdom, retaining representation at Westminster and a devolved legislature at Stormont, Belfast. The Act itself was evidence of the success of the Orange resistence to independence. However, the survival of Ulster as an integral part of Great Britain was not easily maintained in the face of an independent Free State in the South and a one-third Catholic population in the North. Any challenge to the Unionist alliance of urban workers, industrialists, agricultural labor, landowners, and small shopkeepers would undermine the dominance of the official Unionist Party and its bourgeois (mostly local capitalist, landed agriculture) leaders (Mansergh, 1936; J. Harbinson, 1973). Until the early 1960s, the refusal of Westminster to interfere in the internal affairs of Northern Ireland permitted the growth of a patrician state and a continuation of patrimonial relations there.[13] Numerous mechanisms were adopted to insure the stability of the Protestant alliance in the new state.[14] But, the linchpin in the entire system was the degree of localism in government and the existence of a powerful Ulster bourgeoisie, which permitted Unionist Orangemen to play a leading role in sustaining patrimonial relations. In this section of the paper, I will sketch out the ways in which a localist government and economy allowed Unionist leaders to sustain an interclass alliance among Protestants. I will examine the breakup of that coalition in the mid 1960s and the development of a militant ethnic mobilization of Protestant workers. Finally, I will use this examination to evaluate the adequacy of each of our models in predicting this reaction.

After partition, the formal organizational basis for integrating the Protestant population into the new state was the Unionist Party. Although it captured two-thirds of the electoral votes in the first parliamentary election (virtually all Protestant votes), its hegemony was not insured. In the next election (1925), the Unionists faced internal challenges by Labour and Independent Unionists and their share of the votes fell to 55.0% (with 13.7% going to Protestant labor candidates). Fearing a Catholic Nationalist bloc, the Unionist elite sought to ward off all internal conflicts and to adopt electoral mechanisms which would reduce flexibility in voting choice and insure that the constitutional position of Ulster would be the dominant electoral issue. The reforms (single member constituencies and plurality rule rather than proportional representation) were read by Catholics as a mechanism for weakening their power: but, the real effect was felt within the Protestant electorate (Donneson, 1975; J. Harbison, 1973, pp. 1–20). As Tables 2 and 3, indicate, by replacing proportional representation with a plurality system, the Unionists effectively increased the power of local capital in government and reduced the power of internal Protestant opponents.

The bourgeois Unionists also relied heavily on the Orange Order to sustain a coherent Protestant loyalism. The Order was made an integral part of the official Unionist Party, nominating one-fifth of the delegates to the Ulster Unionist Council. Thus, the ordinary Orangeman felt that he had a real voice in party matters.[15] The Orange lodges played their most important role at the local level, moderating the class cleavages that could undermine Unionist solidarity in particular constituencies. Through intervention of lodge officers in local constituency association, Protestants were able to monopolize public housing, public works, and local council employment (Barritt and Carter, 1972; Bell, 1976; Probert, 1978). The decentralized structure of the state supported a quasi-populist localism in which such interventions were more easily accomplished. An equally important function of the Order was symbolic: the reinforcement of Protestant solidarity through ritual marches, songs, and sectarian symbols.[16] However, if Orange loyalism was the formal ideological and informal institutional mechanism for integrating Protestants under the Unionist banner, the costs of that integration were steep. Without the patrimonial contract, the Unionist Party would be vulnerable to Nationalist challenges and to class-based politics. However, they were also trapped by it, unable to disentangle themselves from the embrace of populist sectarianism, even when it interfered with capital development and the modernization of the state. As I shall demonstrate, this exclusive reliance on Orangeism to counter Unionist political weakness during the first 40 years of partition precipitated a political crisis in the late 1960s and ushered in a largely working class and fundamental Protestant neonationalist politics.

At the time of partition, we know that Ulster was the most developed region of

TABLE 2. General parliamentary elections in Northern Ireland, 1921–1969: party by percent vote and members elected (MP)

Election	Unionists		Unofficial unionists[b]		NILP		Independent Labour[c]		National/ Republican[d]		Liberals		Other		For union	Against union
	%	MP	%	MP	%	MP	%	MP	%	MP	%	MP	%	MP		
1921	66.9	40	—	—	—	—	0.6	—	32.3	12	—	—	0.2	—	40	12
1925	55.0	32	9.0	4	4.7	3	—	—	29.1	12	—	—	2.2	1	40	12
1929	50.6	37	14.3	3	8.0	1	0.8	—	13.0	11	6.3	—	7.0	—	41	11
1933	43.1	36	21.4	3	8.6	2	—	—	26.9	11	—	—	—	—	41	11
1938	56.5	39	29.1	3	5.7	1	1.7	1	4.9	8	—	—	2.1	—	43	9
1945	50.4	33	5.0	2	18.6	2	13.3	3	9.2	10	—	—	3.5	2	40	12
1949	62.7	37	0.6	2	7.2	—	2.1	2	27.2	9	—	—	0.2	2	31	11
1953	47.5	38	12.8	1	12.1	—	11.6	3	15.5	9	—	—	0.5	1	40	12
1958	43.6	37	9.0	—	16.0	4	12.7	2	17.5	8	—	—	1.2	1	42	10
1962	48.6	34	—	—	26.0	4	6.8	3	15.4	9	3.2	1	—	1	40	12
1965	59.1	36	—	—	20.4	2	2.4	2	8.4	9	3.9	1	5.8	2	41	11
1969	48.2	36	19.2	3	8.1	2	2.4	2	7.6	6	1.3	—	13.2	3	40	12

[a]From Elliott (1973, pp. 96–97).
[b]Includes Independent Unionists, Progressive Unionists, Protestant Unionists, and Independent O'Neill Unionists.
[c]Includes Independent Labour, Commonwealth Labour, Federation of Labour, Irish Labour, Republican Labour, and Socialist Republicans.
[d]Includes Nationalist, Republican, Sinn Fein, Fianna Fail, and Anti-Partitionists.

TABLE 3. Distortion in votes–
seats relationship, 1929–1938

Election	Difference index[b]
1921	0.101
1925	0.083
1929	0.301
1933	0.302
1938	0.293

[a]From Osborne (1982, p. 143).
[b]Difference index refers to a summary of distortion, with higher scores
indicating greater distortion.

Ireland. However, its industrial base was narrow: workers were concentrated in a few industries (ship building, marine works, textiles, light engineering) and the major industries were small family firms. Over 25% of the labor force was still engaged in agriculture. Dependence on British markets and this thin economic base made Ulster vulnerable to fluctuations in the world economy and British tax policy and subject to chronic depression. After partition, unemployment consistently ran about four times as high as the British average (Probert, 1978: pp. 51–67). Industrialists, during the early years of partition, did little to shore up the paternalist relation with Protestant labor, which they had cultivated during the struggle against Home Rule. The consequence of this failure became apparent during the depression of the 1930s when nonsectarian strikes sprang up in Belfast. Like the earlier strikes of Larkin, these did not constitute a complete turning by the Protestant working class to secular class politics. However, they shook the complacent industrialists into sectarian action. Publicly, the government presented the strikes as a Catholic IRA plot, but privately, government officials urged industry to discriminate against Catholics, if they hoped to break the labor coalition. Indeed, the strike was broken only when the Royal Ulster Constabulary invaded Catholic and not Protestant slums, cut off food supplies, and systematically attacked these neighborhoods (Mansergh, 1936, p. 240; Farrell, 1976, pp. 100–140). Major industrialists learned their lesson well, and concentrated hiring on Protestants.[17]

However, after World War II, a number of social changes threatened the basis of the political order, revealing in the process the internal tensions within Unionism. These included the decline of traditional industries that had been the material base of patrimonial relations; growth of a welfare state in which Catholics began to receive some rewards; and the interest of Great Britain in establishing favorable trade relations with Ireland. With the concentration of capital, the emergence of multinational conglomerates, and increasing automation and land consolidation in the post World War II period, the traditional industries of

Northern Ireland (agriculture, textiles, shipbuilding, and aircraft manufacture) began to steadily decline. In 1948, 40% of all employment in Ulster was in these four industries; by 1968, it had fallen to 22% (and by 1977 to 11%). Between 1949 and 1969, the number of workers fell by 50% in agriculture, 50% in linen, and 17% in shipbuilding. In the postwar period, Northern Ireland was more sensitive than any other U.K. region to cyclical variation in unemployment rates, and by 1963, real income was 25% below the British average and unemployment stood at 9.5% with no sign of falling. When the Northern Ireland Labor Party captured 26% of urban workers' votes in 1962, it was clear that the Unionist Party was in trouble (Probert, 1978, pp. 51–87).

Stormont's dependence on English revenue to support a growing welfare system and provide support for economic planning made the Unionists particularly vulnerable to pressures for rapprochement with the South and for reform of its discriminatory state system. Moreover, the expansion of welfare services and educational opportunities provided resources to Catholics that made them less interested in separatist politics. In 1962, the Nationalist Party entered Stormont for the first time as a loyal opposition and began a moderate movement toward political cooperation and reform of the state. Thus, they undermined one of the basic rationales for the Protestant Ascendancy, i.e., the purported disloyalty of the Catholic population. As a result, the single-claim Unionist party organization was threatened. Thus multiple forces were working on Unionists: externally, Westminster was pressing for reforms that would eliminate the ethnic communal gap and would facilitate economic diversification; internally, labor was pressing for economic reform and employment growth for Protestant workers and Catholics were pressing for political reform and civil rights. The Unionist response to these pressures was to adopt a program of "modernization": cautious political reform, industrial diversification, and centralized economic planning. Under the leadership of Terence O'Neill, Stormont offered generous inducements to foreign investment, initiated trade negotiations with Ireland for the first time in history, and turned to Westminster for increased support of planned development (Farrell, 1976, pp. 239–242).

The evidence suggests that Stormont's economic development shcemes did not alter the relative employment disadvantages of Catholics. In fact, a study of aggregate employment accessibility rates indicates that in the period of 1959–1972, the differential between Catholic and Protestant access to jobs increased. Throughout that period, Protestant areas were favored for manufacturing growth and all sponsored development (Farrell, 1976, pp. 239–242). However, centralized planning and British intervention did threaten the *base* of Unionist hegemony. Foreign-owned chain stores displaced small shops; capital-intensive multinational industries slowed the growth rate in new jobs. Discrimination against Catholics was challenged, occasionally quite effectively in those arenas of the public sector that were governed by metropolitan rules of appointment and services (e.g., family allowances, medical insurance, aid for education). In border areas (those with a high proportion of Catholics), where there was some competition for jobs and housing and where unemployment rates were particularly high, erosion of local control would further undermine the position of working and lower middle class Protestants (Gibbon, 1967, pp. 20–41; Bew, Gibbon, and Patterson, 1979, pp. 163–175; Daugherty, 1982, pp. 225–247). Thus any action by Stormont that was not overtly favorable to Protestants could be read as an assault on the loyalist covenant. Yet overt favoritism would be opposed by Westminster and widely denounced by the civil rights activists.

Under pressure from Westminster, then, the Unionist government began to adopt a public appearance of nonsectarian politics. Mostly symbolic gestures (visits by the Prime Minister to Catholic schools), even minor overtures were unprecedented and constituted a violation of the code of Orangeism. Hence when Terence O'Neill met with the Irish Prime Minister in an economic summit in 1965, Ian Paisley, minister of a small evangelical sect in Belfast, called on Protestants to stop the "Romeward Trend" of the Unionist Party and its "fur-coat brigade" (Rose, 1971, p. 101).[18] Paisley's anti-elitist, anti-Catholic denunciations appealed strongly to Protestant workers in rural areas, to whom reform meant the end of preferential treatment in land sales, housing, and local employment. However, Paisley also appealed to the fundamentalist Protestants, a small but highly committed sector of the population (about 13% on a 1968 study). Civil rights demands were presented by Paisley as mere cloaks for confessional interests. And in a society defined by ethnic territoriality, a march through any "Protestant" area was a sectarian challenge and spawned violent reactions on both sides. Reluctant to embrace reform, yet unable to control the Protestant populace, the Unionist Party began to fragment. A study of support for the government in 1968 indicated the extent of this fragmentation. Although 85% of the Protestant respondents identified themselves as Unionist, they were quite divided over Unionist policy. About one-third of Protestant respondents supported reform of the state; half wanted no change; and 11% wanted to increase the power of the Unionist Party (Rose, 1971).

The political schisms within the loyalist population were significant, and the next 4 years were marked by escalating violence, controversy, and dramatic changes in the party structure as the fissures within Unionism became more evident. From 1969 to 1972, new party fractions emerged, and numerous militant vigilante groups, defense associations, and platoons sprang up in urban areas, each with its own self-styled leadership and its own understandings of Orange loyalism (Boserup, 1972, pp. 157–192; Boulton, 1973; Burton, 1978; Hepburn, 1980; Miller, 1978; Rose, 1976; Sunday Times Insight Team, 1972). The imposition of direct rule in 1972 laid bare the ideological fiction on which Unionist alliance had been based: that Protestant ascendancy was coincident with metropolitan interests and that God and Crown were the unchanging principles of state formation. The Protestant God clearly had less to say than the modern Crown. The Unionist Party declined even further under direct rule. In 1973, when Westminster proposed constitutional reforms that would permit a coalition-based regional executive, with a power-sharing government and a Council of Ireland, the election was contested by four different groups of loyalists (and an equal number of Catholic-based parties). The support for the right wing, Orangeist approach is evident in Table 4, where the Official Unionists captured only 26.5% of the votes and antireformist groups (the Vanguard Unionist Loyalist Coalition, the Democratic Unionist Loyalist Coalition, and the Anti-white Paper Unionists) secured 33.7%

Successive initiatives by the British governments have failed to resolve the conflicts: from the 1974 Ulster Workers' Council strike, which forced the end of a brief power-sharing government, onward, the troubles escalated and the Unionist Party has foundered. The fragmentation of the Unionist Party has been exacerbated by the intensification of differences between Catholics and Protestants on the question of the Constitution. The difference index between them was about 34% in 1968; in surveys since direct rule, it has averaged 56% (Osborne, 1982) The demise of the Unionist patrimony, together with the failure of liberal reformers to develop an effective substitute for the archaic ideologies of Orangeism and Irish republican nationalism, have renewed the prescriptive power of those ideologies at the very moment that their social base has eroded.

In this section, I have concentrated on two major periods of crisis during partition in order to test out the claims of our four models. In the first period, the depression of the 1930s, urban workers began mobilize along nonsectarian lines

TABLE 4. Results of the 1973 assembly elections[a]

Party	Percent of vote	Seats in proportion to votes	Seats
V.U.L.C.	10.5	8.2	7
D.U.L.C.	10.8	8.4	8
A.W.P.U.	12.4	9.7	10
Other Loyalist	1.6	1.2	2
Official Unionist	26.5	20.7	23
Alliance	9.2	7.2	8
N.I.L.P.	2.6	2.0	1
S.D.L.P.	22.1	17.2	19
Republican Clubs	1.8	1.4	0
Other Nationalist	1.4	1.1	0
Others	0.9	0.7	0

[a]From Osborne (1982, p. 156).
[b]V.U.L.C., Vanguard Unionist Loyalist Coalition; D.U.L.C., Democratic Unionist Loyalist Coalition; A.W.P.U., Anti-White Paper Unionist; N.I.L.P., Northern Ireland Labour Party; S.D.L.P., Social Democratic Labour Party.

but were short-circuited by local capital. The data from this period clearly support Nairn's claims about the patrimonial alliance forged by Ulster's industry and tolerated by Westminster in order to deflect class conflict. However, the postwar capitalist investment patterns, development of a welfare state, and more central state planning, combined with shifts in Catholic politics, undermined the material base of this alliance. These developments raised Catholic expectations of reform and shifted their political sights from nationalism toward civil rights. When official Unionist leaders began to make even symbolic concessions and overtures to Catholics, they were perceived, particularly by Protestant industrial labor, rural workers, and evangelical fundamentalists, as violating the loyalist covenant. The decline of local control and challenge to an assumed Orange covenant threatened the privileges of Protestant working class, fragmented this interclass ethnic coalition, and helped precipitate the resurgence of "the troubles." During this period, we find support for both uneven development claims and even more clearly for the postulates of the resource competition model.

V. CONCLUSION: A REASSESSMENT OF THEORIES OF ETHNIC MOBILIZATION

As we have seen, the uneven development model is an essential starting point for understanding the history and bases for ethnic conflict in Northern Ireland. The metropolitan state and its dominant class shaped the resources and interests of Ulster's Protestants. The patrimonial relations between tenant farmers and Anglican landlords retarded the development of a secular Irish nationalism. And during the period of the Union, some of Ulster's working class, particularly the skilled workers, directly benefited from overseas imperialism. Since partition, the decline of indigenous capital in the postwar period, which eroded the base of this interclass alliance, contributed significantly to the present troubles.

However, this model does not adequately explain the contours of the patrimonial relationship, particularly the extent to which workers themselves constructed the rules of the game, insisting that their loyalism was conditioned on exclusive ethnic privileges. To understand the process of building a patrimonial relationship, then, it is useful to turn to split labor market theory. Protestant labor itself played a major role in creating the contours of the class and ethnic relations; their conditional loyalty was evident during both colonialism and Union (in the rural outbursts against renting land to Catholic tenant farmers, in the smashing of Catholic looms, in the exclusion of Catholics from the shipyards). They set ethnic limits on the dominance of capital and in so doing reproduced a class structure based on an ethnic division of labor. However, the historical relation between Protestant capital and labor is more complex than either of these models allows. Sometimes something approximating a split labor market was apparent. At other times (as in the nineteenth-century arming of Protestants to collect tithes) it was capitalists who sought to ''play the Orange hand,'' in order to break down possible interethnic labor alliance. Equally important, this analysis should demonstrate that neither patrimonial class relations nor a split labor market will fully explain Protestant "loyalism." For throughout the Union and partition we have identified major instances of ethnic conflict that were unrelated to labor market factors or to class relations, based instead on competition for political resources or on displays of ethnic dominance. Indeed, nearly every instance of ethnic riots in nineteenth-century Belfast was a reaction to provocative politics, invasions of ethnic residential turf, which is clear support of resource competition claims. Nor does the analysis of the final period support the claim of split labor market thesis that the current "troubles" are rooted in displacement of the Protestant labor force as a result of a corporate search for cheap labor. As I have pointed out, the wage labor situation of Ulster workers within Great Britain as well as vis-à-vis Catholics have been relatively stable since partition. It is their political privileges that are challenged. This ethnic "class fraction" has organized against a secularizing state bureaucracy, which would erode the base of differential advantages, not all of which are economic. In short, both of these theories can be used to elucidate aspects of the Northern Ireland situation. However, neither considers sufficiently the range of competitive situations or the role of institutions and ideologies in reinforcing ethnic political identity.

The internal colonial model has serious limitation as an explanation of the patterning of ethnic relations in Ulster. Hechter's claim that ethnic mobilization is associated with the coincidence of relative economic deprivation and a high degree of cultural difference in a preindustrial setting can certainly be supported when we consider eighteenth-century rural Ireland. Language and religious differences, combined with the ethnic division of labor, precipitated continuous ethnic skirmishes. The rural Orange societies sustained these differences and functioned as an institutional base for communal politics. However, the shift of ethnic antagonism in Ulster, from the rural areas to Belfast and Londonderry, indicates that industrialization actually reinforced ethnic boundaries and communal segregation. Thus, the predictive power of the internal colonial model is challenged.

We have seen, as resource mobilization and competition theories predict, that industrialization exacerbated ethnic conflict as Catholics migrated to urban areas and as competition for political and economic resources escalated. Settlement in ethnic ghettoes reinforced their reliance on ethnic institutions to provide the language and symbols around which people mobilized politically. Orange Lodges, local churches, and segregated neighborhoods cultivated the psychological terrain in which ethnic loyalties took root, and they provided a base for organizing. The British state fostered (during colonialism and Union) and then tolerated (during partition) the traditional role of "loyalist" institutions in Ulster's ethnic politics. Moreover, as this model postulates, the development of impersonal bureaucracies of the modern welfare state has undermined the patronage system and helped spawn the reactive loyalism of the recent period. In short, the case of modern Ulster does support the resource competition prediction that industrialization and expansion of the state sectors generate the conditions for ethnically circumscribed competition and conflict. However, it also illustrates the important mediating role of cultural attitudes and beliefs, apart from concrete resource competition.

If my consideration of the patterning of ethnic and class relations among Protestants in Northern Ireland points out the limitations of our current conceptual paradigms, it also underscores their utility. Together, they point in the direction of a more unitary approach, one that is grounded in appreciation for the complex interaction of ethnic and class structures and processes.

ACKNOWLEDGMENTS

I would like to thank the Rockefeller Foundation and the Center for the Study of Human Rights, Columbia University, for the support provided at a crucial stage of this research project. I wish also to express my appreciation to Allen Batteau, Leonard Isaacs, Joane Nagel, Susan Olzak, and Kenneth Waltzer for their valuable comments and suggestions on various drafts of this chapter.

NOTES

[1]This argument draws from world system theory and neo-Marxist analyses of state development, especially the work of Anderson (1975).

[2]Among the laws were those passed in 1665, in which export of dairy products to England was banned; in 1680, a regulation was passed requiring that Irish trade take place on English ships; in 1699, Irish woolens were excluded from English markets; and after 1720 all brewers were required to purchase hops in England (Cullen, 1972, pp. 16–36).

[3]In County Armagh, the Peep O' Day Boys banded together to prevent Catholics from bidding for Protestant farms and succeeded in driving 500 Catholic families out of the area in 1795 (Strauss, 1957, p. 25; also see Cullen, 1972; Lecky, 1972). Not all agrarian outbursts were sectarian. In Antrim and Down, Presbyterian tenants used secret societies to pressure for the abolition of tithes, county cess taxes, and other state impositions. Nor were these associations exclusively political. For a good discussion of the development of these societies, see Gibbon (1975).

[4]Industrial workers in the south declined from 1.7 million in 1821 to 1.6 million in 1841, while agricultural workers increased from 2.8 to 2.5 million. In the first half of the nineteenth century, imperial policies encouraged subdivisions in the land, rackrenting, and a shift from stock farming to tillage (generating unproductive use of land, rural unemployment, and peasant discontent). In the latter half of the century, a shift in policies to favor livestock forced landlords to consolidate their holdings and displaced huge numbers of peasants from the land (Pomfret, 1930, pp. 7–8; Strauss 1957, pp. 134–137; Marx and Engels, 1971, pp. 121–138; Kee, 1972; Lyons, 1972; O'Tuaithaighs, 1972).

[5]Despite its less fertile soil, an acre of crop land in prefamine Ulster yielded an average value of £6, 3s, whereas the yield in the south was only £5, 18s (Pomfret, 1930, pp. 54–56).

[6]Small farms decreased from 100,000 in 1841 to 30,000 in 1851 (Budge and O'Leary, 1973, pp. 28, 30).

[7]It may be this pattern of Orange reciprocity that best explains the absence of rural Protestant participation in the land wars of the late nineteenth century. For Catholics, land reform meant "land for the people," a return of the land taken during colonization, and a demand for national sovereignty. For Protestant tenants, the Catholic-led land reform was interpreted to mean erosion of the Ulster Custom, threat to ethnoreligious status, and immersion in a sea of politically and religiously dangerous papists. It worked: patrimonialism ensured that there were few challenges to the hegemony of the Anglican landed gentry on the part of the rural Protestant populace. However, it should be evident that this modern patrimonialism was due not to Protestant tenant farmers' mobilizing to protect a high-wage position, but to the calculated efforts of landed capital to avert any possibility of nonsectarian populism and to the powerful appeal of evangelical fundamentalism as a vehicle for ethnic solidarity.

[8]The population of Belfast increased dramatically and with it the proportion of Catholics. In 1784, Catholics represented only 8% of the city's populace; at the time of the Union, this had doubled to 16%—but by 1861, they constituted 33.9% of the residents (Budge and O'Leary, 1973, p. 28).

[9]According to contemporary sources, those Catholics who migrated to Belfast between 1811 and 1860 were largely unskilled workers from the South and West, where the Irish language was still strong. They carved out ethnic enclaves, clustered in traditionally Irish sections of Belfast (Edwards, 1970, p. 129).

[10]To the extent that Parliamentary elections, with Home Rule candidates, were presented as a threat to Protestant workers, then we can find some support for an economic interpretation of these conflicts. However, that movement was not effectively mounted until the 1870s (Budge and O'Leary, 1973, pp. 89–90).

[11]Appeals by Tory leaders called on Orangemen in city and country to prove that "all those ceremonies and forms which are practiced in Orange lodges are really living symbols or only meaningless ceremonies" (Edwards, 1970, p. 85).

[12]To recruit working-class opposition, the Ulster Unionist Club Council was formed; its central executive consisted of six industrial capitalists, two landowners, a clergyman, a solicitor, and a "private gentlemen." However, its appeal was to Protestant labor in the city and rural areas. At the Ulster Unionist Convention in 1912, 473,000 of Ulster's 500,000 adult male Protestants subscribed to a Solemn League and Covenant to "defeat Home Rule by any means necessary" (Gibbon, 1975, pp. 136–137).

[13]Westminster reserved to imperial control those matters that would affect the conditions for the development of capital: issues of war, peace, international treaties, external aid, revenue matters (raising taxes, income levels, excess profit and corporate taxes, customs and excise duties), a preservation that would contine Northern Ireland's status as an internal colony.

[14]These included some gerrymandering of electoral boundaries to contain the power of Catholic votes, the development of an entirely Protestant police force, passage of laws that restricted civil liberties, and patronage in public sector jobs. The dominance of Ulster's bourgeois elite was sustained by such mechanisms as a business premises franchise in local elections.

[15]Between 1921 and 1969, 87 of the 95 Unionist Cabinet members, every Stormont senator, and 54 of the 56 Unionists elected to Westminster were Orangemen. In nearly every case, the exceptions were women who could not join the patriarchal Orange Order (J. Harbison, 1973, pp. 18–25).

[16]Challenges to the notion of privilege and to myths about Catholics were few within the Protestant community, and reinforcements were many: territorial segregation, separate social institutions and networks—even in rural areas, segregated schooling—all mitigated against interethnic contact (Barritt and Carter, 1972; R. Harbinson, 1968; Harris, 1972; Holland, 1981).

[17]Although it is difficult to secure data (given census failures to collect this information until recently and the refusal of private firms to give estimates of the religous distribution of the labor force), studies of industrial segregation and inferences from unemployment data and income and occupational figures by residential location show a historical pattern of clear Protestant advantage. The structure of the economy and the predominance of local capital and family firms through the late

1950s permitted this (Aunger, 1975; Barritt and Carter, 1972, pp. 93–108; G. Bell, 1976, pp. 20–29; Probert, 1978, pp. 5–53).

[18]It is difficult to ascertain the extent to which these differential attitudes are correlated with class positions or economic interests. Analysis of this data by Thompson (1983) compared regression models that took religiosity (support for a series of evangelical fundamentalist attitude measures), class, and economic nonclass factors (employment sector location, family income, education, unemployment, home ownership, residence, region) into account to explain likely support for reform of the Unionist Party. His findings indicate that the economic factors covering a range of competitive situations, were not as strong a predictor as religiosity in explaining opposition to reform. This is not to deny the importance of economic competition in understanding the difficulties that the Unionist Party faced, but to emphasize that where "religious values are rooted in relatively autonomous social institutions, they are likely to have a substantial political impact independent of economic factors," and that religious conviction is not a "cover" for class or other economic interests (Thompson, 1983, pp. 127–152).

REFERENCES

ANDERSON, PERRY (1975). *Lineages of the absolutist state.* London: New Left Books.
AUNGER, EDMUND A. (1975). Religious and occupational class in Northern Ireland. *The Economic and Social Review* **7**(No. 1):1–17.
BANTON, MICHAEL (1983). *Racial and ethnic competition.* Cambridge: Cambridge University Press.
BARRITT, DENNIS P.,and CARTER, CHARLES (1972). *The Northern Ireland problem: A study in group relations.* London: Oxford University.
BECKETT, J. C. (1969). *The making of modern Ireland.* London: Faber.
BECKETT, J. C., and GLASSOCK, R. G. (1967). *Belfast: The origin and growth of an industrial city.* London: B. B. C. Publications.
BELL, DANIEL (1975). Ethnicity and social change. In *Ethnicity: Theory and Experience* (Nathan Glazer and Daniel Patrick Moynihan, eds.), pp. 141–176. Cambridge: Harvard University Press.
BELL, GEOFFREY (1976). *The Protestants of Ulster.* London: Pluto Press.
BEW, PETER, GIBBON, PETER, and PATTERSON, H. (1979). *The State in Northern Ireland. 1921–1972.* Manchester: Manchester University Press.
BONACICH, EDNA (1972). A theory of ethnic antagonism: The split labor market. *American Sociological Review* **37**:547–559.
BONACICH, EDNA (1979). The past, present and future of split labor market theory. In *Research in Race and Ethnic Relations* (Cheryl Leggon and Cora Marrett, eds.), pp. 17–64. Greenwich, Connecticut: JAI Press.
BOSERUP, ANDERS (1972). Contradictions and struggles in Northern Ireland. *Socialist Register* **9**:157–192.
BOULTON, DAVID (1973). *The UVF, an anatomy of loyalist rebellion.* Dublin: Torc Books.
BUDGE, IAN, and O'LEARY, CORNELIUS (1973). *Approach to crisis: A study of Belfast politics. 1613–1970.* New York: Macmillan.
BURTON, FRANK (1978). *The politics of legitimacy.* London: Routledge and Kegan Paul.
CULLEN, L. M. (1969). *The formation of the Irish economy.* Cork: Mercier Press.
CULLEN, L. M. (1972). *An economic history of Ireland since 1660.* London: Batsford.
DAUGHERTY, PAUL (1982). The Geography of unemployment. In *Integration and division: Geographical perspectives on the Northern Ireland problem* (Frederick W. Boal and J. Neville H. Douglas, eds.), pp. 225–247. New York: Academic.

244   KATHERINE O'SULLIVAN SEE

DePAOR, LIAM (1970). *Divided Ulster*. Hammondsworth, England: Penguin.
DONNESON, DAVID (1975). Civil servants and religion at Stormont. *New Society*, 2–5.
EDWARDS, OWEN DUDLEY (1970). *The sins of our fathers*. Dublin: Gill and Macmillan.
ELLIOTT, SYDNEY (1973). *Northern Ireland parliamentary election results. 1921–1972*. Chichester: Political Reference Publications.
ELLIS, P. BERRESFORD (1972). *A History of the Irish Working Class*. London: Victor Gollancz.
ENLOE, CYNTHIA (1973). *Ethnic conflict and political development*. Boston: Beacon.
FARRELL, MICHAEL (1976). *Northern Ireland: The Orange State*. London: Pluto Press.
FITZGIBBON, CONSTANTINE (1972). *Red Hand: The Ulster colony*. New York: Doubleday.
FOX, RICHARD, AULL, CHARLOTTE F., and CIMINO, LOUIS (1981). Ethnic nationalism and the welfare state. In *Ethnic Change* (Charles F. Keves, ed.), pp. 198–245. Seattle: University of Washington Press.
GIBBON, PETER (1967). The dialectic of religion and class in Ulster. *New Left Review* **55**:20–41.
GIBBON, PETER (1975). *The origins of Ulster unionism*. Manchester: Manchester University Press.
HARBISON, JOHN F. (1973). *The Ulster Unionist party, 1882–1973*. Belfast: Blackstaff.
HARBINSON, ROBERT (1968). *No surrender*. London: Times Books.
HARRIS, ROSEMARY (1972). *Prejudice and tolerance in Ulster*. Manchester: Manchester University Press.
HECHTER, MICHAEL (1975). *Internal colonialism: The Celtic fringe in British national development*. Berkeley: University of California.
HECHTER, MICHAEL, and LEVI, MARGARET (1979). The comparative analysis of ethnoregional movements. *Ethnic and Racial Studies* **2**:260–274.
HEPBURN, A. C. (1980). *The conflict of nationality in Northern Ireland*. London: Edward Arnold.
HOLLAND, JACK (1981). *Too long a sacrifice* New York: Dodd Mead.
KEE, RICHARD (1972). *The green flag*. New York: Delacorte.
LECKY, W. E. H. (1972). *A history of Ireland in the eighteenth century*. Chicago: University of Chicago Press.
LYONS, F. S. L. (1972). *Ireland since the famine*. London: Weidenfeld and Nicholson.
MACDONALD, MICHAEL (1982). Colonialism in Ireland. Paper presented at Comparative and International Studies Seminar. University of California at Santa Cruz, March.
MANSERGH, N. S. (1936). *The government of Northern Ireland*. London: Allen and Unwin.
MARX, KARL, and ENGELS, FREDERICK (1971). *Ireland and the Irish question*. New York: International Publishers.
MILLER, DAVID W. (1978). *Queen's rebels: Ulster loyalism in historical perspective*. Dublin: Gill and MacMillan.
MOODY, T. W., and MARTIN, F. X. (1967). *The course of Irish history*. Cork: Mercier Press.
NAGEL, JOANE, and OLZARK, SUSAN (1983). Ethnic mobilization in new and old states: An extension of the competition model. *Social Problems* **30**:127–143.
NAIRN, TOM (1977). *The break up of Britain: Crisis and neo nationalism*. London: New Left Books.
OLZAK, SUSAN (1983). Contemporary ethnic mobilization. *American Review of Sociology* **9**:355–374.
OSBORNE, ROBERT (1982). Voting behavior in Northern Ireland, 1921–1977. In *Integration and division: Geographical perspectives on the Northern Ireland problem* (Frederick W. Boal and J. Neville H. Douglas, eds.), pp. 137–166. New York: Academic.
O'TUAITHAIGHS, GERARD (1972). *Ireland before the famine. 1798–1848*. Dublin: Gill and Macmillan.
POMFRET, JOHN E. (1930). *The struggle for land in Ireland. 1800–1823*. Princeton: Princeton University Press.
PROBERT, BELINDA (1978). *Beyond Orange and Green: The political economy of the Northern Ireland crisis*. London: Zed Press.

QUINN, DAVID BEERS (1966). *The Elizabethans and the Irish.* Ithaca, New York: Cornell University Press.
ROBINSON, PHILIP (1982). Plantation and colonisation: The historical background. In *Integration and division: Geographical perspectives on the Northern Ireland problem* (Frederick W. Boal and J. Neville H. Douglas, eds.), pp. 19–47. New York: Academic.
ROSE, RICHARD (1971). *Governing without concensus: An Irish perspective.* Boston: Beacon Press.
ROSE, RICHARD (1976). *Northern Ireland: A time of choice.* London: Macmillan.
ROTHSCHILD, JOSEPH (1981). *Ethnopolitics: A conceptual framework.* New York: Columbia University Press.
STONE, JOHN (1979). Internal colonialism in comparative perspective. *Ethnic and Racial Studies* 2:255–259.
STRAUSS, ERIC (1957). *Irish nationalism and British democracy.* New York: Columbia University.
SUNDAY TIMES INSIGHT TEAM (1972). *Ulster.* London: Deutsch.
THOMPSON, JOHN (1983). The plural society approach to class and ethnic political mobilization. *Ethnic and Racial Studies* 6:127–152.
WILSON, THOMAS (1950). *Ulster under home rule. A study of the political and economic problems of Northern Ireland.* London: Oxford University.
YOUNG, CRAWFORD (1983). The temple of ethnicity. *World Politics* 35:652–62.

Index

247